EMILY WU & LARRY ENGELMANN

Feather in the Storm

Emily Wu's stories have appeared in both Chinese and American publications. She is one of the featured subjects in the film *Up to the Mountain, Down to the Village*. She lives with her two children in Cupertino, California.

Larry Engelmann is the author of five previous books, including *Daughter of China*. His writing has appeared in many publications, including *American Heritage*, *Smithsonian*, and the magazines of both the *Los Angeles Times* and *The Washington Post*. He lives in San Jose, California.

Feather in the Storm

A Childhood Lost in Chaos

EMILY WU &
LARRY ENGELMANN

ANCHOR BOOKS
A DIVISION OF RANDOM HOUSE, INC.
NEW YORK

FIRST ANCHOR BOOKS EDITION, JANUARY 2008

Copyright © 2006 by Emily Wu and Larry Engelmann

All rights reserved. Published in the United States by Anchor Books,
a division of Random House, Inc., New York, and in Canada by Random House
of Canada Limited, Toronto. Originally published in hardcover in the United States
by Pantheon Books, a division of Random House, Inc., New York, in 2006.

Anchor Books and colophon are registered trademarks of Random House, Inc.

The Library of Congress has cataloged the Pantheon edition as follows:
Wu, Emily.
Feather in the storm: a childhood lost in chaos / Emily Wu and Larry Engelmann.
p.   cm.
1. China—History—Cultural Revolution, 1966–1976—Personal narratives.
I. Engelmann, Larry.   II. Title
DS778.7.W723   2006
951'.225—dc22   2006041772
[B]

Anchor ISBN: 978-0-307-27662-9

Photograph of Emily Wu © Anchee Min
Photograph of Larry Engelmann © Jane Ling
Book design by Soonyoung Kwon

www.anchorbooks.com

Printed in the United States of America
10 9 8 7 6 5 4 3 2 1

For my beloved children

Jasmine and Erik

and for the children lost in the Chaos
and those who loved them

We've lived in a time of chaos, when it is impossible to love.

—MAO ZEDONG (1893–1976)

Author's Note

That was a long time ago, but it's wrong what they say about the past, I've learned, about how you can bury it. Because the past claws its way out.

—KHALED HOSSEINI, *The Kite Runner* (2003)

Feather in the Storm is my story and the story of my family. It is also the story of millions of children like me whose stories have never been told. We had the misfortune to be born and raised in a time of revolutionary upheaval, brutality, and inhumanity. Only recently, after returning to China several times to visit the towns and villages where I was raised, and interviewing my aunts and uncles and my dearest childhood friend, Qin Xiaolan, was I able to write about those times.

The conversations recorded here from my youth may be qualified with the phrase "to the best of our memory" when the conversation involved more than one individual. Certain events, such as the visit to my father, were retold to me by both my mother and father and the precise words and facts were theirs. Their personal memories informed my own memory. Some conversations, such as those with the Sun children,

I can still clearly hear in my mind, as they pounded on the school door and threatened me, and I remember the sound of their feet as they pursued me. As I grew older and attended school, made home visits, lived in the countryside, and formed close friendships, I did not have to go back as far to remember what was said, how it was said, and what my reaction and response was.

This is, therefore, a work of nonfiction, though some names have been changed to protect the identity of an individual or a family. I researched with others the events described here. I went back to the places where I had lived. I read and reread lengthy diaries and journals I had kept. I talked to my old friends and detractors who still lived in China. I opened doors to rooms I had not entered in decades. I went inside. I sat, thought and remembered. I heard again the voices I heard there when I was a girl. I heard the laughter and the cries. I remembered the things I describe—events, people, places, sounds and smells. Like anyone recalling distant events in faraway places, my memories are personal, and the words I remember may vary from what someone else remembers. But like everyone who passes through a long, traumatic series of events, I remember those events more accurately than if my childhood days had been uneventful. This is what I still see and hear when I close my eyes and those times descend on me again.

Over the years I have come to believe in the basic goodness of people and the fundamental dignity and strength of humanity. But there was a time in my life when such a belief was impossible. Ironically, that was when I was most vulnerable, most innocent, and most in need of compassion. Those were the years of my childhood—a childhood that was lost too soon.

I survived the years of revolutionary chaos in China. Millions did not. Many of those who did not survive were children. And many of those children were my friends. We were all innocent and often unseen victims of a dark and indecent time.

It is my hope that this memoir may serve as a reminder and a memorial to all of the children who were lost in the Chaos and to all of those who, even though they survived, were robbed of their birthright—innocence and happiness. Perhaps in telling my story, I can help assure that other children will never be forced to relive it.

Emily Wu
Cupertino, California

Feather in the Storm

Visitors

When I was a small boy, my grandmother told me about a distant uncle who was living in China during the Cultural Revolution. He promised to send a picture of himself to his relatives in America. If conditions were good, he said, he would be standing. If they were bad, he would be sitting. In the photo he sent us, my grandmother whispered, he was lying down.

—DAVID HENRY HWANG (1997)

The concentration camp is six miles from the train station. There is no public transportation. Visitors must walk to the camp. The woman carrying me shifts me to her side, asks if I'm comfortable, and sets out on the last leg of our journey. She stops to rest. There are no benches, no trees, no grass, not even weeds. All around us is a dull, parched, lifeless landscape under a withering and unforgiving sun. It is Saturday, June 3, 1961. My third birthday. I am on my way to meet my father for the first time.

We pass several places not far from the road where the earth is ruffled with rows of low mounds. A wooden stake with a number scratched on it protrudes from each mound. These are graves of the prisoners—men, women and children. The government does not want prisoners to waste time burying the dead. Relatives are summoned to dig the graves and to collect the belongings of the deceased. People pass us. They are like shadows carrying shovels and small sacks, moving slowly to and from the camp. They glance up with sad, hollow eyes.

After an hour we are only halfway to the camp. The woman stops and puts me down. She looks into the distance and wonders if she can make it before the brief visiting period is over.

An old man approaches on a horse-drawn cart. He wears drab rags and a frayed cap. His skin is dark and leathery from the sun. He's toothless, and his face is shrunken and small. The cart is piled high with straw. The horse is skin and bones and moves as if each step is its last. The woman moves to the middle of the road and waves for the man to stop. He draws back on the reins, pauses and looks at us impatiently but says nothing.

"Can you give us a ride to the camp?" the woman pleads. "I'm exhausted. I don't want to be late. I'm taking my daughter to meet her father for the first time."

The man looks at his horse, thinks for a second about her request and then turns back to us. "My horse is sick and weak," he says. "He can't pull any more."

"Please," the woman begs. "Just carry my daughter. I'll walk and hold her on. It would make it much easier for me. And we've little time."

"All right," the man answers. "Put her on."

She parts the hay to make a place for me and lifts me onto the cart. My legs dangle over the side. When we are ready, the man makes a clicking noise, and the horse resumes his sluggish pace.

The woman rests her hand on my leg as we go along. After several minutes the driver turns and asks, "Where are you from?"

"Anhui Province," she says.

"You've come a long way," he responds.

"Yes."

"How old is your little girl?"

"She is three years old today."

He turns around and looks at me. "What's your name?" he asks.

I don't answer.

"She is called Yimao," the woman says. "A feather. Her father named her after a poem by Du Fu. Do you know it? 'A Feather in Heaven Forever'?"

"Yes," the driver answers and turns back to the horse. "I read Du Fu also. Long ago."

"Do you live near here?"

"Not *near* here. I live *here*."

"What did you do before you came here?"

"I was an elementary school teacher," he says.

"Have you been here long?"

"Eight years."

"Do you have children?"

"Yes."

"Will you go home soon?"

He turns and gives her a long look as if to ask with his eyes whether her question is serious. Finally, he answers, "No. I won't."

The answer bothers the woman. She stops asking questions.

"Your husband," the driver says, "the girl's father—what about him? What did he do?"

"A professor. In Beijing."

"A professor!" the driver repeats and nods. "And what did he profess?"

"English. He studied in a university in America."

"He studied in a university in America. And now the professor's here," the driver says, watching the road. "There are many professors in here. And over there, too," he says and turns toward a cluster of mounds and numbered stakes.

As we near a slight rise in the road the driver stops. "This is as far as

I can take you," he says. "They'd be angry if they knew I let your daughter ride. Better walk the rest of the way."

"Is it far?" the woman asks.

"Not far," he says, pointing ahead.

The woman takes me down and thanks the driver. "You're a kind man," she says. "What's your name?"

"My name? My name is 905131." He smiles sadly, makes the clicking sound again, and moves on.

When we arrive at the crest of the low hill, a massive structure looms up in the distance. Its tall redbrick walls are topped with coils of glistening barbed wire. Watchtowers rise at the corners of the walls.

The woman stops to take in the scene. Then she sighs and says, "Let's go see Papa now, Maomao."

As we proceed toward the camp, guards in the nearest tower turn to watch us through binoculars. They keep us in their sights, studying us until we arrive at the shed just outside the main gate where visitors are required to register.

In a distant field hundreds of tiny figures are moving about. Their activity produces a haze of brown dust that hangs in the air over them. They are dressed alike and are too far away for the woman to distinguish men from women, let alone to identify her husband.

She anxiously hands her papers to a guard. "We're not too late, are we?" she asks.

PART I

THE CHAOS

I saw China in the form of an old hag so decrepit and brainsick that she would devour her children to sustain herself. Insatiable, she had eaten many tender lives before, was gobbling new flesh and blood now, and would surely swallow more. Unable to suppress the horrible vision, all day I said to myself, "China is an old bitch that eats her own puppies!"

—HA JIN, *The Crazed* (2002)

I

In the fourth winter of the famine I was returned to my family. It was the final week of January, a few days before the Lunar New Year. I was three and a half years old.

We lived in a large house in Tianjin. I slept beside my grandmother in a bedroom on the first floor. My mother, father and three sisters slept in an adjoining room. On the floors above us lived the families of three uncles and aunts. Nine adults and twelve children shared the house.

On my last morning in the house I was awakened before dawn by a gentle touch. Papa stood beside the bed, his finger to his lips to indicate that he did not want me to disturb Grandma. He carried me from the room and put me down on a stool in the corridor and then he gathered some of my clothing and my only toy—a doll—and put them in a bag. He helped me into my winter coat, tied my wool cap under my chin and wrapped a scarf around my neck. Finally, he helped me pull on my mittens and winter shoes. He put on his coat, picked up the bag of clothing and took my mittened hand in his. With hardly a sound, he unlatched the door, opened it just enough for us to squeeze through, and closed and locked it behind us. ●

The morning was cold and quiet. The air was filled with snowflakes. The courtyard was buried beneath a blanket of new snow. When Papa noticed it was difficult for me to get a footing on the slippery cobblestones, he stooped and lifted me in his arms. As he straightened up, a light came on in the bedroom where I'd been sleeping with Grandma. There was a muffled cry—"Maomao!"

I twisted in Papa's arms and was about to shout, "I'm here, Grandma." But Papa whispered, "Be quiet!" He hurried through the gate and out onto Happiness Lane. The anxious voice continued to call, "Maomao! Where are you?"

Papa rushed down the lane. Two blocks from the house he stopped to catch his breath. I wrapped my arms around his neck and laid my head on his shoulder.

We waited on the corner until a bus stopped for us. We rode silently through the sleeping city to the train station.

After buying our tickets Papa carried me into a crowded concourse. I pulled his ear and asked, "Where are we going?"

"I'm taking you home," he replied.

"But we *are* home, Papa."

He raised his finger to his lips.

———

An abrupt restlessness in the crowd startled me. Several shrill blasts from a whistle were followed by commands to begin boarding. We were carried along as the bustling mass of people moved toward the platform.

Papa held me tightly. When the crowd thinned he ran along the line of waiting cars watching in the windows for empty seats. After passing a dozen packed cars he bolted up the stairs into a car and hurried toward a single empty seat. A woman struggling with two big bags in one arm and a child in the other approached from the far end of the aisle. She snagged her bags on the back of a seat and stopped to pull them loose. Papa dropped into the vacant seat a few steps ahead of her. She looked around anxiously. A crowd converged on her from either end of the car and made an exit impossible.

After catching his breath Papa rose and hoisted our bag onto an overhead shelf. Then he sat down and pulled me onto his knee. The woman next to us held a girl about my age. The girl's face was flushed and her nose was running. Her watery eyes remained fixed on me.

An explosion of shouting and whistles sent people racing frantically back and forth across the platform. The cars shuddered and banged on their couplings. Those people standing in the aisles grabbed for overhead grips or the backs of seats as they tumbled against one another. Protests and cursing rose from one end of the car to the other. As we picked up speed the grumbling of disgruntled passengers faded to a low, steady hum of conversation.

The train made many stops. At each new station people crowded the platform. Most were peasants making their way to the cities to sell goods on the black market. They clutched baskets or carried nets and crates of live animals. They pushed past those trying to leave the car, filling every vacant space while further compressing unfortunate passengers remaining in the aisles.

At each stop the air was infused anew with a stench of soot, tobacco and animals. People shouted, scolded children and complained while climbing over one another. To this was added the noise of chickens and piglets. I watched the confusion of commerce and discomfort from my perch on Papa's lap.

Before long hunger pangs reminded me that I hadn't eaten breakfast or lunch. "Papa," I said, "I'm hungry."

He reached into his pocket and withdrew an old newspaper page tied with a string. Inside were two hard-boiled eggs. He handed me one and returned the other to his pocket. I pulled off my mittens and peeled the egg, letting the shell fragments fall to the floor. A whine sounded beside me. The girl in her mother's arms was reaching out, begging for my egg. I paused before taking a bite. The girl screamed. Several people in the aisle, emaciated and hungry-looking, watched me.

I cupped the egg in my hands. The girl's mother whispered in her ear and she quieted. I decided not to eat but, rather, to sleep.

I awakened later and became aware of the quiet around me. I opened my cupped hands and found . . . nothing. No egg! I searched on the floor and found bits of eggshell. I looked up at the little girl. She was asleep. On her chin I noticed a tiny speck of egg yolk.

I whispered to Papa that I was still hungry. He handed me the remaining egg. I quickly peeled it and gulped it down.

I asked Papa to get my doll from our bag. I told her all about our trip and how crowded the cars were and how hungry I had been. I promised I'd give her an egg when we got home.

"Do you like her?" Papa asked.

"Yes."

"She is a gift from your mama."

"No, she is not," I said.

Papa was about to add something but stopped himself and turned to stare out the window.

I remembered receiving the doll months earlier. A woman had come to our house accompanied by a boy. She spoke with Grandma and Papa. Early one morning she took me with her, and we traveled on the train to a place filled with very scary people. I cried and hid behind a bench and screamed that I wanted to go home.

Before she left with the boy, the woman gave me the doll and told me it was a birthday present.

The doll was little more than rags stitched together and stuffed with cotton. It was without a face or clothing. Papa, however, made her beautiful for me. He found a piece of plastic and cut it to fit the front of the head. He painted wide black eyes, rosy cheeks, and red lips on it. I watched him work as he brought her face to life. Grandma made a dress and slippers of matching material and presented the completed doll to me.

I played with her so much that her painted face chipped and faded. I examined her and noticed cracks in her face and a tear in one corner where the stitching had come undone. I told her I'd have Papa give her a new face when we got home.

2

Our journey ended shortly after daybreak the next morning. A voice on the loudspeaker announced that we had arrived in Hefei.

"You are almost home now, Maomao," Papa said. He pulled our bag from the rack, grasped me tightly and asked, "Are you ready?"

"Yes," I replied. Yet I had no idea what I was supposed to be ready for, except to see Grandma and Mama and my sisters.

Papa had me lock my arms around his neck as he pushed his way out of the car, through the station and onto the street.

In the brisk winter wind, I felt a cold draft on my feet. I suddenly remembered removing my shoes during the night and letting them fall to the floor. I'd forgotten them there.

I pulled Papa's collar and told him, "My shoes are on the train."

"What?" he asked in disbelief and looked at my bare feet. He glanced at the crowded station and sighed. "We'll just have to get you new ones." He undid a button on his jacket and had me stick my feet inside to keep them warm.

We boarded a bus and stood in the aisle for half an hour before getting off near a cluster of buildings. We approached one of them.

Papa read a number over the entrance and said, "Your mama and papa live here with your brother. You will live here, too."

I was frightened by his words. "No," I said. "They don't. I know where Mama and Papa live."

"Let's go meet them," he replied.

"I want to go home," I said in a tremulous voice. "Take me to Grandma."

"Maomao," he said, "listen to me. Don't call me Papa anymore. I am not your papa. I am your *second uncle.*"

I searched his eyes, confused. I waited for him to say this was a game.

"From now on you must call me Second Uncle," he said.

Tears spilled down my face. I wrapped my arms tightly around his neck. "No," I cried. "Don't give me away, Papa. I'll be a good girl. I won't say I'm hungry again. No . . . no . . . no."

I clung to him, sobbing. He patted my back and said, "It's okay, Maomao. It's okay."

———

Papa carried me up the stairs to the second floor and knocked on a door. It swung open and a boy stood before us. Papa gave his name, and a moment later there was a flurry of footsteps and a man and a woman appeared at the door. The woman gasped, "What a surprise!" I buried my face in Papa's coat.

She touched my arm and said, "Maomao, come to Mama."

She sounded kind. The man beside her watched me through thick black-rimmed glasses. "Little Maomao, do you remember me?" he asked.

I shook my head.

"I am your papa," he said.

I studied the two adults and the boy, confused and apprehensive. The woman said, "Come in. You must be hungry and tired." She knelt and picked up my doll—without noticing, I'd dropped her. Before handing it to me, she said, "I gave you this doll, Maomao. Do you remember?"

"She's afraid," Papa said. "And she's shy."

He carried me down the hall to a room where a table was set up with stools around it.

"Where is Grandma?" I asked. There was no answer to my question. The woman said, "Maomao, come here." Papa handed me to her. I struggled to hang on to him, but he pried my arms loose. As she pulled me to her, she saw my bare feet and asked, "Where are her shoes?"

"I'm afraid we lost them on the train," Papa said.

"I'll find something for her," the woman said. She carried me into a small adjoining room. She sat me on the bed and put a pair of slippers on my feet. She told me, "Maomao, walk slowly and they'll stay on and keep your feet warm."

She took my hand and helped me slide from the bed. I stayed close to her but as we walked from the room my feet came out of the slippers. I stopped and reached back with each foot, felt around with my toes, and put the slippers on without using my hands.

She laughed. Side by side and hand in hand, taking small steps so my slippers stayed on, we joined the others.

3

I didn't realize how hungry I was until I was seated at the table and food was placed before me. I eagerly devoured my entire serving. When I held up my bowl and asked for more, everyone looked at me. "There is no more, Maomao," Mama said. And then, "Listen to that Tianjin accent! Other children here are not going to understand her."

That evening Second Uncle and Papa set up a white wooden crib. Mama put me in it. My new brother, whose name was Yiding, slept with my parents in their bed and Second Uncle slept in a bed beside the crib.

I lay in my crib and listened to the adults in the next room.

"I remember when you brought her to Tianjin," Second Uncle said.

"February 1960," Mama said. "It broke my heart, but . . . what could I do? If I'd kept her with me, we would have all starved."

"I know." Second Uncle sighed.

"She was one and a half," Mama said.

"She has been with us for two years," Second Uncle said. "We're the only family she knows. She'll need time to adjust."

I heard the scratch of a match and smelled cigarette smoke.

"Our mother starved herself for Maomao," Second Uncle said. "I tried to stop her, tried to get Mother to eat her food, but she found a way to give it to Maomao. We talked about it—the brothers and sisters. We concluded that the best solution was to bring Maomao back to you."

His words reminded me of an episode a few days earlier. I had been playing hide-and-seek with my sisters. I crept into my bedroom and hid behind the clothing inside a large wardrobe. I heard footsteps. A moment later Grandma and Second Uncle started talking a few feet from me.

"She is killing you," Second Uncle said.

"No," Grandma replied. "She's no trouble. She's a blessing."

"I know what I see," Second Uncle said. After a pause and a rustling of paper he said, "I bought these at the black market. You give her most of your food. She's healthy and you are not. Promise me you'll eat these."

"I will," she promised.

Second Uncle left. I stepped from the wardrobe. Grandma looked up and smiled. "Come here," she whispered. I hurried to her, and she said, "Eat these, quickly!" She held out a small pack of roasted peanuts wrapped in newspaper.

I stuffed some in my mouth. Grandma held the others as I chewed and swallowed, and she urged, "Quickly!"

Before I was finished, Second Uncle returned. "What's this?" he asked. He smelled my breath.

"Maomao is my granddaughter," Grandmother said, as if that explained everything.

"This cannot continue," Second Uncle said. Then he left the room.

Grandma fed me the remaining peanuts one at a time. She watched as I savored them. Her expression changed from delight to melancholy. She pulled me to her and stroked my hair and cried. She rocked me back and forth and repeated, "I don't want them to take you away, Maomao."

As she whispered the words, I cried. "I don't want them to take me away, Grandma. I want to stay with you." I was unsure who "them" were and where they might take me. But I was afraid and I clung to her.

After several minutes she brushed away her tears and wiped my face clean. "Go play with your sisters," she said. "Grandma needs her rest."

Voices from the next room interrupted my memory of Tianjin.

"I'm sorry," Mama said.

"Mother lost weight. She became listless. We brought in a doctor to examine her. He said she had edema as a result of malnutrition. Most of her food was going into Maomao's mouth. We could not let her die for her granddaughter."

"You did the right thing," Papa said.

"How did Mother react when you said you were bringing Maomao here?" Mama asked.

"We couldn't tell her."

"So . . . you . . . said nothing?" Mama asked.

"Yikai," Second Uncle said, "we decided they'd break the news later. She'll cry and sulk. But in time she'll accept it. Then she'll start eating and regain her health."

"How serious are the food shortages in Tianjin?" Mama asked.

"We don't have enough," Second Uncle said. "Nobody does. But we're alive. It's the same everywhere. This famine," he went on in a lower voice. "Four years of it. Four long years! Peasants come into Tianjin. They sell what they have. They beg. They sell their children. And when they can't find a buyer . . . I don't like to think about it. We find them on the street. Along the rivers. On the train tracks."

"It's the same here," Mama said. "The black market is all that separates us from starvation. Nothing else. The three of us—I mean the four of us now—the four of us have to live on my salary."

"Will you work again, Ningkun?" Second Uncle asked Papa.

"I don't know," Papa answered. "No work. No salary. No medical care."

"How many have died?" Mama asked.

Papa said, "Many millions. Many. That's what I've heard and I believe it."

"I've heard it, too," Second Uncle said.

"Why?" Mama asked. "Can you explain it?"

"Haven't you heard? It's the weather," Second Uncle said. "That's the *official* explanation."

"What about the weather?" Mama asked.

"Has your weather changed?" Second Uncle asked. "Is there a flood here? A drought?"

"No," Mama and Papa answered at the same time.

"It's not the weather," Second Uncle said.

"Will it ever end?" Mama asked.

"We can hope," Second Uncle said.

"All we have left is hope." Mama sighed.

"Yes," Second Uncle responded.

There was a long silence. Then the light was switched off, and Second Uncle came into the room and lay down on the bed beside my crib.

"Papa?" I said.

"Maomao," he answered. "You're still awake?"

"Are we going to see Grandma tomorrow?"

"Maomao," he said, "I am Second Uncle, remember?"

"Second Uncle," I said, "aren't we going to see Grandma tomorrow?"

"No. We are not."

"Are we going to stay here?"

"This is your home. You are going to live here."

"But I want Grandma," I cried. "Take me home to Grandma, please. I promise I will never eat her peanuts again."

"Go to sleep, Maomao," he said. "Good night." He turned away and covered himself with a blanket.

The next morning the man who had been my papa and become my second uncle was gone. I was alone with my new family.

4

Mama gave me a bowl of rice porridge for breakfast. "You're going to be happy here," she assured me. "Today we will do something special. Just Maomao and Mama." She smiled and brushed my hair out of my eyes. "You're coming to work with me."

Mama was a typist in the university's Foreign Languages Department. She was forbidden from teaching, despite her fluency in English, because of Papa's political crimes. In the office her colleagues swarmed around me and agreed I was a very pretty girl.

"Go ahead, tell them your name. Tell them how old you are," Mama said.

"My name is Maomao," I said. "And I am . . . almost four."

The women giggled. "Listen to that accent!" one of them clucked as she cupped a hand to her ear. "How old did you say you are?" another asked, leaning close to me in wide-eyed anticipation.

"Almost four," I answered, and the two women repeated my words, imitating my accent and laughing.

Mama smiled and patted me affectionately.

That evening Mama said that I would stay with Papa each day

while my brother was sent to the university's child care center. "We simply can't afford to send both of you," she explained.

After Mama left for work, Papa swept the apartment. After he'd finished the daily shopping, he cooked lunch for us. After that, when the weather permitted, he took me for a walk around campus. Sometimes Papa played hide-and-seek with me or told me stories. But after a while he'd tire and read his books. His spirits revived when he retrieved my brother from the child care center.

Our apartment was small—three rooms and a kitchen. One room served as a bedroom for my brother and me. Another functioned as a living room and dining room as well as a bedroom for our parents. A third room, about the size of a Ping-Pong table, was used for storage. Our few pieces of furniture were rented from the university, with the exception of the crib, which had been passed down through two generations of Mama's family.

After dinner my brother practiced writing Chinese characters at the desk and Papa sat nearby on a stool using a chair as his desk. When my brother had finished his homework, Papa moved to the desk where he worked late into the night.

I listened to Papa typing, adjusting his chair and paging through his books and papers. Mama fell asleep while he worked translating English novels into Chinese. Now and then he came to the door of the bedroom and stood silently watching us sleep. "Papa?" I'd whisper, and he always responded, "Go to sleep, Maomao. You'll wake up your brother."

Papa smoked cheap cigarettes, Big Iron Bridge brand, which he bought for nine fen per pack. They left an acrid aroma lingering in the air and a permanent amber residue on Papa's fingertips. They also left a memorable impression in the wool rug under the desk, a wedding gift from Grandma.

Late one night I was startled by an unusual commotion and cries of alarm from the next room. The apartment began to fill with smoke. Papa had fallen asleep at his desk and let his cigarette drop to the rug. It eventually ignited in flames. Mama extinguished the fire quickly with a thermos of water but not before a hole had been burned in the rug.

Our table, on the other hand, was special because we gathered around it for our meals and often played games on it. Through yet another blunder, Papa left his special mark on the table as well.

Papa often took me to the street markets with him. Sometimes we walked to them, and other times, if they were far away, he propped me in front of him on our old bicycle and we rode. The rationing of food and the fact that Papa had no income limited our choices.

Food was scarce and money was more scarce. Mama was paid in cash once a month. There were mandatory deductions from her pay—rent for our apartment, rent for the furniture, and fees for water, electricity, coal and union dues, and the child care center for my brother. Her salary was fifty-nine yuan per month, or about 196 fen per day. Eggs cost fifty to sixty fen each on the black market, so our budget was the equivalent of less than four eggs for the entire family of four each day, before deductions.

One morning Papa found a merchant selling tiny fish. They were each about half an inch long. In normal times these were food for cats. Papa bought two pounds for us. Later, I watched him meticulously clean each fish with the tip of a knife. "They are a bargain and they are rich in protein," he pointed out. "They are good for our health. Sometimes little is good."

"Like little Maomao?" I asked.

He grinned and said, "Ah, you understand. Yes, like little Maomao."

As he cleaned the fish, Papa taught me how to count and corrected my pronunciation, helping me lose my accent. He laid the fish out on the table. There were just over four hundred. He showed me how to arrange them in perfect rows twenty by twenty, all facing the same direction, until they formed a square. The half dozen that remained he placed in a line along the bottom of the square. He stepped back and observed his work proudly and told me, "When they're dry, we'll have a banquet!"

They dried quickly. But there was to be no banquet. By the time Papa tried to remove them, the skin of each fish had bonded to the red paint of the table. As he peeled them off, a small impression in the image of each little creature remained on the tabletop. It looked as if a master craftsman had etched the table with an intricate pattern. A school of four hundred tiny fish—all swimming in the same direction in an orderly square with a few stragglers at the bottom—covered our table like perfect fossils in shale. When my brother and I ran our fingertips over the tabletop we could feel the slight impression where each fish had dried. We were delighted, even though Papa had to clean the fish again, peeling away the skin and paint so that nearly nothing was left to eat.

My brother and I turned the tabletop into a maze for some of our games. We also used it for counting and math. My brother was able to use part of the design as a chessboard. The table provided us with endless hours of games and diversions. The joy the fish brought us in drying was far greater than our joy from eating what little remained of them.

5

In the summer of 1962 Papa was given permission to teach at Anhui University. He was accepted back into the academic fold as a man whose partial redemption had been achieved through three and a half years of labor in a concentration camp. He was assigned two classes— one in English composition and another in reading English texts. He was not restored to the position he had held in Beijing as a professor. He was classified as a temporary employee and his contract was reviewed every three months. He remained politically suspect and he still wore two "caps" or labels. In the eyes of the state and the university, he was both "ultra-rightist" and "an element under corrective education." His salary of sixty yuan per month was less than one third his previous pay. He was not granted fringe benefits such as medical care or use of the university pharmacy.

I was enrolled in the child care center that autumn, and my brother was enrolled in the first grade at Meishanlu Elementary School. Shortly before classes began, Papa's stepmother moved in with us. She had lived with Mama and Papa previously in Beijing. She shared the small bedroom with my brother and me.

Papa was a wonderful lecturer. Students and teachers from Anhui University and nearby universities came to his classes. His lecture room filled early and eager students spilled into the hallway. Others gathered to listen outside the windows. Some students began writing notes telling him how much they enjoyed his lectures and how he opened their minds to the wonders of literature. Papa destroyed the notes and warned the students never to write to him because it could get them all in trouble.

Within a few weeks, as a result of the jealousy of other faculty, Papa's classes were restricted. Only faculty members and students from Anhui University were allowed to attend. A few junior faculty were ordered to monitor the political content of his presentations and to keep a detailed record of every word he said.

Mama worried about Papa's popularity. She reminded him that "a big tree catches the wind" and that he should seek security in anonymity. Papa acknowledged that his passion for his work attracted the critical attention of faculty and administrators, and along with the attention came risk. He was "skating on thin ice," he said. Yet he believed that in time his detractors might accept the simple fact that his intention was to enlighten and inspire his students. He forgot that thin ice cracks and breaks with only a slight rise in the temperature.

A young faculty member oversaw Papa's thought reform and instructed him in Communist Party doctrine. In turn, he received instruction in English literature from Papa. It was a strange situation for each of them. The young man composed book reviews and literary essays for Papa, and Papa wrote political essays and self-criticism for him.

After two years of outstanding teaching, the Party secretary notified Papa that his political status would be revised. His two caps—"ultra-rightist" and "element under corrective education"—were to be removed, and a political instructor would no longer be assigned to him.

On July 4, 1964, the third anniversary of his return from the concentration camp, Papa was officially "decapped" and he was "returned to the ranks of the people." But this was not really true. Instead of becoming a citizen and faculty member in good standing he was merely a "decapped rightist and element under corrective education." He exchanged one derogatory label for another. And it was understood that caps were held in reserve by "the people"—meaning the authorities. They had the right to replace them whenever they wished.

Papa was told that his changed status came with substantial financial compensation. And it meant that Mama was allowed to teach English to the non–English majors in the university. The job reassignment for Mama took effect immediately, but the announcement of the new salary was postponed until the last week of the year. Papa was notified that in recognition of his "progress in thought reform" and excellence in teaching, he was awarded a raise of ten yuan per month. It was disappointing. We had hoped that we'd be eating better. Yet Mama said we should be grateful for small blessings. "Ten yuan," she reminded us, "is better than nothing." It meant a few more eggs each month and a little more meat now and then.

6

The university campus was surrounded by a high wall. Four gates provided access to the campus. Within the wall were several classroom and administration buildings; living quarters for the faculty, staff and students; a clinic; stores for the university community and a child care center.

The center was a single-story concrete structure at the north end of the campus. Nearly two hundred children attended the facility. They ranged from infants to seven-year-olds—the last age before children transferred to the elementary school outside the university wall, a fifteen-minute walk from campus. Mama enrolled me there in the autumn of 1962, when I was four.

Children were separated by age in the center and assigned to one of four classrooms. Each classroom was tended by two teachers. In addition to the classrooms, there was a kitchen where a daily meal was prepared. The children were served food in the classrooms. The teachers and supervisors were all women. The only man in the building was the cook, whom we called Uncle Liu.

Our day was devoted primarily to simple academic exercises—

learning to read and write Chinese characters, basic math problems, drawing, and crafts such as paper folding. Part of each day was also allotted to organized games on the playground. The children three and under played tag or amused themselves on the slide or merry-go-round or dug and built in the sandpit. The children aged four to seven played Chinese jump rope, which required improvisation, since we had no real rope. Children brought rubber bands to school and wove them into a single thick line that served as our rope. Whenever our rubber rope frayed and broke we wove it together again with newer rubber bands.

I learned to chant and count on the playground and gradually became adept at skipping over the rubber line. Soon I could skip over it without actually seeing it, by merely watching the movement of children in front of me. We learned to jump in unison and avoid getting out of step and being snagged. The play seemed nothing more than an enjoyable diversion at first. Yet in time I found that our game was an ideal preparation for what was expected of us in this world of socialist uniformity into which we had been born.

When I was enrolled in the center, I had three problems.

First, I spoke with a distinct Tianjin accent. Students and teachers were sent into fits of laughter when I spoke.

My second problem was equally distressing. I threw a ball, picked up my chopsticks and wrote with my left hand. This was forbidden. As in almost every facet of life under Communist rule, uniformity was required, even in the hand one used for activities. Everyone was required to use the right hand. Being left-handed was considered a "wrong choice" and had to be corrected. The teachers spotted my deviance. At first they removed the writing brush or chopsticks from my left hand and put them in my right, but invariably I returned them to my left hand. They started slapping my hand. "Stop that, Wu Yimao!" the teachers snapped over my shoulder. "Why can't you learn? Why can't you be like everyone else?"

Finally, in their exasperation, the teachers assigned another girl,

Qin Xiaolan, to sit beside me and watch during lunch or writing exercises. When I tried to use my left hand, she whispered, "You're doing it again, Maomao." She was patient and persistent, and gradually, with her reminders, I developed facility with my right hand. But I was never very good at calligraphy, and I have difficulty to this day manipulating chopsticks with my right hand.

My third problem could not be corrected. I was from a "black" family. Children from black families—those accused of rightist or reformist or anti-revolutionary leanings—bore the guilt of their parents. We were quarantined in our own peculiar circles. I did not become aware of my membership in this group until I first heard the words whispered by students at the center. The teachers knew my family background and carefully steered me into the circles of children from other black families. We understood we were bad seeds. Being from a black family was like carrying a contagious disease that could contaminate others through social or physical contact.

Children of "red" families—those of Party members and high-ranking university officials—formed their own closed group. They sat next to each other in classes, played together on the playground, ate together during lunch, and walked back and forth to the center together. Xiaolan was assigned to help me not simply because she was a diligent student but because she was from a black family, and it was deemed acceptable for her to have a close association with me.

I slowly overcame my initial difficulties. I learned to use my right hand to write and to hold chopsticks, and I lost my accent. I knew my family was black and there was nothing I could do about it. I accepted my new parents and my brother as my real family. When my new grandmother arrived from Beijing, I accepted her, too.

But I never forgot my Tianjin family. I thought of my grandma often. In my dreams, for a long time, I was back on Happiness Lane in Tianjin.

7

My second brother was born on July 2, 1963. Papa named him Yicun, meaning "one village." His name was taken from a poem by the classical poet Lu You. In the poem, the "one village" signified renewed hope.

The birth of another brother meant I was relegated to a less important position in the family. My father entertained a traditional Chinese conceit valuing boys more than girls. His sons were his pride and joy. His daughter was another child. He cared for me, but not as much as for my brothers.

Papa devotedly helped my older brother with his homework and doted on my younger brother. I was never asked how I was doing in school or what had happened to me each day. I wasn't questioned about my playmates. It was expected that I should fill a role of secondary importance to my brothers, that I should watch over them, take care of them, do household chores, and serve them and my parents and grandmother.

Mama taught me to sweep the floor and to wash and dry the dishes and to set the table. Papa taught me how to shop and bargain. My first solitary task was purchasing eggs and carrying them home. Papa handed me one yuan and sent me off to the nearby street markets. On the way home I watched where I walked to avoid tripping on paving stones. When I returned with unbroken eggs and a bit of change, Papa congratulated me and assigned me additional shopping duties.

I collected the milk ration for Yicun each morning. At dawn an elderly vendor riding a bicycle pulled up outside our apartment building and called out, "MILK! POUR YOUR MILK!"

When I heard the milkman's cry, I rushed downstairs carrying a small pot. I put my pot on the ground, and he handed me two bottles of milk. The top of each bottle was covered with blue-and-white waxed paper. A rubber band held the paper in place. I removed the rubber band and slipped it over my wrist and pulled off the waxed paper. Under it was a small cardboard disk sealing the mouth of the bottle. The underside of the disk was coated with slick rich cream. I removed the disk and licked it clean. I poured the milk into my pot, put the lid and paper back on the bottle and returned them to the milkman. The rubber bands I kept to make jump ropes.

Sometimes the old milkman asked wryly, "Didn't you miss a drop, little girl?" I'd stop and examine the bottle to make sure nothing more could be shaken from it, and he'd laugh. I carried the full pot up a flight of stairs, never spilling any. I learned how to light the fire in our stove with kindling and coal in order to heat the milk.

In the afternoons after I'd finished sweeping and cleaning the pots and pans, I played outside. There was a shallow sandpit beside the sports field, and I built little cities and canals and my own miniature Great Wall in the sand. I met other girls from the neighborhood who came to the sandpit, and we played together. We talked about our parents and our brothers, and I discovered they had lives like mine—the same inattention and expectations, the same duties and the same diminished status relative to our brothers. We became friends.

When I returned home from the child care center, I sometimes saw Grandmother outside watering or weeding a small vegetable garden of tomatoes, beans and turnips that she had planted between the apartment buildings. I recognized her because of the way she walked. Her movements were slow. Her feet had been bound when she was a child. This was the traditional Chinese practice of breaking and tightly wrapping a girl's feet in cotton bandages in order to keep them as small as possible. As a consequence, she hobbled around the garden with a peculiar rolling gait.

One evening when she was washing her little feet, I noticed she had six toes on her left foot. "Grandmother, why do you have six toes?" I asked her. I stared at her remarkable foot.

"It means good luck," she told me.

I examined my own feet and found only five toes. I felt along the edge of one foot to see if I might sprout another toe when I grew older, but I found nothing. I concluded I was not lucky. I asked Papa about it.

"It's an old superstition," he told me. "It means nothing, Maomao. Nothing at all."

I remembered the phrase and again asked Grandmother about it. "I know it means good luck," she insisted. "I am living with my son and his two sons. That is good luck, Maomao. That is six-toes good luck."

I asked Xiaolan and she said her mother had told her it did not mean good luck at all. "It means a cruel fate," she said.

My Hefei grandmother was not at all like my Tianjin grandma. When she came to our home, the famine was ending but there was still a food shortage. Each morning Grandmother was given an egg—a rare treat in those times—because she had diabetes and Papa said it was essential for her health. After warming the milk for my brother, I fried one egg for Grandmother. This stood the world as I'd known it in Tianjin on its head. There, Grandma had been my protector and had denied herself food in order to feed me. My mouth watered as I watched Grandmother eat.

One morning when my parents were at work and my brothers and I were home with Grandmother, I fixed her an egg and stood across from her at the table. Instead of eating it, she called my brother Yiding.

She asked him to sit beside her, and then she cut her egg into small pieces and fed them to him while I watched. I could almost taste the egg. I had leaned forward to see better when, suddenly, Grandmother stopped, looked at me sternly and snapped, "Go to the other room. This is not for girls."

It was unfair. But I learned that the best food, the best everything, in our household and others like it, was for the boys first and for the girls last.

8

Four days after Papa's decapping, on July 8, 1964, we received a telegram from Second Uncle in Tianjin. It read: "Mother sick. Come now. Hurry. Bring Maomao."

I was excited by this unexpected chance to see Grandma for the first time since my return to Hefei. I had asked often if I might visit Grandma or she might visit us. Mama responded by telling me how expensive such a trip was—costing nearly a month's salary for a single ticket—and how difficult it was for Grandma to make a long journey at her age.

We had received letters each month from Grandma and Second Uncle. Sometimes Mama called me to her side when she read them and told me, "Grandma says she misses you, Maomao." My heart skipped a beat when I heard that, and I replied, "Tell Grandma I miss her and tell her to eat all her peanuts!"

Mama packed a few items, and the next morning we boarded the train to Tianjin.

I could not stop talking during the journey. I told Mama every-thing I planned to say to Grandma, the songs I would sing to her and

FEATHER IN THE STORM

the games we would play. Mama's thoughts were elsewhere, however, and she only nodded at my words. I stayed awake most of the night looking out the window, watching the other passengers, talking to my doll, making plans for Tianjin.

We arrived at the house on Happiness Lane the next morning. Second Uncle somberly greeted us. I made my way to my old bedroom to look for Grandma. The bed was tidily made and Grandma's clothes were stacked neatly in the old wardrobe, but there was no sign of Grandma. I glanced at myself in the ancient flaking mirror and smiled and spun around, the way I used to do. I recognized the sandalwood scent of the place and the creak of the plank floor when I crossed the room.

I returned to Mama and the others, who were gathered in the foyer. Second Uncle said that Grandma had been in great pain and was taken to the hospital. She had immediately gone into surgery. "The doctor found she had liver cancer and it had spread," he said. "She was bleeding internally and the doctor said there was little he could do except try to alleviate her pain. After I heard that I sent the telegram."

Mama cried.

At the hospital, Second Uncle said, Grandma asked for me and made him promise that Mama would bring me to see her.

"It was so sudden," my second aunt added. "She was sitting talking with us, feeling fine. She was telling funny stories about Maomao. And just an hour later she was in such pain!"

A telegram had been sent to Mama's sister in faraway Changsha, Second Uncle said, summoning her to Tianjin. But a return telegram said she was unable to travel because she was about to have a baby.

———

I learned what had happened that day when my mother recounted it for me years later. Grandma had aged much in two years. She was thin and pale, her hair had turned white and she was so feeble she could barely move. She was so heavily sedated, she had difficulty keeping her eyes open.

"You're here," she whispered weakly when she recognized my mother. "Where is Maomao?"

Mama held her hand and told her I was at home, exhausted after the long train ride. "She's asleep in your bed, Mother," Mama said, her voice breaking.

"I want to see her," Grandma said.

"I'll bring her tomorrow," Mama promised.

"And how is she? Does she miss Grandma?"

"She cries for you every night."

"Does she have enough to eat?"

"Yes, Mother, she does. She has grown. She is healthy."

Mama shared the news of Papa's restoration as a teacher. Grandma was relieved. Mama said that her sister could not come from Changsha because she had given birth to a big healthy baby boy. Grandma smiled.

The day was hot and humid. The hospital had no air-conditioning or electric fans. A nurse suggested that Mama buy ice for her mother in a nearby market.

Mama left for a short time and brought back a big bowl of chipped ice. She held each piece of ice to Grandma's lips and touched it to her forehead and her arms. Mama stayed with Grandma all afternoon and evening, returning to the street two more times for ice.

At about four in the morning, Second Uncle arrived and took Mama's place at Grandma's side. I was up before anyone else that morning. I dressed and brushed my hair and washed my face and waited for Mama to get up.

Second Uncle came in the door. His eyes were swollen and red. He noticed me sitting with my doll in the early-morning light. He passed us without saying a word and hurried to the room where Mama was sleeping. There was a brief exchange and suddenly Mama screamed, "No! No! No!"

Others in the house awakened, and before long, there was crying from every room. I found Mama slumped on the edge of the bed, holding her head in her hands, sobbing.

"Can we see Grandma now?" I asked.

"No," Mama said. "We can't. Grandma passed away this morning."

I did not understand what "passed away" meant. Mama pulled me to her and held me tightly and sobbed.

I did not know what death meant. I was unaware of its finality. I'd heard Papa say to Mama that he'd "returned from the dead" when he came back from the concentration camp. I believed, therefore, that death was a temporary condition of separation. I cried with everyone else. But I hoped that soon there would be no more tears and I'd see Grandma, that she'd return from the hospital and hold me and play games with me. I waited for that day. Only slowly did I realize that I would never see her again.

A memorial service was held. We learned that my auntie in Changsha had given birth to a girl. My uncles and aunts thought this might have disappointed Grandma, which is why Mama had told her it was a boy. But I knew she would have loved another granddaughter. I knew it in my heart.

We returned to Hefei in late August. I resumed my chores in the household and was enrolled again in the child care center. Mama went back to work and Grandmother cared for my younger brother. Papa taught his classes in the university. Yiding went to school. I soon came to believe I lived in a secure world and that day followed day and season followed season without unusual disruption or disappointment. I thought if I did what was asked of me and did it well, if I was a good and obedient daughter, that the world could be a good place, even without Grandma in it.

9

In the summer of 1965, a few weeks after my seventh birthday, I began to suffer from frequent severe headaches. My joints ached and I lost my appetite. For over a week, I endured these discomforts and afflictions without complaint.

One warm afternoon, while I played with Xiaolan in the sandpit near our apartment, I was struck by a throbbing headache so severe that it made me dizzy. I pressed my hands to my head to make the pain stop. I was terrified and began to cry. Xiaolan took my hand and led me to our apartment. She ran to summon my mother from work. I crawled into my bed, pulled the mosquito net closed and waited for the pain to stop.

By the time Mama came home, the headache was accompanied by a high fever. Mama felt my forehead and asked me several questions. She bathed me with a damp cloth to bring down my temperature. I felt too sick to eat. During the night the pain decreased but the fever lingered. Early the next morning Mama dressed me and took me to the university clinic.

After a long wait a doctor examined me and told Mama, "It's just a minor viral infection. You have nothing to worry about." He prescribed an herbal medicine and sent us home. The medicine didn't work. The headaches and pain persisted and my temperature fluctuated. I told Mama I didn't feel well enough to get the milk in the morning. My brother went in my place.

When she touched my face to see if I still had a fever, I murmured, "I feel bad."

"Let's go to the clinic," she said with growing concern.

I had difficulty walking. When I got to the bottom of the stairs I began to cry. I sat on the bottom step and rested my head in my hands. "I can't go on, Mama," I said.

She retrieved a small stool from our apartment. I walked beside her for a few steps, and we stopped and Mama put the stool down and I sat on it. I walked another few steps and sat again. In this plodding fashion, we made our way to the clinic.

The doctor was unhappy to see us again and, after a cursory examination, prescribed more herbal medicine. I took the medicine to no effect, and we returned to the clinic the next day and every day after that for a week. The doctor insisted it was nothing serious. He was more annoyed with my repeated appearances than with my illness. My physical condition declined and I lost weight until I was little more than skin and bones.

One afternoon we went to the clinic and I rested on my stool in the lobby while Mama registered me. We waited until a nurse called us into an examination room where the same doctor was waiting. He frowned. "Not you again!"

Mama told him I still had difficulty eating and that my bowel movements had become white. She added that she'd heard at work that a teacher's child had contracted hepatitis B. She said she suspected I'd contracted it, too.

The doctor glared at her. "What do you know?" he huffed, his voice edged with cold indignation. "Are you a physician?"

Mama reddened.

"I'm the only one who can tell you what this little girl has," he said. "*I* am the doctor!"

Mama was quiet. I was frightened by his outburst. I wanted to leave.

The doctor dropped to his stool and proceeded to examine my body, my eyes, my ears and the inside of my mouth and my throat, and listened to my heart and my breathing.

"Look at me," he said, and I raised my face to him. "Her skin and the whites of her eyes are turning yellow. She has hepatitis B. I'm referring her to the Dashushan Contagious Disease Hospital. Take her there immediately."

"Yes," Mama said.

The doctor filled out a referral document, handed it to Mama and left.

The journey home was slow and painful. People passed us and gawked and asked, "Did you see how thin she is?" But they continued on without another word. Several times I felt I might faint and had to hold on tight to Mama's hand.

I waited at the bottom of the stairs as Mama ran to our apartment and packed clean clothes and my doll in a bag. She was required to report to work, so Papa took me to the hospital.

"Let's leave the stool here," he said. He helped me stand.

"Papa," I whispered, "I can't walk anymore."

"It's all right," he said. "I will carry you."

He knelt and told me to wrap my arms around his neck and my legs around his waist. He slung my bag over his shoulder and locked his hands together behind him to support me. He rose and leaned over so I lay at a comfortable angle on his back and I did not need to hang on tightly.

"Are you all right, Maomao?" he asked.

"I think so, Papa," I told him. "But go slowly. I hurt all over."

He set out hunched over like a man with a cumbersome bundle on his back rather than a sickly child. He carried me to the bus stop an hour's walk from our home. All the seats on the bus were taken and no one offered us one. Papa held me in his arms during the forty-minute ride. I clung to him as tightly as I could and closed my eyes. The weather was warm and I felt as if I were on fire.

The bus deposited us a short distance from Dashushan Contagious Disease Hospital, several miles outside the city, where patients were isolated from the general population.

Papa carried me into the lobby. He put me on a bench, showed the referral document to a clerk and waited.

Half an hour later a doctor appeared. He looked at me carefully, turned my face to his, looked into my eyes and mouth, and felt my neck and arms and legs. He turned and glowered at Papa. "What kind of parent are you?" he snapped.

"What do you mean?" Papa asked timidly. Others in the lobby stopped what they were doing and stared.

"I mean," he said, slowing his speech and giving emphasis to each word, "this little girl is very sick. Why didn't you bring her here earlier? How could you let your own child deteriorate to this pathetic state?"

"We took her to the university clinic every day," Papa said. "They looked at her and gave her herbal medicines and sent us home."

"Oh, don't blame someone else," the doctor grumbled: "She's your daughter. You're responsible."

"We can't do anything without a transfer permit from the clinic," Papa said, his voice rising.

The doctor paused for a moment, thought about Papa's remark and shook his head. "Okay," he said, sighing. "But I tell you . . . somebody should have known better. This is . . . not good!"

I slumped over, weak, listening to the doctor's bitter words echo up and down the hall. I was shocked and ashamed. The doctor was wrong. He didn't realize Papa had carried me on his back all the way to the hospital. My sickness wasn't Papa's fault. I had not come to the hospital earlier because of the rudeness of another doctor. It was *his* fault. If this doctor only knew the truth, if there were some way for me to tell him, I was sure he would never talk to Papa that way.

"I'll do what I can for her. But I can't promise much," the doctor said with something that sounded like sympathy. "At best, her stay here will be a long one. You can go."

Papa reached out and touched my hand. He started to say something but hesitated and bit his lip. I wanted to tell him I was sorry for getting sick. I wanted to tell him I tried to be a good daughter and not a burden. I wanted to tell him I was sorry I could not walk to the bus. But I had no energy and I could not speak. And even if I could, I really didn't know how to give voice to my pity and guilt. So I simply looked into his eyes and forced a hint of a smile.

Before Papa left, he reached into the bag and pulled out my doll and handed her to me. "Mama and I will come back soon to visit you, Maomao," he said, his voice wavering. "Be a good girl and do what they tell you."

I nodded. I listened to Papa's footsteps as he walked away, and I heard the door open and close. The doctor summoned a nurse and told her to carry me to a room.

10

The nurse took me to a small second-floor room crowded with four beds. She put me on the bed and covered me with a sheet. Three other girls in the room stared at me and whispered to one another.

The doctor told the nurse I was in the fourth stage of the disease. "I hope we can save her," he said.

I could hardly speak or swallow food when I was admitted to the hospital. For two weeks I was fed through an IV. I was given daily shots and powders and pills and tests. I took my medicine as directed and slowly regained my strength, my appetite and my voice.

Soon I found I could painlessly pull a needle from my arm when an IV bottle was empty. The other girls in the room, squeamish and averse to needles, loved to watch me remove a needle without grimacing. Sometimes, when I did, I watched their faces and smiled as they stared incredulously or shut their eyes. They came to believe I was either unusually courageous or absolutely unfeeling. I enjoyed the attention and their astonishment when they huddled around my bed and watched me deftly do the job of the doctors and nurses.

Two weeks later I was eating solid food. Not long after that I could stand and make my way to the bathroom. The nurses called me "Little Cat" because, they pointed out, I was the smallest child in the hospital; I never made a noise when I padded around, and my name sounded like the Mandarin word for "cat."

I liked the name. The doctors and nurses used it affectionately. Whenever one of them entered the room I responded to their greeting of "How's Little Cat today?" with a soft "meow."

Visitations were allowed only on Sundays. Mama and Papa took turns visiting me. They tried to bring a special treat when they came. One time Mama brought me a box of Hefei Hong cookies, which were prized for their rich taste and texture. I tasted one and found it irresistible. I might have eaten them all at that moment, but Mama asked me to save them and to eat them over the next several days. I said I would. Yet no sooner had she left than I succumbed to the temptation to eat another.

As I was about to remove one from the box, a nurse came to take my temperature and stuck the thermometer in my mouth. When she left, I pulled out a cookie and tried to bite it with the thermometer in my mouth. When I did, the thermometer shattered. I hurriedly tried to pick the slivers of glass from my mouth and spit cookie and glass and mercury onto the floor. The other girls shouted for help. When the nurse realized what I'd done, she was more alarmed than I was.

After she removed the mercury and glass from my mouth and was sure I had not swallowed anything, the nurse joked with the other girls, telling them that they had better watch me because I had become so hungry I was even eating thermometers. "You are an unusual little cat," she said. "You pull out your needles and you eat thermometers and you are hungry all the time."

I responded, naturally, with my customary "meow."

I made friends with some of the adult patients once I was able to walk around the ward. They were happy to see me and sometimes gave me treats and told me stories. I explored the hospital and found it to be incredibly filthy, just like my room. Each time I moved a tray or a towel, cockroaches scurried out. The cockroaches, however, were not as frightening as the rats that came out in the dark. Late one night the other girls in the room awakened me with terrified screaming. I bolted upright and saw all three girls huddled in one bed, the sheets pulled up high around their faces. They pointed to the far side of the room where I saw, in the moonlight, a score of fat rats moving in an orderly column along the wall and out the door. They were so bold, even the screams didn't faze them. They proceeded with military precision, each a few inches behind the one in front of him, just as if they were supposed to be in the room—as if they were landlords and we were intruders.

"Don't be afraid," I said, "they're just rats. Leave them alone and they'll leave us alone. We had lots of them in our basement in Tianjin."

One of the older girls said, "Of course you're not afraid. You're a little cat and cats are not afraid of rats."

"You're right," I said and let out a loud meow toward the rats. The girls clung to one another and giggled nervously. But after several seconds they lost a bit of their fear and scooted together to the foot of the bed, leaned far over the rail and, following my example, meowed. Our kitten quartet grew louder. Occasionally a rat paused and flicked an annoyed glance our way. When that happened, the other girls stiffened and went silent, but not me. I meowed even louder. The rats sensed nothing ominous in the noise and went on with their business.

We stayed awake for a while waiting to see if they might reappear. And they did. The same little long-tailed gang materialized at the door carrying pieces of food or garbage or dragging a dirty bandage behind them. They crossed the room defiantly and made their way through a crack near the bottom of the wall and disappeared.

I attempted to talk the other girls into overcoming their fear. But they remained terrified whenever they spotted the nocturnal trespassers and insisted that I take command of the defense of our room. My fearlessness never failed to restore their courage.

What did disturb me during my stay in the hospital and remained with me was the dead body I saw one warm Saturday afternoon.

My roommates and I were wandering around our ward when we heard a commotion followed by screaming and wailing downstairs. We ran to the stairwell to see what was happening. We saw a man lying on a table in the lobby. Several doctors and nurses surrounded him. They were frantically pushing on his chest and clearing his mouth and shouting at him. Around the doctors and nurses was another circle—this one of children, all of them small, crying and screaming hysterically. We began to descend the stairs to get a better look, but a nurse ordered us to go back to our room. We scurried up the stairs to the landing and huddled together and watched.

I saw a woman about my mother's age. She was crying and screaming louder than anyone else. The doctors worked on the man for perhaps fifteen minutes, then stopped and looked at one another and shook their heads. They covered him with a sheet. The woman and the children moaned and screamed, and the woman attempted to touch the man, but she was pulled away from him and led from the lobby. One of the nurses wheeled the table with the body down the hall.

Later that day, when we asked a nurse what had happened, she told us that there was a reservoir near the hospital. Two boys had been swimming there with their father. A part of the dam that formed the reservoir had come loose. The hole in the dam created a strong undercurrent. When the children swam near the hole, they were pulled under the water and held against the stones. Their father rushed to rescue them and pulled the children to safety, but he was too exhausted to save himself. He was sucked against the dam and drowned.

It was the first time I'd seen a dead person. The man looked peaceful, as if he were asleep. And what slowly registered in my mind was the dedication of this man for his children. He'd given his life for them. When I asked the nurse further about the incident, she said, "He died for his sons."

I was deeply affected by the episode and for many days afterward could hear the children—the little boys and girls wailing for their poor drowned father.

My roommates and I talked about it. One girl said she'd seen a nurse sitting on a chair in the lobby crying later that afternoon. When I saw how hard the doctors and nurses worked to help people, I liked them more, even the doctor who had scolded Papa. I remembered that no one would give me a seat on the bus when I came to the hospital. The anger of the doctor at Papa, I concluded, came not so much from his dislike of Papa as from his concern for my health. This was new to me. My roommates and I came to share a deep affection for the doctors and nurses who cared for us. We felt almost like a family with them. Perhaps that was why, as my health improved, I did not really look forward to leaving the hospital.

One by one my roommates were discharged. Finally, after sixty days, it was my turn. The doctor said I was well enough to leave. Papa came to get me. As we left, the nurses came to say goodbye to their "Little Cat." I wanted to cry. Instead, I just waved to them. Then, in my sadness, I remembered something. Just before the door swung closed behind me, I turned and gave a very long and gentle "meooooooow."

All the doctors and nurses clapped their hands and laughed.

II

That autumn I was enrolled in first grade at Meishanlu Elementary School. When I was not working or studying, I played with Xiaolan and other friends and told them about my stay in the hospital.

One thing was delightfully different at home after my return from the hospital. In my absence, Papa had initiated a nightly ritual of telling stories to my brothers. He placed my younger brother in the crib and pulled a chair next to it, and my older brother sat on a stool beside him. Papa turned off the light and told his tales in the dark.

I brought a stool to sit next to him. But Papa refused to let me stay. "This is for the boys, Maomao," he said. "Go to your room."

I strained to listen from the next room. Grandmother and Mama sat on my brother's bed talking or reading. Some nights Mama fell asleep waiting for Papa to finish his tales, and he gently awakened her and laid my brother in his bed and led Mama from the room.

After a while I discovered a way to get closer to the nighttime ritual. After washing the dishes and putting them away, while my older brother was studying and Papa was working, I took my blanket and crawled under my brother's crib. There, huddled tightly against the wall, wrapped in the blanket, I remained still and nobody noticed my presence.

Papa was a superb storyteller. I was enthralled by his sonorous recitations, his voice rising and falling and his tone changing as he created compelling narratives for his sons. Sometimes, when a story was funny, I clamped my hand over my mouth to smother a laugh, while my brothers hooted uncontrollably an arm's length away. In the shaft of light from the next room, I watched Papa's slippers dance and saw my older brother's feet shift back and forth. Above me was the intermittent squeak of the crib springs as my younger brother rolled from side to side. We were enchanted, especially when Papa spoke in the voice of a character. We fell helplessly and blissfully under his magical spell.

Some of Papa's stories were traditional Chinese tales that we heard in school, but never as compelling as he told them. *The Journey to the West,* the saga of the Monkey King, was a favorite. But my brothers and I loved most the stories he brought back from his student years in America. What was spellbinding about them was not so much the characters' adventures as their strange and funny-sounding names.

One of my early favorites was "The Pearl." He'd translated the story from English into Chinese, and his translation was widely used in classrooms in China. "Once upon a time," he began, "there was a happy family. A papa named Kino, a mama named Juana, and a little baby named Coyotito."

As he said each name, my brothers giggled.

"Say the names again, Papa," my older brother begged.

"Kino and Juana and Coyotito, the baby."

We did not understand the story but we loved the names, especially Coyotito. I had no idea what a pearl was or why it should be of great value or cause people to be happy or unhappy. But that made no difference. I adored any story about a happy family with funny names.

Papa could shorten or lengthen a story as he wished, depending on when in the evening he began it. Not until years later did I learn that

"The Pearl" did not have a happy ending and that little Coyotito died. Papa left that out. In fact, he left a lot out; he used only the names from the book and made adventures we might easily understand. With stories like that, all three of us slept peacefully in a world of happy endings.

When he was finished with a story, Papa would put my older brother back in our room. I would scurry from beneath the crib and wait in the darkness of the kitchen or against the wall in the hallway while he returned with Mama to his room and I found my way to my bed in the dark.

Papa also told us tales from *David Copperfield* and *Oliver Twist,* which enchanted us. But my favorite, by far, was *Huckleberry Finn.* I loved the story more than any other because it was about a black man and his family. We were a black family. We were mistreated and distrusted and watched, and when anything went amiss, we were blamed. I did not understand, but there was no need to understand any more than there was a need to understand hunger or disease or death. They just were.

The stories we heard in school were about red families and heroes. But at home, Papa told us about a heroic black man and his black family. I was so delighted by this that I repeated the stories about Huckleberry Finn and Black Jim to Xiaolan, who was inspired by them, too.

Papa described Huckleberry and Black Jim floating on a raft down the Mississippi River in America. We loved words like Huckleberry, Polly, Jim, and, of course, that most magical and musical of all words, Mississippi. My brothers asked Papa to say every unfamiliar word again and again, and each time he did, they'd laugh. I smothered my own giggles until tears ran down my cheeks.

When Papa described the boy and the black man on a raft on the river, I imagined it was the story of a boy with a father who was very much like Papa, escaping from somewhere bad to somewhere good, and I delighted in that familiar theme. I wanted the story to go on forever. One night Papa said the raft finally carried Huckleberry and Jim all the way to Chicago, where they went ashore and enrolled in the University of Chicago.

That thrilled me. I loved the way Papa translated the word "Chicago." He pronounced it *zhi jia ge,* which in Mandarin literally means "Big Brother." The words warmed me and made that distant city sound like a nice person. My big brother, Yiding, and I were developing a special bond. He accompanied me around the campus, played with me in the sandpit and on the playground. So it comforted me to learn that Huckleberry found a big brother at that university as well. The selection of Chicago was not mere whimsy. Papa had lived there for three years while he worked on his Ph.D. at the University of Chicago. He sometimes talked about the city with affection and pride.

Papa went on and on, often losing himself in his words. There were nights after my brothers had fallen asleep when he'd continue his recitation as if he knew I was under the crib listening. At other times Papa sat quietly and didn't say anything for a long time. On those nights I lay on the floor unseen, hearing my younger brother breathing above me. After a while, Papa would move his chair away from the crib. I'd hear the paper crinkle as he fished a cigarette from a pack, and I'd hear him remove a wooden match from a small box and strike it. After lighting his cigarette, Papa would pour himself a cup of wine and sit smoking and drinking.

From my hiding place I followed the glow of the cigarette dancing in the dark like a lazy firefly. Papa would smoke one cigarette after another and rock back and forth in his chair. After drinking several glasses of wine he'd hum or sing softly, slurring his words. When he tired of this, he'd sit quietly. Then the silence would be broken by sudden sobbing. Sometimes he recited the names of men he knew during his years in the concentration camp. I knew the names because I'd heard him telling Mama about the men. "I helped bury them," he told her. "I can never forget them. I put each of them in the frozen earth in the dead of winter."

He told Mama they came back to him in his dreams. They called to him, and he could hear their voices and see their frozen tears when they spoke of their families far away. "They were younger and stronger than me," he moaned. "But they died and I lived . . . Why? So much of life makes no sense."

If Papa had known I was in the room, he would have spanked me. He didn't want me to hear his stories and he didn't want me to know his private pain. But I did hear and know. Just me. Night after night.

I understood little except that this was another face of Papa. When he thought he was alone at night, he removed the mask he wore in the light and I saw him not only as Papa but also as a secretly sad and haunted man.

One phrase that he repeated mystified me. I wanted to ask him about it but could not without revealing I'd been in the room with him. The phrase was "It's not over. It's coming . . . I see it." Sometimes he said it with resignation. Sometimes with regret. Sometimes with fear, and sometimes with something like humor, but in a strange unfunny way.

I imagined that Papa looked out the window one evening and saw someone in the street outside. Whoever it was looked up and saw him before he stepped away from the window. Now this person knew where we lived. Now maybe he was crouching at the bottom of the stairs. Waiting.

I wanted to scream and run away. I had no idea what to do. Even worse, I concluded, neither did Papa.

I told Xiaolan what Papa said. I asked what she thought it meant. She said she'd never heard her parents use the phrase but she didn't think it was about anything bad.

Papa didn't know that during those nights he had a secret sharer listening to his stories, his memories, his sorrows, his songs and his sobs. He never knew that his daughter lay beneath his son's crib, like a trapped angel or a cornered god, unable to do anything but listen and wonder.

12

On the night of January 20, 1966, Papa toasted the arrival of the Year of the Horse. He raised his cup of wine and proclaimed, "To a year of changes. Everything is going to get better." The rest of us at the table responded by raising our teacups and chorusing agreement.

"The Year of the Horse—that means . . . happy times," Mama added.

We took turns describing the changes we wished for. But Grandmother cautioned, "The Year of the Horse also bring chaos and turbulence. We must not forget that." Her words cast a momentary pall over our celebration. But Papa responded, "This may be true, Mother. But we will hope for the best."

Yiding jumped to his feet, poked me in the ribs and shouted, "Happy times! Happy times!" and ran away. I leaped from my stool and chased him down the corridor while Yicun, laughing loudly, followed close on my heels. We ran in and out of the bedroom and chased one another in a circle until we fell in a heap on the floor, tickling one another and laughing uncontrollably.

At midnight we went outside and ignited a string of firecrackers. We giggled and screamed and covered our ears as red and yellow flashes punctured the darkness and explosions echoed off nearby buildings. Our neighbors were also outside celebrating. I saw Xiaolan and her parents huddled together nearby, lighting firecrackers. I waved and shouted "Happy New Year" during a lapse in the noise. She heard me and did a playful little dance and waved back.

In mid-May the Central Committee of the Communist Party issued a call for a Great Proletarian Cultural Revolution. Chairman Mao denounced Party officials who were "following the capitalist road" and cautioned against "counterrevolutionary revisionists" within the Party. The moment had come for purging the Party, he said, for eliminating enemies of the state and their ideas.

A huge poster was put up on a wall on the campus of Beijing University, calling on all students to "resolutely, thoroughly, cleanly and completely eliminate all demons and monsters, and counter-revolutionary revisionists." The *People's Daily*, official organ of the Communist Party, printed the text of the poster and called on true revolutionaries to embrace the leadership of Chairman Mao. Those who opposed him, the paper declared, must be struck down.

Students in other universities and high schools rallied in support. They accused teachers and administrators and local government officials of opposition to Chairman Mao. Revolutionary committees were organized to coordinate and carry out a new revolution.

Our hopes for better times faded as quickly as the pop of firecrackers on New Year's Eve.

On the morning of June 1, following the radio broadcast describing the excitement in Beijing, students at Anhui University suspended classes, formed revolutionary committees and seized control of the campus.

Papa walked to his literature seminar early that morning to find an empty classroom. He went upstairs searching for his students. He found them packed into a room heatedly debating "revolution" and composing posters.

He reported the situation to the chairman of his department. The chairman advised, "The only thing to do is to wait in your classroom for the students to return. If they don't return today, they will tomorrow, and if not tomorrow, then next week. Be patient. This whole thing will blow over in a short time."

Papa returned to his classroom and sat at a desk. Overhead he heard the thunder of footsteps rushing back and forth and excited outbursts of singing and strident chanting. He gazed out the window and listened and worried. He paged through his lecture notes and replaced them in a folder. At the end of the hour he came home.

The next morning he proceeded to his classroom, and his students did not appear. He came home before the full hour passed.

On Friday he did not go to his class.

Classes were suspended for the next several years at Anhui University. The only times Papa faced his students after June 1 were when they dragged him from our apartment to beat him and denounce him or cage him up with other faculty members in dormitory rooms from which they extracted him periodically for further abuse.

The Great Proletarian Cultural Revolution had come to Hefei.

13

On the morning of June 4—a Saturday and the day after my eighth birthday—I arose early and went to a nearby market to do the family grocery shopping. Despite the early hour, scores of students scurried about, huddled in small groups and conferring excitedly. Several large posters had been affixed to the walls of campus buildings and students gathered in front of them.

When I returned home, several thousand students and outsiders crowded the campus sidewalks and lawns, shouting, singing and reading aloud. The disturbances that began on Wednesday had become a mania. A typhoon of noise and activity swirled around me. Students rushed by, their eyes fixed on the walls where posters had just been displayed or where people were congregating. I recognized some of Papa's students.

Posters were pasted on every building, tree and utility pole on campus. The wall around the campus had been transformed into an unbroken palisade of posters. Wire and rope had been strung between trees, poles and buildings. Reed mats were tied to them and posters affixed to the mats. Most posters were the size of two or three newspaper pages. But some were as big as bedsheets, constructed from a dozen newspaper pages. Each was filled from top to bottom with bold red-and-black slogans, discourses, accusations, revelations, caricatures and cartoons.

I navigated my way through the turbulent sea of enthusiasts and carried the groceries to our apartment. After I'd put away the food I returned to campus and wandered through the crowd looking, reading and listening.

I was jostled by students eager to get closer to some poster or to move on to another. Students gushed in a steady stream from buildings where they constructed and composed posters, the ink dripping from the trailing paper and sprinkling the sidewalks, grass and bystanders. My bare feet were soon speckled with red and black. The shirts and trousers of students were doused in ink, and their forearms and hands were stained. A group wedged its way through the mass, crying frantically, "Out of the way! Out of the way!" They held a freshly composed poster high above their heads. Once they found an open slot, they hurriedly put up their composition and began reading it to the crowd.

At first I thought everyone participating in this activity must be having fun. It looked and sounded like a gigantic playground for adults. But soon I was struck by the fact that none of the participants was smiling or laughing. When students at my school made posters, it was fun.

Many posters proclaimed devotion to Chairman Mao and demanded implementation of the new Party policy of eradicating the Four Olds—old thought, old culture, old customs and old habits. Others, more strident, demanded that the people "sweep away all cow demons and snake spirits"—a phrase resurrected from Chinese myth to describe enemies of the people. The new demons and spirits were landlords, rich peasants, reactionaries, bad elements, rightists, traitors, spies, capitalist roaders and the running dogs who supported them. Prominent among running dogs were academics, who, it was revealed, used classrooms and the press to undermine the revolution in order to restore the rule of the Nationalists and capitalist exploiters. "The intelligentsia fancy themselves the nation's brain," one poster proclaimed. "In fact, they are not the brain but the shit."

After an hour of watching students tear down old posters and put up new ones, I found myself standing before a poster that struck me with dread. My heart began beating so hard I feared those standing around me might hear it. The poster showed a large crouching tiger with a man's face and long fangs. Blood dripped from the open mouth. The caption proclaimed, WU NINGKUN, THE PAPER TIGER ISN'T DEAD.

The drawing exaggerated Papa's black-rimmed spectacles and the mane of hair combed straight across his forehead. An American flag was painted on his cheek. I quickly stepped to the next poster only to find yet another ugly caricature of Papa. One accused him of undermining the socialist spirit of his students by assigning bourgeois texts. Yet another condemned his use of *Gulliver's Travels* and *The Great Gatsby*.

An entire series of posters alleged that Papa used radio broadcasts to undermine student faith in the Communist Party. He had indeed been given clearance to use excerpts of broadcasts from the BBC and VOA in addition to Radio Beijing for listening comprehension courses. Because it was a crime to listen to "enemy broadcasts," the local Bureau of Public Security had to extend special permission for Papa to make recordings from the broadcasts. He was the only former "enemy of the people" in Hefei granted such permission. Yet now he was under suspicion for making the recordings, and the administrators who had helped him gain access were also in trouble.

Beneath the smiling tiger caricature was an explanation of why Papa, despite his decapping, remained an enemy of the people. "Wu Ningkun," it read, "has a criminal past. As early as 1943 he worked as an interpreter for the Imperial American Flying Tigers and the Nationalist Air Force. During his eight-year stay in the United States he was secretly trained as a spy. Under the disguise of a professor of English, he came back to teach at Yenching University in 1951. His crime was exposed when he was denounced as an ultra-rightist and sent to prison on April 17, 1958."

I had known only that Papa was away when I was small and that he had spent three years in concentration camps in northeast China. I was not even sure what a concentration camp was.

I glanced around as I read, fearing that someone might recognize me and point me out as the daughter of the man on the poster, raise an accusatory finger and detain me. I wanted a gust of wind to blow away these posters. I wanted a rainstorm to wash out the hateful words and pictures. I wanted everyone around me to stop reading and go home and forget what they'd seen. As I slipped toward the rear of the crowd, I could not hold back my tears. I shielded my eyes with my open hand. Suddenly, out of nowhere, someone grasped my shoulder. I looked up to see one of Papa's students, a young man who had visited our apartment. Half a dozen others stood with him in a semicircle, watching me. They were all smiling.

"You can read this, can't you?" asked the student holding me. He pointed to the nearest poster.

"No," I responded timidly.

He pointed to the characters near the bottom of the poster and read them aloud: OUR GREAT LEADER CHAIRMAN MAO SAID THE U.S. IMPERIALISTS AND REACTIONARIES ARE PAPER TIGERS.

I stared at the poster and said nothing.

"Don't be afraid," he said, and the others chimed in. "We are your friends. Wu Ningkun is your enemy."

The lead student spoke solicitously. "You love Chairman Mao. We love Chairman Mao. We are comrades. All of us."

Another whispered into his ear, and he beamed and said, "Come with us. We'll help you make a poster like this. You'd like that, wouldn't you?"

I was too frightened to say no.

A student took my hand firmly in hers and led me through the crowd. Those escorting me chattered enthusiastically about the poster they planned to construct. One of them asked, "Are you a revolutionary or an anti-revolutionary?"

I knew the only correct answer to that question and responded meekly, "A revolutionary."

Everyone laughed.

On the second floor of their dormitory stood a tall stack of old newspapers. Someone had lined up several large pots of black and red ink. The student leader said, "Yimao, little revolutionary, you are going to make a poster denouncing your father."

"I don't know how to do that," I said, my voice quivering.

"We'll show you," he said.

The students unfolded newspaper pages and pasted them together into a single large sheet. One student dipped a brush in the black ink and handed it to me. "I'll help you," he said and grasped my wrist and guided the movement of my hand to make the large characters. As our locked hands made each stroke of a character, he pronounced it. Together we wrote, DOWN WITH THE COW DEMON, SNAKE SPIRIT, COUNTERREVOLUTIONARY, SMILING PAPER TIGER, ULTRA-RIGHTIST, U.S. SPY, WU NINGKUN! LONG LIVE THE GREAT LEADER CHAIRMAN MAO!

At the bottom of the poster we signed my name, Wu Yimao.

The other students read it aloud approvingly.

Two students carefully picked up the poster, and we proceeded out onto campus. They put up my poster. A crowd quickly gathered to read it.

The students lost interest in me, and I pushed my way through the crowd and returned home, troubled by what had happened. I prayed that Papa and Mama would not see my poster and that no one would tell them about it. I hoped someone would soon paste another over it.

At dinner Yiding said he had seen the posters on campus, and he asked Papa what snake spirits and cow demons were. Papa explained, "They're nothing. You shouldn't worry about them."

I sensed at that moment that my father had seen my poster. I wanted to confess everything, to tell him all I'd done and that I was sorry, and that they had made me do it. But I did not have the courage. I stared at the table and clenched my teeth.

14

Mass rallies were held every night. Students sang revolutionary songs and marched through campus pounding on drums and cymbals while chanting slogans. The incessant nocturnal cacophony kept us awake. The admiring and attentive students who once crowded Papa's classes and called him "Mr. Chips" seemed transformed overnight into a crowing and hateful herd. The nearby thunder of their rallies sent chills of fear through me.

Before long, militant students became bolder and began seizing those they termed "class enemies," dragging them to the university's athletic grounds for public interrogation and punishment. They vowed to expose every enemy of the people.

They came for Papa on the night of June 6.

As their boisterous procession neared our building, the windows rattled with the resonance of their poisonous invective and bluster. Then, all of a sudden, the shouting and drumming ceased. A single voice barked out orders. The crowd exploded with a cry: "DOWN WITH WU NINGKUN. DOWN WITH THE U.S. SPY."

The monster I'd imagined, the one Papa cried about night after night, was now downstairs screaming his name. The door to the building crashed open, followed by a rumble of footsteps rushing up the stairs. I wanted to run and hide. Where? I wanted to fly away. How? There was pounding on our door. Several voices cried together, "Let us in or we'll break your door down, you filthy American spy!"

Grandmother parted her mosquito net, slipped from her bed and hobbled through the dark to the door. The moment she unbolted the door, it was flung open as if by a blast of wind. Students scrambled through the door and ran down the hall. A student switched on the light in our room and screamed, "Where is the bastard Wu Ningkun?"

I recognized Chen Congde. He'd visited our apartment many times to speak with Papa and receive tutoring. Papa told us he was from a "good peasant" background but was slow, so he'd been assigned to Papa for special help. Our eyes met for a moment. He was a startling contrast to that of the deferential self-conscious student I'd known. "I am the head of the Cultural Revolution Committee," he shrieked. "Where is that archcriminal Wu Ningkun hiding?"

From the next room came a cry: "We have him!"

Chen Congde rushed to the next room. Two students seized Papa by the arms and hair and shouted, "Come with us, you spy!"

Papa appeared at the door, held tightly by students. He was wearing only boxer shorts and a T-shirt. He was barefoot.

My throat constricted, and I let out a long desperate cry: "*Papa!*" My brother clung to me tightly, crying. Grandmother stood pinned against the wall by an enraged student. All the color had drained from her face. Her lips moved but her words stuck in her throat.

"Don't be afraid, Maomao," Papa said, turning to me. "I will be back soon."

He forced a brave smile just before a student grasped the back of his neck and gave him a violent push. Papa stumbled out of my sight. There was an eruption of shouting and cheering outside when those who'd invaded our apartment appeared with Papa. A dozen professors who had been seized earlier were held by the crowd. Papa joined the group and the mob departed, pounding their drums and cymbals and triumphantly bearing the professors as their prizes.

They proceeded to the university athletic grounds where nearly four thousand students had gathered for the spectacle. The professors were lined up on the basketball court and forced to their knees. They were spat upon, slapped, slugged, kicked and punched by their tormentors. Chen Congde frequently interrupted the rough treatment to proclaim his contempt for Papa. He finished each of his diatribes by slapping Papa hard across the face.

Papa and his colleagues were designated "cow demons" by their captors. Chen Congde proclaimed in a piercing voice that it was beyond question that the cow demons had conspired to overthrow the socialist revolution and the dictatorship of the proletariat. But their plans had been foiled when the students joined together and rose up to crush the counterrevolution.

The hysteria of the denunciations increased by the minute. Then, almost as quickly as it began, it ended. The students broke into the chant: "Long live the great leader Chairman Mao! Long, long live the great leader Chairman Mao!" Chen Congde led the cheer and pumped his fist in the air with each repetition. When he was finished, he smirked at the kneeling professors and then sauntered away.

The students dispersed and left the cow demons kneeling on the ground. One by one they stood, some with difficulty. Without a word to one another, they, too, trudged through the night back to their apartments.

———

I lay staring into the darkness, listening to the voices and drums in the distance. When they stopped, I could hear the beating of my heart. Mama came to my bedside, holding my little brother, to assure us that everything would be all right. A short time later, I heard shuffling outside and then through the mesh of my mosquito net saw Papa's hunched shadow.

"What happened?" Mama asked.

"Nothing," he said and gave a tired chuckle. "I have to show up for political study tomorrow morning at eight. But I'm not alone anymore. The entire department consists of criminals and suspects now. We are all equally cow demons."

The next morning I watched Papa as he prepared to depart. The side of his face was swollen and bruised, and he had difficulty walking, as if his feet had been bound when he was young.

Forty faculty members were herded into a classroom to hear a Party official warn them of the grave nature of their crimes. The official waved his fist and proclaimed, "The student action last night was warranted. You brought this down on yourselves. Your plans to restore a bourgeois society have been revealed and smashed."

His harangue was met by cowed silence. The accused were commanded to go home and compose confessions telling how the beatings by the students had touched them "to their very souls" and to reveal why they were deserving of the beatings. "The students rescued you from the commission of additional crimes. They deserve your praise. Bring your confessions tomorrow at eight a.m."

Papa went empty-handed to the next session. The other professors had obediently composed long confessions. These were not collected. The Party official asked for a discussion of what had happened on the basketball court. One after another, professors agreed that what had happened was wonderful. "The students woke us up and reminded us of how heinous our crimes are," said one elderly professor. The others—with the exception of Papa—chorused assent. Another volunteered, "We are all criminals. The students were correct to do what they did. In fact, they were far more lenient than they should have been, and I am grateful for that."

Papa listened with increasing despondency.

"In fact," the confessing professor gushed, "we deserve to be shot! Each and every one of us deserves to be shot!"

His words were followed by a cry of agreement from the others.

Some were clearly dismayed that they had not been the first to offer to be shot.

"We must make up for our crimes against the people," a female professor interjected. "We must make up for our crimes and . . . and . . . make up for the fact that we have failed the students and . . . and we have failed the people."

"Yes! Yes!" the others exclaimed.

The Party official commended their self-condemnation. "Very good. Excellent, in fact. Just excellent."

The meeting was interrupted by an announcement over the public address system that university officials had been relieved of their duties and the administration of the school was to be taken over by a working committee of the People's Liberation Army (PLA).

Before dismissing the professors, the Party official directed, "You all did very well today. Now go home and write down your confessions." He'd forgotten that he'd already given that assignment. The next day the professors gathered, but the Party official did not show up. Each professor, with the exception of Papa, carried his expanded confession and expressed eagerness to present it.

Mama's work group also devoted itself to daily political study and confessions. Routine academic activities were suspended and forgotten. In the following days a large number of soldiers moved onto campus and assumed administration of the university. Soldiers also moved into posts throughout the city of Hefei and took charge of the government.

With the onset of summer vacation, however, nearly all the students departed from campus, and the flame of revolution in Hefei seemed to have been nearly extinguished.

15

Students crowded onto trains that summer, as transportation was free. They traveled around the country visiting historic revolutionary sites and seeing how students were making revolution in other parts of China. Some young red faculty members joined them. A mandatory destination was Beijing, where the Cultural Revolution was born and where Chairman Mao, the "reddest, reddest sun of our hearts," presided. The students rallied there by the hundreds of thousands, read and composed posters, exchanged ideas and stoked their enthusiasm for revolution.

Papa was "recapped" as a rightist. He told Mama that all faculty members and administrators were suspect. Capped or uncapped, no one knew what fate awaited him. My parents spoke in lower tones, as if they feared being overheard by someone listening in the hallway or outside. Grandmother was tense and nervous. She jumped at the slightest noise. At night she sat on her bed and stared at the wall, lost in confusion and fear.

My older brother spent hours playing chess against himself. Some-times I watched him and envied his ability to lose himself so completely in the game. My younger brother constantly clung to our father or mother.

I feared our home might be invaded again. I had nightmares.

The soldiers on campus and in the city provided some sense of security. The PLA was the champion of the people. The sight of a soldier was always reassuring. They could be depended upon, I believed, to maintain order and prevent injustice. I was taught that soldiers were heroes. I envied children from red families who might someday become PLA soldiers.

During the third week of June I began to suffer from a severe toothache. I didn't want to bother Mama or Papa with my problem. I examined my mouth in the mirror and found a blackened tooth at the back with the gum swollen around it. I tried to pull the tooth out with my fingers but it would not budge. I asked Xiaolan to help me, but she was unable to extract it. I decided to visit a dentist.

The next morning I set out for the city's only dental hospital. It was several miles away, in the downtown area of Hefei. I had only enough money for a one-way bus ride. I decided to take the bus to the dental hospital to make sure I got in line early for treatment. I planned to walk home. After asking around, I located the large facility. I hurried inside, waited in line, paid my five-fen fee, and after an hour was summoned to a cavernous room with many dental chairs, nurses and dentists. I'd dressed nicely that morning in my red-and-black-checked blouse and black trousers. I wanted to look like a responsible girl.

"Why are you here?" the nurse asked.

"My tooth hurts," I said, opening my mouth and pointing inside. She said a dentist would take care of it.

I was surrounded by patients being tended by dentists. Some of them were moaning as the dentists worked on them. I began to feel anxious. A dentist came to my chair. He examined the tooth. "It's rotting away," he concluded. "I should remove it."

"That's okay," I assured him.

He cautioned, "This will hurt. You can come back another time with your mother."

"I'd like it fixed now," I insisted.

"You're a brave girl," he said with surprise. He told the nurse to give me a shot of Novocain, and he waited for it to take effect. Neither the dentist nor the nurse was skilled. Several times they tried and failed to pull out the tooth. The dentist moved from one side of the chair to the other and traded places with the nurse. He tried to get the tooth from the new angle and, after another failure, finally succeeded. I didn't make a sound. The dentist held up the extracted tooth for me to see.

"Keep the area around the tooth clean," he instructed me. The nurse told me to rinse my mouth over a basin and put a cotton ball in the hole to stop the bleeding. Before I left, she gave me a small bag of clean cotton balls to use later. I was dizzy. I sat down outside the clinic for several minutes before I began my long walk home. I often felt inside my mouth to see if the cotton was saturated. Whenever it was I replaced it.

The day had become hot and humid, and heavy dark clouds hung in the summer sky. I was surprised by the ominous rumble of thunder and glanced up to see a single iridescent strand of lightning silver the air. I hurried, hoping to get home before the storm broke. I was caught in a heavy downpour. People darted past me, covering their heads with folded newspapers. My sandals sloshed and splashed as I walked along the flooded sidewalk.

I remembered a shortcut on a path through a wooded area. I decided to take it. I turned on to one of the dirt paths leading through the area, staying close to the edge so the tall pines shielded me from the rain. As I neared the university I started singing a popular tune praising the PLA.

Uncle PLA is good!
Carries long guns.
Shoots big cannons.

Trains to fight,
Day and night.
Defend securely,
Motherland's gate.

As I hurried along, jumping over puddles, I was startled by a man—a PLA soldier—who appeared suddenly out of nowhere. One moment I was walking alone, and the next he was beside me. He was tall and somber. He held out an umbrella to shield me from the rain. I was surprised but not afraid because he was a soldier and he served the people.

"I heard you singing," he said. "Where did you learn that song, little friend?"

"In school," I replied, looking up at him and brushing rain-drenched hair out of my eyes.

"That's good," he said and patted me on the head. "Where are you going?"

"I am on my way home, Uncle PLA."

"And do your parents know where you are?"

"No, Uncle PLA."

He glanced around as if looking for someone.

"How old are you?"

"Eight."

He was silent for several seconds. At last he said, "I may have something for a revolutionary little singer." He reached into his pocket and pulled out a large metal disk. "Do you like this?"

It was a badge with a raised silver profile of the Great Leader Chairman Mao Zedong. Badges like this had become popular during recent weeks. They were highly prized. I'd seen ones like it on the shirts of the students and faculty and red-family children. But this one was bigger and more ornate than any I'd seen before.

"I like it very much, Uncle PLA."

"Would you like to keep it?" he asked and thrust it into my hand.

"Yes, I would, Uncle PLA," I said. "But I have no—" A clap of thunder interrupted my words.

"You don't have what?" he asked, cupping his hand to his ear and leaning closer.

"Money!" I said.

"You don't have money?" he asked. "Well, what can be done about that?"

I didn't know what to say, so I waited for him to answer his own question.

"Come here." He took me by the arm and led me off the path and into the trees, where we were better protected from the rain by a thick canopy of branches. He folded his umbrella and put it down. "Now, that's better," he said. "You want this beautiful Chairman Mao badge but you don't have money for it, is that right?"

"Yes."

He leaned closer, his face nearly touching mine, and stared into my eyes. I felt uncomfortable with his closeness and with the breeze of his breath on my face. I turned my head aside and looked at the trees.

"What is wrong with your mouth?" he asked.

"I had my tooth pulled."

"Let me see," he said, taking my wrist and leading me a few steps farther into the trees. "Show me where the bad tooth was." He dropped to his knees on the pine needles. I opened my mouth wide and pointed to the space where the rotten tooth had been.

He put his hand on my shoulder and peered into my mouth. "That looks all right," he said. "But is the rest of you all right?"

"I think so," I said.

"Well, let's see," he said.

"What—?" I began to ask. But quickly, deftly, before I knew what he was doing, he untied my trousers and let them drop, pulled my underwear aside and slipped his fingers between my legs. His other hand darted from my shoulder to my neck and his fingers tightened around my throat. "Don't make a sound," he hissed. "I need to see if you are all right."

I tried to pull away but he held me fast. Fear exploded inside me. His grip on my throat choked me, and his fingers between my legs hurt me. I squirmed and squeezed my legs together tightly and attempted to free myself. I couldn't breathe. My face flushed hot. My eyes burned and my vision clouded. The more I struggled, the tighter he grasped my neck.

I managed a desperate squeal. I flailed and struck his wrist and clawed desperately at the sleeve of his tunic.

"Ouch!" he shouted and released me. He looked in disbelief at his wrist, which was streaked with blood.

I stumbled back and clutched my trousers but before I could tie them, his hand shot out and grabbed my shirt and jerked me to him. He pressed his hand over my mouth and ordered, "Don't move!"

I whimpered and gasped for air. I was sobbing, terrified. The soldier stood, towering over me. The knees of his trousers were damp and soiled. Blood covered his hand and fingers. He pulled out a handkerchief and wiped it away. He glowered at me menacingly as I tugged at my trousers and rubbed my throat. He held out his bloody hand and said, "Look what you did to Uncle PLA!"

"You hurt me," I sobbed.

"Don't say anything about this to anybody," he said in an oddly gentle voice. "Because if you do . . ." Here his voice became steely. "I will find you. Don't ever forget that. Do you understand me?"

"Yes," I choked.

"I'll go get you a Popsicle," he said. "That will make your tooth feel better. Wait here until I come back."

"Okay," I said.

I watched his feet back away from me and move out of the shadows and onto the dirt path. I waited and listened. Soon I heard only the hiss of the rain in the treetops. I could not stop crying. I felt between my legs, where I hurt badly. My throat was burning.

I guardedly stepped to the edge of the path, peered out and saw the soldier walking away in the distance. The rain obscured him, but I recognized the umbrella and the green uniform.

Still crying, I tightened the drawstring on my trousers and felt a sharp pain in my palm. I turned my hand over and saw a puncture wound. I noticed a shining object in the pine needles at my feet. It was the Chairman Mao badge. I had been holding it when Uncle PLA grabbed me and undid my trousers. I'd hit his hand repeatedly while holding the disk, gashing him and cutting myself with the sharp pin before I lost my grip and dropped it. I picked it up. Chairman Mao's semi-smiling face was smeared with blood.

I slipped the badge into my pocket and stepped out into the downpour. I tasted blood in my mouth, felt around with my tongue and realized the cotton ball was gone. I'd swallowed it. I looked around on the ground and found the cotton balls. Many were soiled, but a few were still clean. I stuck a clean one in the back of my mouth.

I looked up and down the path. There was no one in sight. I ran home as fast as I could.

Mama was surprised when I burst into our apartment wet and out of breath. "Where have you been?" she asked. She approached me and noticed right away that my face was red and swollen. "What happened?" she asked with alarm.

"I had my tooth pulled."

"Where?"

"At the dental hospital downtown."

"Where did you get these scratches?" she asked and leaned closer to examine marks on my neck and face.

I hesitated for a moment before I lied, "The nurse held me there when the dentist pulled my tooth. It wouldn't come out." I looked away from her as I spoke, lest my eyes betray me.

My words seemed to hang in the air as Mama examined the bruises. "How unusual," she exclaimed. "The nurse did this?"

"Yes."

"You've been crying, Maomao. Why?"

"It hurt."

"Is that all?" she asked, her eyes softening as she watched my expression.

"Yes."

She touched my neck and I was tempted to tell her what had really happened. But I was afraid if I did, the soldier would find out and he would find me and hurt me even more. I said nothing about Uncle PLA to anyone. Yet I could not forget his voice and his eyes and the feel of his hand choking me and his fingers between my legs. Never.

I took the Chairman Mao badge from my pocket. I was unsure what to do with it. I pushed it under my pillow. I awakened abruptly in the middle of the night when I dreamed I heard the voice of Uncle PLA. I was trembling. I lay awake until dawn, thinking about what he'd done. When I heard the call of the milkman, I got out of bed. As I dressed, I noticed spots of blood on the sheet and on my underwear. I put on clean underwear and hid the bloody pair, fearing Mama might ask me about it. That afternoon, when my parents were away, I washed the sheet and the underwear.

Later that week, Mama had our photo taken—me and my two brothers—in a small inexpensive studio near our home. She had us put on our finest clothing; I wore the same red-and-black-checked blouse I'd worn to the dental hospital. To demonstrate our love of Chairman Mao, each of us wore a badge. My brothers had small ones. I pinned on my large one and told Mama I'd found it on the street near the dentist.

Mama picked up the photograph two weeks later and put it in our family album. In the picture I am standing between my brothers smiling broadly, and my Chairman Mao badge is prominent. Papa and Mama said the picture was very good. I looked at it once when Mama brought it home. I wanted to see if the marks on my neck were visible. They weren't. I didn't look at it again for a very long time.

More PLA soldiers arrived in Hefei in the next weeks. Everyone continued to tell heroic tales about them. I listened to the stories and repeated lines we were taught about their courage and selflessness. I sang songs praising Uncle PLA. Yet when I saw the soldiers, I looked for the face of the man who hurt me.

16

That summer students formed Red Guard units, a militant organization that vowed absolute allegiance to Chairman Mao. The Red Guards were the violent vanguard of the Cultural Revolution. They wore green military uniforms and red armbands. Members carried a small red plastic-bound copy of the *Quotations of Chairman Mao,* which became the holy book of the whole country.

Beijing burned with revolutionary fervor. In mid-August Chairman Mao appeared before a rally of more than a million Red Guards in Tiananmen Square and accepted the title of Red Guard general. Defense Minister Lin Biao appeared at the rally and admonished the Red Guards to be resolute in destroying the Four Olds.

The public security minister proclaimed the existing laws of the People's Republic of China no longer binding. He ordered the police not to interfere with the Red Guards. "Police should stand with the Red Guards," he proclaimed, and supply them with information and let them know who the black families were. Following his announcement, Red Guards initiated the Red Terror. They invaded the homes of black families. They went on a rampage in a village near Beijing and murdered hundreds of people. The Cultural Revolution had found its method, its madness and its executioners.

Word spread quickly as to what the Red Guards were doing. Mama concluded that our exile from Beijing to Hefei, which had been ordered in 1958 after Papa was sent to the concentration camp, had been a blessing in disguise. There was little doubt, she said, that had we remained in Beijing, our names would have been high on the Red Guard list of enemies and we might have been butchered.

I watched middle and elementary school students from red families assemble on street corners and in parks in their new uniforms, waving Little Red Books and chanting revolutionary slogans. Xiaolan and I applied for admission to the Little Red Guards. "Why would we allow enemies of the people in our ranks?" a group leader responded. "Keep your distance." He tore up the applications and threw them on the ground.

When local Red Guards came back to Hefei in September, they initiated house searches, seeking evidence of the Four Olds and counterrevolutionary conspiracies. Suspicious property was destroyed on the spot or seized and carted away to be held in quarantine. Books, manuscripts and art judged to be part of the Four Olds were thrown to the street to be burned or hauled to the dump. Anything the Red Guards said they needed in order to make revolution was expropriated. Resistance brought arrest, beating, imprisonment and, in many cases, execution.

Passionate and dramatic public demonstrations were reinstituted as a requisite prelude to unmasking and destroying class enemies. The Red Guards held massive rallies morning, noon and night, exhorting and inciting and arousing loyal citizens. The call to arms was constant. Black families cowered and hoped this storm might pass or change direction before it consumed them. Yet each day it increased in fury. Orders were issued over the campus loudspeakers for the cow demons and snake spirits of the university to assemble on the university's athletic grounds, where they had been denounced and beaten in June.

When Papa arrived, he found a battalion of Red Guards and several thousand of their supporters already there. A huge dunce cap was put on his head and a sign was hung around his neck describing his crimes. The apartments of some of those summoned had been ransacked the previous evening and the prizes confiscated by the Red Guards were piled around the basketball courts. The booty included radios, clothing, photographs, academic certificates, books, records and magazines. Some materials—clothing and shoes or underwear of fine material— were confiscated because, Red Guards insisted, they were carryovers from a decadent bourgeois life.

After berating the academics and warning them of the consequences of resistance, the Red Guard commander announced that their pay was too high. They were "unjustly compensated" by being paid more than the cream of society—the workers and the peasants. "A pay adjustment is in order," he said.

Papa's salary was seventy yuan per month, much less than that of his fellow faculty members. He listened as one after another of his colleagues volunteered to have his pay sliced in half. When Papa's turn came the Red Guard leader leaned forward until his nose nearly touched Papa's. "Well?" he sneered.

"Thirty yuan per month," Papa said softly.

"Yes!" the leader exclaimed. "Very good." He moved on to his next victim.

Papa returned home dispirited and depressed. He dropped his dunce cap and sign next to his desk. He studied them with an expression of exasperation and embarrassment before seating himself at the table.

He told Mama all that had happened. "Thirty yuan a month!" He sighed. "How can we get by on that?" He'd managed to put a political problem on hold while creating a serious economic one. "There's more," he said, his voice breaking. "So much more. Yesterday afternoon a prominent elderly scholar from the Chinese Language Department committed suicide by jumping out a second-story window after Red Guards ransacked his home. They confiscated three thousand volumes of classical Chinese literature and burned them in front of his house."

"When will this end?" Mama asked.

17

The next morning I was awakened by shouting and pounding on our door. The moment Mama opened it a mob of hysterical Red Guards burst in. A tall young man—another of Papa's former students—demanded that Mama and Papa stand before them. "Chairman Mao teaches us 'Revolution is violence,' " he proclaimed. " 'It is the violent action of one class overthrowing another.' Long live Chairman Mao!"

"Long live Chairman Mao!" the others shouted and thrust their Little Red Books into the air.

"Revolutionary Comrades," the young man said to his followers, "we are here to take action. Seize the day! Don't let any incriminating evidence of the Four Olds escape your search."

I sat up, pulled aside my mosquito net and rubbed my eyes in a daze.

"Wu Ningkun," the leader said, "turn over all of your correspondence with foreign spies."

"Revolutionary Comrade," Papa responded calmly, "I have no such thing."

"Don't deny your anti-revolutionary actions," the young man

yelled. "Sit down. Make a list of everyone in the enemy country you have corresponded with since you returned to China in 1951 from the imperial United States."

Papa dutifully seated himself at his desk and began to write. The Red Guards spread out through our apartment and began their search, opening drawers, boxes and photo albums and unceremoniously dumping the contents onto the floor. They crawled under the beds and tapped up and down the walls, floors and ceilings, seeking secret compartments.

The leader and a female Red Guard were intrigued by Papa's books, which were stacked on his desk and stored in boxes around it. They crouched on the floor beside the boxes and began paging through the books. When they finished each one, they threw it off to the side or put it in a box. Finally the leader pointed to the filled boxes and announced, "These are bourgeois propaganda. Burn them!" At his words, two Red Guards slid the boxes into the corridor.

Oh, please don't burn Papa's books! I cried out in my heart.

As if he heard my thought, the leader motioned for Mama, my brothers, grandmother and me to leave. "All of you get out," he commanded. "Go into the corridor. Leave the door open so I can see you."

We huddled around the boxes of books. I saw among them Papa's treasures—Hugo, Zola, Du Fu, Li Bai, Lawrence, Stendhal, Dumas, Cao Xueqing, Balzac and Shakespeare. I wanted to cry. The fat volume of *Jean-Christophe* by Romain Rolland lay on top of one of the boxes, close to my feet. The novel had been translated from French by Papa's dear friend Fu Lei, who, along with his wife, had recently been driven to suicide by Red Guard harassment. The book was autographed. Papa kept it on the corner of his desk. Many times when he was writing, I saw him pause and page through it, then read a passage to himself.

While the Red Guards were absorbed with ransacking our apartment, I slid closer to the box. I was trembling as I reached over and furtively snatched *Jean-Christophe*. I sneaked a quick glance inside the apartment to make sure no one saw me, put the book under my shirt and leaned back against the wall.

A Red Guard wheeled Mama's bicycle past us. "I need it to make revolution," he snarled. Mama bit her lower lip and averted her eyes.

I watched two female Red Guards sitting on the floor of my bedroom, going through the clothing, bedding and toys. One picked up the small mirror I kept under the bed. She examined it, looked up to make sure the other girl was not watching and smiled at herself in the mirror. She turned her head from side to side, pursed her lips, frowned and combed through her hair with her fingers. When she was finished preening, she slipped the mirror into her uniform pocket and resumed searching.

The other Red Guard found the Chairman Mao badge the soldier had given me. She admired it briefly before dropping it into her pocket.

The Red Guards confiscated everything they deemed bourgeois, Four Olds or counterrevolutionary. Papa's Smith-Corona typewriter, Kodak camera, RCA phonograph, neckties, pictures he'd brought from his years in the United States, and a hundred-watt lightbulb they said wasted electricity were relegated to piles of goods to be removed. When they departed, they had Papa carry several boxes of books outside for them.

The moment they were gone I hurried to the bathroom. I pulled out the book, which had stuck to my sweaty back. The sweat left a dark stain on the cover.

I heard shouts and chanting outside, and I peered through the bathroom window. The Red Guards and a crowd of their followers were gathered in a tight circle around a fire. Papa, standing near the middle of the circle, was feeding his books to the flames. Each time a volume ignited, the crowd cheered and chanted. I felt tears well up in my eyes. "Do not cry!" I said to myself.

When Papa returned, he sat at his desk, sad and silent. I approached timidly and stood beside him. "My books," he moaned. "All gone." He struggled not to break down in front of me.

I carefully laid the copy of *Jean-Christophe* on the desk. "I'm so sorry I made the cover wet, Papa," I said.

I went downstairs and outside. Although they had burned most of Papa's books, two boxes sat off to the side, undamaged. I carried them back to the apartment. We picked up all the things the Red Guards left strewn throughout the apartment and put them away. Mama discovered that among the bourgeois materials they'd confiscated was our grocery money, which she kept in an envelope in the desk drawer.

In the weeks following the search, Papa attended daily meetings with his fellow professors to study the works of Chairman Mao and confess personal crimes. When supervising Red Guards became bored, Papa and his colleagues were herded outside to do manual labor.

One task the Red Guards enjoyed assigning was gathering night soil from the public toilets and transporting it to garden plots for use as fertilizer. Each academic, regardless of age or gender, used a wooden dipper to scoop the excrement from the latrines and drop it in the buckets. Once the buckets were full, the academics strapped them to a shoulder pole and lugged them from one plot to another while Red Guards upbraided them. They demanded that the cow demons shout slogans of self-denunciation as they trudged around bent low by the weight of their loads.

If a professor stumbled or fell and spilled his buckets, several Red Guards swooped down on him and forced him to pick up what he could with his hands and put it back in the bucket. Such moments provided an interlude of hilarity for the Red Guards. They laughed uproariously and slapped their thighs in merriment while witnessing the utter degradation of their former instructors.

18

Classes remained suspended in the fall of 1966 and university students spent their time making revolution. Middle schools and primary schools resumed their regular schedule. My older brother and I returned to our school, and my little brother, Yicun, was sent to the child care center. But the Cultural Revolution increasingly affected our lives. Children from black families were singled out for even greater segregation, harassment and punishment. The teachers turned a blind eye to the activities of the red students or collaborated with them. The persecuted black students found safety and solace only in one another. Even three-year-old Yicun was a target for hate. He became quiet at home and was reluctant to go to the center. He clung to our mother and cried when she dropped him off.

One morning she returned to the center and peeked inside. She watched, sickened with dismay, as a teacher led Yicun to a potty chair in the corner of the room. He was ordered to take off his pants and stay there. After that, the teacher paid no attention to him, and none of the other children played with him. Our parents gave Yicun special attention at home to make up for his mistreatment at the center. But there was no one in a position of authority to whom they could complain.

My parents didn't know what happened to me at school, and I could only guess what my older brother experienced. He played chess against himself each afternoon and evening when he'd finished his homework. On weekends he'd sit quietly, hour after hour, moving methodically from one side of the table to the other, lost in his game.

I had a companion in misery—my best friend Xiaolan. At school we shared a common label: daughters of the damned. Her father was labeled a "historic anti-revolutionary" for having served in the Nationalist Army during the war against the Japanese. Xiaolan's name meant "little magnolia," and it fit her perfectly. She was moonfaced, with thick black hair that she wore in long braids. Her skin seemed to glow every time she smiled. She looked like those children who appeared in propaganda posters illustrating the glory of China.

When Xiaolan and I began third grade together that autumn, the hatred of other students for us— "little cow demons and snake spirits"—initially took the form of teasing. Students, older and younger, sneered and called us names. Sometimes one of them threw a rock at us when our backs were turned. When we looked to see who had done it, a group of students stared back at us and snickered and made defiant gestures.

The boys pulled our hair or tried to pull down our trousers and underwear. Quickly, they became bolder. I arrived at school one morning, opened my desk and found a large dead rat inside. I was horrified and jumped back. The students watched my reaction with glee. I picked up the rat by its long tail and walked out of the room and threw it into the school yard. In the next days other dead animals—sparrows, mice and toads—were left inside my desk.

When I pretended the pranks didn't bother me, it infuriated them. They realized from watching Red Guards that escalation of harassment was warranted when someone refused to be cowed. The teachers and other students saw what was happening. The teachers looked the other way. The red students were delighted. They called themselves Little Red Guards, and in their sentiments and lust for inflicting pain on others, they were like grown-ups. They turned when I entered the room, watched as I opened my desk, and giggled or guffawed when I stepped back after finding what was inside. They leered as I walked from the room, waiting for the pleasure of seeing me lose my composure. The other black children stared down at their desks, fearing they might be next. Xiaolan was subject to similar indignities. Like me, she struggled to remain strong.

One day I found a lump of human excrement wrapped in paper in my desk. I gagged. Students near me grabbed their noses and hooted and pointed and backed away. I put down my books, took the edges of the paper, walked out the door, and deposited the mess in the latrine. I paused for a moment to fight back tears. Xiaolan appeared. She hugged me and said, "Don't cry. It will only make them happy." I returned to my desk and dutifully joined in the recitation of the quotations of Chairman Mao.

The world is yours, as well as ours, but in the last analysis, it is yours. You young people, full of vigor and vitality, are in the bloom of life, like the sun at eight or nine in the morning. Our hope is placed on you. The world belongs to you. China's future belongs to you.

The teacher recited a few words, and we shouted them back at her. We did this each day until we had committed hundreds of quotations to memory.

We can learn what we did not know. We are not only good at destroying the old world, we are also good at building the new.

The teasing and attacks moved from the school to the street. The red children began waiting for me after class and followed me chanting "little rightist" and "little stinking ninth." There were nine categories of class enemies: landlords, rich peasants, counterrevolutionaries, bad elements, rightists, traitors, spies, capitalist roaders and the ninth and worst category—intellectuals. Intellectuals were referred to by Mao as the "stinking ninth."

I stared straight ahead and kept walking. My rigid indifference only emboldened my detractors. They walked closer, surrounding me, crowding me. Some spat on me.

As the Cultural Revolution became more violent among the adults, so did the attacks by children on children. On the way home each afternoon, I watched Red Guards leading lines of men and women like cattle—Red Guards berated them, beat them, knocked them to their knees and commanded them to recite quotations from Chairman Mao or make self-condemnations. Crowds of adults and children watched this wretched carnival of misery with what seemed to be gleeful contempt and enraptured detachment.

One afternoon I was followed by a group of students taunting me. A boy ran up to me and punched me hard in the back. It took my breath away.

"Stinking rightist! Stinking rightist!" a girl shouted as she ran circles around me.

A boy charged and struck me in the back of the head. "Stupid girl," he yelled. "Stay away from our classroom."

My ears were ringing. The street seemed to undulate under my feet. I looked at the boy and saw the hate and rapture in his face.

A girl grabbed my schoolbag and threw my notebook, books and papers onto the street. I picked up the bag and ran to gather the spilled contents. One paper floated out of my reach each time I stooped to pick it up.

"Just look at that dancing idiot," a boy screamed and the others doubled over in laughter. Another girl, her face flushed with hate, hurried over, stepped on the paper and grabbed a fistful of my hair. I fell to the cement. I got to my feet and stuffed the soiled papers into my bag.

The girl and her friends gathered close around me, legs spread, hands on hips, jaws jutting out, defying me to break their circle. I stepped in one direction and a boy blocked my way. They began to chant, "Little black bitch, little black bitch, little black bitch."

Something snapped. I lashed out with my bag, catching a boy in the face. I leaped forward and grabbed a girl by the hair, jerked her head down and pulled it from side to side as she howled. In a flash the others were on my back, pummeling me, pulling my hair, punching my arms. I held on to the girl's hair like someone possessed.

I was unafraid. As the others beat and battered me, I swung my bag and punched wildly with my fist. I bared my teeth and snapped at them. Finally someone tripped me, and I stumbled and fell flat on my back. Stunned, I paused for my head to clear. They stood over me, uncertain what to do next. The girl screamed for them to kill me, but she had edged away several safe feet.

The biggest boy, panting, fists clenched at his sides, looked down at me and spat, "Stupid little rightist bitch!" He turned and wrapped his arm around his weeping companion. The group moved on, singing songs of Chairman Mao's quotations.

My arms, legs and face were scraped and bruised. I was crying and trembling so I could hardly stand. I sat on the curb, gasping for air. I clasped my hands together tightly to steady them. What happened? I asked myself. Where had my strength, my courage, my incredible rage come from?

At home I washed my soiled clothing and sewed up the tear in my shirt before Mama saw it. I examined my scalp in the mirror and found a bald spot where the hair had been pulled out. I gathered my hair around the spot and used a rubber band to make a ponytail. I told Xiaolan what had happened. She laughed about my fighting back but warned, "Maomao, now you're really going to get it."

Together we conspired to postpone their retribution. We circled the campus searching for a way to get out without going through the main gate. We found a weak spot in the campus wall, concealed partially by shrubbery. The mortar had disintegrated and bricks had come loose. We pulled out several bricks near the base of the wall and made a hole large enough for each of us to squeeze through. We crawled out the hole and took a new route to school.

Nobody followed us that day. The next morning we met outside Xiaolan's apartment building and hurried to our secret exit. After we'd slipped through it we looked down the street toward the main gate and saw several of the students who'd chased me lingering in the street. I pointed them out to Xiaolan, and we had to cover our mouths to stifle our laughter. We ran through alleys and down side streets we'd never taken before to get to school. This became our regular route. We eventually gave the crescent-shaped hole in the wall a name—Moon Gate.

We evaded our tormentors for the next few weeks. We hoped they'd tire of looking for us.

But before long we got into trouble with another group.

19

One of our most malicious classmates was a tall, temperamental girl named Sun Maomao. Her father had been provost of the university. He was a powerful man who freely used his position for personal advantage. His family lived a life of luxury. Even in hard times, they ate well.

My parents were high on his hate list. At a political meeting of the university faculty and staff a few years earlier, the provost gave a long speech—a directive as well as a criticism—about birth control. My parents had two children at the time and my mother was expecting a third. Looking straight at her, he said that the best policy for black families was a one-child policy. "Having more than one child," said the father of six, "is irresponsible and unpatriotic for a black family. Such people who produce more than one child will suffer dire consequences."

One morning Xiaolan and I were playing quietly in a corner of the school yard before class started. We found that when we pulled up a clump of crabgrass and cleaned off the roots, we could chew them and extract a sweet-tasting juice. While we chewed the roots, we wove the blades of grass into a bird's nest. Perched on our knees on the ground, we talked about the birds that would come and lay eggs in our nest. We imagined how they would look, their wonderful colors, the size and color of the eggs and the number of baby birds we could watch. There were almost no birds in the city. Eight years earlier, a fanatical campaign had succeeded in exterminating wild birds in the cities and the countryside because Chairman Mao believed they were pests that ate crops that might otherwise be consumed by people.

Xiaolan was wearing a new white blouse with tiny blue flowers printed on it. Her mother had made it and Xiaolan was quite pleased with it. The bell rang. We ran to class. Xiaolan held the nest in her hands. She didn't want to drop it, and she would get into trouble if she brought it inside the classroom. She shouted, "Maomao! Look!"

I turned to see her fling it high into the air, as though it were a bird, rather than a nest, and would take flight. As it left her hands it came apart into wet roots and blades of grass. Behind us came Sun Maomao. The disintegrating nest rained down on her. She was furious. She sprang at Xiaolan, grabbed her by the collar, slapped her twice across the face and shrieked, "How dare you, you rotten little historic antirevolutionary!"

As Xiaolan tried to pull away, Sun Maomao jerked her forward. They struggled, and Sun Maomao tore off Xiaolan's blouse. I stepped between them and pushed Sun Maomao away. She tripped over her own feet. "You rightist bitch," she screamed. She was about to charge me when Xiaolan jumped in front of me. She was half naked; Sun Maomao still clutched the remnants of her new blouse. In a flash Xiaolan was clawing furiously at Sun Maomao's face like a ferocious cat. Sun Maomao screamed, dropped the blouse and covered her face. "My eyes!" she cried. "You hurt my eyes!" Xiaolan broke off her attack, snatched up her torn blouse and ran home. Sun Maomao cowered nearby.

All five of Sun Maomao's siblings attended our school and the nearby middle school. They planned their vengeance methodically, just as the adults did.

The next afternoon Xiaolan and I participated in a rehearsal for our school's Mao Zedong Thought Propaganda Team. The best singers and dancers in the school were selected to be part of the team and perform on the streets and for other classes and schools. After an hour of singing and dancing, the students and teachers left. Xiaolan and I stayed to sweep the floor and clean the blackboard. We had not yet been forbidden from participating in rehearsals but we were required to perform extra labor. When we were finished, we gathered up our books and walked to the door and spotted Sun Maomao and her brothers and sisters—the entire Sun brood—waiting for us outside.

"There they are!" Sun Maomao shouted when she saw us. They rushed the door. We scampered back into the classroom, slammed the door shut and blocked it with a desk. We braced our backs against the desk and held the door closed. The Suns pounded and kicked the door, cursing and making threats. Each time they succeeded in pushing the door open an inch we pushed back with all of our might. Slowly the opening became smaller until, to the sound of expletives and threats from the other side, it clicked shut.

"Are there just two of them? Are you absolutely sure?" we heard one of the Suns ask. Our desperation gave us the strength of many.

"We have all the time in the world, you little black bitches," one of the Sun boys shouted. "The longer we wait out here, the worse it is going to be for you. Come out and face your punishment."

We had no intention of facing them. Eventually Sun Maomao's big brother announced, "We'll sit here as long as you are in there, and we'll save our strength for beating the shit out of you." After a long silence, Sun Maomao screamed, "You filthy black bitches had better come out of there, or . . . or I'll have my brothers . . . set fire to the building. I'll see you bitches burn."

We didn't know what they might do if we went out, but our imaginations were vivid. So we waited quietly while the Suns brayed outside.

Hours passed. We heard them whispering and creeping up to the door to test it. The light faded. We soon found ourselves enveloped in darkness, whispering to each other, wondering if our parents might come looking for us.

Finally there was no sound outside. We pulled the door open a crack and peeked out. We could see no one. We opened it farther, to see if that might lure the Suns out of hiding. There was no movement. We decided to make a run for it. We stepped outside and stood very still, watching and listening. The Suns had lost their patience that day. But we knew they would return. They had only postponed our punishment.

Xiaolan and I raced to our apartment buildings. We heard chilling chants from a gathering far away. Big character posters, pasted on walls and hanging from ropes and wires, blew lazily in the breeze like flags or shrouds. The gaunt caricatures on the posters looked down on us like a gallery of ghosts as we hurriedly passed.

As I was on my way home from the market one Sunday morning, Sun Maomao and her siblings stepped from an alley and surrounded me. Sun Maomao grabbed my hair, and her brothers and sisters kicked and punched me. The food I was carrying spilled to the ground and the eggs broke. The oldest boy proclaimed loudly, "You are Xiaolan's friend. For every hair Xiaolan pulled from my sister, you will pay with ten."

They pulled out my hair and kicked me until I stopped resisting and they tired of beating me. They picked up the vegetables scattered around me and ran away, laughing and shouting, "Long live the Great Proletarian Cultural Revolution!"

Xiaolan and I continued to watch out for the Suns. On several afternoons we were ambushed and chased. Caught alone on the street once, Xiaolan was beaten badly.

My only consolation was that Xiaolan and I remained loyal and kind to each other. When I saw Xiaolan each morning, her face was freshly scrubbed, and her clothes had been washed and sewn or patched if they'd been torn. She was always happy to see me. We slipped through our very own Moon Gate and out into the hostile world together, sister victims in the world of the big revolution.

As we ran to school, sheets and shredded fragments of paper blew around us—loosened scraps from old weather-worn political posters. Sometimes a breeze tore off a corner or an entire poster came loose and flipped and flew down the street. We found ourselves racing it as it twirled and twisted along in the drafts, or several tattered shreds skittered across our path. At times the characters were decipherable—ENEMY. RIGHTIST. TRAITOR. DEATH. KILL. Or a partial accusation, interrupted by a rip in midsentence. Fragments of posters caught on our legs, and we giggled and jumped or halted and kicked our feet in a little dance, trying to free ourselves of the ribbons of soiled and crinkled paper.

Then we ran on to school, clutching our book bags while the condemnations swirled past us, shredding, balling up, tearing apart, snagging in the branches of trees or the spokes of bicycles. Adults avoided these remnants of posters as if they were a poison or carried a curse. But Xiaolan and I dashed fearlessly through them.

When it rained the ink on the posters blotted and ran, and the characters were transformed into flowers and clouds and bleeding spots and collages of color, beautiful to see. Sometimes we saw in the blotches human or animal faces that we tried to identify. Sometimes we saw monsters forming in the running ink, and we screamed and ran from them in mock fright as we played our game pursued by colorful paper.

We spent much of our time that autumn and winter playing and planning ways to remain out of harm's way, and to find some bit of security, some companionship, beyond the reach of the Sun siblings.

One morning after the winter chill began, I waited for Xiaolan outside her apartment for our walk to school. When she appeared, she looked sad.

"What's wrong?" I asked.

"Papa told me I could no longer walk to school with you. He said I cannot talk to you or play with you," she answered.

"Why?" I asked, shocked.

"Because, Maomao. Just because." She fidgeted with her book bag.

"Papa said that if people see us talking or playing together, they will say we are exchanging information from our parents."

"But we don't," I said.

"Sun Maomao's father warned Papa. So . . . we have to stop being friends."

It was useless to argue. "Okay, Xiaolan," I said, my voice breaking. "I'll stay away. But I'll always be your friend. You know that, don't you?"

"Goodbye, Maomao." She sighed and hurried away. I watched her slip through the Moon Gate. She didn't look back.

From that day on we faced the Suns alone.

In November the political ground shifted. Sun Maomao's father came under intense criticism by Red Guards. He was labeled a "capitalist roader in power." He was stripped of his title and position and lost his authority, privileges and status. Overnight he and his family went from red to black. The hunters became the hunted. Sun Maomao and her siblings became fair game for children of red families. I stopped worrying about them. I almost felt sorry for them.

As I was coming home from school one day, I saw her father standing on a platform in the street. He was wearing a dunce cap and his head was bowed. He was being denounced and punched by former students and colleagues who, in time, would be stars on the same stage. The next day I saw boys chasing Sun Maomao's brothers down a street, flinging rocks at them. Another time I watched with amusement as Sun Maomao furtively squeezed through our Moon Gate and ran home.

Yet something about the Sun family made them different from my family and Xiaolan's. They could not bear suffering. They could only inflict it.

One afternoon while Sun Maomao's father was being pulled around the campus like a dog on a leash, he collapsed. The Red Guards thought he was faking an ailment. They kicked him, pulled him to his feet, slapped his face and doused him with buckets of water but were unable to bring him to his senses. In frustration, they dragged him by the feet to his apartment building and left him. It took his wife over an hour to summon help and get him to a hospital. The doctors concluded it was not exhaustion that had caused his collapse but a stroke.

When he regained consciousness he was unable to move or speak. He was taken home to be cared for by his family. Within a few weeks he became pale and thin. His eyes clouded and his hair turned white and fell out. Each day he sat strapped in a chair staring vacantly at the floor.

Sun Maomao's eldest brother got out of bed one night and walked to the nearby pond. He stepped into the water, disappeared beneath the surface and drowned. The next morning Red Guards discovered his body, denounced him and fed his remains to wild dogs outside the city wall.

With the fall of the Suns, it was safe for Xiaolan and me to see each other. We resumed playing together and walking to school hand in hand. One morning we passed Sun Maomao seated on a little stool in front of her apartment building. She was singing nonsense rhymes in a loud, shrill voice. When she spotted us, she stopped singing and stared as if she had never seen us before. We moved past her and she followed us with her eyes. She erupted in ear-piercing shrieks of hysteria and started pulling at her own hair. Xiaolan and I broke into a run and Sun Maomao's cries faded behind us.

Sun Maomao was never reunited with her sanity.

20

One afternoon I heard another mob approaching our apartment. I listened to the familiar chorus of hate as it drew closer and increased in volume.

They were chanting, "DOWN WITH JIANG ZHONGJIE!"

Jiang Zhongjie, my grandmother, was sitting on the bed next to mine, holding my little brother on her lap. I looked at her, and she averted her eyes to the door. My brother sat still as a stone on her lap.

The crash of the building's front door being flung open was followed by a thunder of fists hammering on our door and shouts of "Open up!"

Papa hurried to comply. The moment he released the lock, Red Guards rushed into our apartment bellowing, "Down with landlord Jiang Zhongjie. Where is she? Where is the criminal?" They had discovered that her family had owned property in Yangzhou before the Communists seized power in 1949.

Two girls saw Grandmother and bolted across the room, grabbed her by the arms and held her tightly. "Move!" one of them yelled at my brother, and he dropped from her lap to the floor with a whimper. The Red Guards jerked Grandmother to her feet.

She managed to ask meekly, "May I go to the bathroom . . . please?"

"Are you trying to play for time, you landlord dog?" a Red Guard yelled.

Mama appeared and explained that Grandmother suffered from diabetes and had to use the bathroom often. "I will help her go to the bathroom," she said. There was a public toilet on each floor of our building. The Red Guard leader, a mean-looking girl with narrow, snakelike eyes and a face flat as a plate, asked, "Will you guarantee that this landlord will not jump out the window and kill herself to escape revolutionary justice?"

"I do," Mama replied. "She will go with you. But with her bound feet she cannot go far."

Mama helped Grandmother to the bathroom. I watched as three Red Guards stationed themselves outside the door to prevent an escape.

Minutes later Grandmother hobbled out. She disappeared in the mass of the howling uniformed boys and girls.

I didn't move. My little brother sobbed, "I want Grandmother!" Mama hurried over and held him. Nobody seemed to know what to do.

Nearly three hours later I heard the familiar sound of Grandmother slowly ascending the stairs.

Her hair, which she kept carefully knotted in a bun at the back of her head, had come undone and was tangled and disheveled. Her blouse was torn. Her face shone with perspiration. Papa helped her sit down and handed her a cup of water.

"They took me to the sports field," she said slowly, as if waking from a nightmare. "Other elderly people were there. They had us stand in a line and put dunce caps on us. The Red Guards slapped us and the crowd shouted and denounced us. They unknotted my hair and threatened to cut it all off."

Grandmother tried to sip her water, but her hands were shaking so badly she could not hold it to her lips without spilling it. Mama took the cup and helped her drink.

"They ordered us to leave Hefei within twenty-four hours," Grandmother continued. She began to cry. "What will I do?" she sobbed. "What did I do to deserve this at the age of seventy?"

There was a banging on our door. Papa jumped up and timidly opened it. He returned to the room followed by a tall, muscular Red Guard in a clean, smartly tailored uniform. He pointed an accusing finger at Grandmother and announced, "Members of the landlord class may no longer live on the campus of Anhui University. If she is not gone by tomorrow night, this entire family will pay a price." His gaze was steely and unwavering and his tone angry. He looked at each of us before abruptly turning and walking out, leaving the door ajar.

Mama and Papa tried to think of a way to allow her to stay with us. Mama decided to go directly to the local headquarters of the Red Guard and make a personal appeal. She had to go alone. Papa's presence was likely to inflame the Red Guards.

She arrived at the headquarters only to find that the same young man who had just left our apartment was in charge. When he saw Mama, he groaned, "You! Have you come here to waste my time?"

Mama steadied her nerves and quietly presented Grandmother's case. "My mother-in-law is very old and a severe diabetic," she said. "She has lived with her son and been supported by him since 1951. She cannot survive without us."

"Enough!" the commander cut her off and smacked the desk with his open hand. "Shut up!"

Mama stopped talking and stood subserviently before him.

"She is a class enemy," he sputtered. "You . . . get out!"

When she got home, Mama told us what had happened. We listened in sadness and fear.

It was decided that Grandmother must move to Yangzhou, Jiangsu Province, where she had been born and grown up. When the political turmoil ended, Papa comforted her, he would bring her back to us. "It is just a matter of time," he said.

The next morning Mama made arrangements to cancel Grandmother's residency permit. Papa helped her pack. He put her belongings in cardboard boxes. My brothers and I tied the boxes with string and, despite our heavy hearts, did what we could to cheer her up.

Mama and Papa waited until dark to leave, to avoid Red Guards who might spot them and harass them. Yiding was asleep when Grandmother left. I watched her go. She cried quietly and lovingly caressed Yiding's forehead. She held my younger brother's hand and put her arm around my shoulder and said goodbye. She hobbled on those tiny bound six-toed feet across the room, out the door and was gone.

Papa summoned a pedicab to take them to the train station. He had wired his distant cousin to meet her in Yangzhou and look after her. He asked Grandmother to write after she was settled.

The cousin met Grandmother's train the next morning. He took her to the office of the local Party secretary, who was in charge of residency permits.

The secretary was irascible and unsympathetic. "You are a landlord," he said. "Why are you in Yangzhou? Anhui Province does not want you. Jiangsu Province does not want you, either."

"I lived in Yangzhou in the past," she answered in a quivering voice. "This was my home."

"Damn it, didn't you hear me, old thing?" the Party secretary roared. "Are you deaf?"

"But I have nowhere to go," Grandmother pleaded.

"That is your problem," he replied. And with a wave of his hand, he dismissed them.

Despite this setback, the cousin was able to help Grandmother. He had lived in Yangzhou many years and knew which Party officials could be influenced by special favors. A small payment in gold was discreetly made to the Party secretary, and a silver bracelet was delivered to his son. Grandmother received her residency permit two days later. Another secret transaction secured her food ration coupons.

Grandmother was assigned a room in the same large house where she had grown up. It had been confiscated by the government and subdivided into quarters for ten families. The other residents treated her with contempt, refusing to talk to her or offer any assistance. Grandmother was familiar with her tiny room. It had been constructed when her great-grandfather transformed a space at the end of a hallway into a family shrine. A small round window facing east provided the only light. A stonemason had been commissioned to engrave a granite block with the family tree—going back eighteen generations. The stone was two meters tall, one meter wide and half a meter thick. It was set on a black granite pedestal. Paintings of several ancestors had once adorned the walls of the shrine.

When the house was subdivided, the paintings were taken away, but the stone proved impossible to move without destroying the walls. So government officials closed and locked the room and left the stone where it was. At the start of the Cultural Revolution, Red Guards attempted to haul the monument into the street, but it was far too heavy for them. So they toppled it and chiseled away a few of the names before abandoning it. The fallen granite slab nearly covered the entire floor. The partially obstructed door to the room could be opened only a few inches. Grandmother had to squeeze her way through it. There was no furniture in the room and she used the stone as her bed.

She lived in fear. She was afraid of the other residents of the house. She was afraid of the Red Guards. She was afraid of local officials. She was afraid that the insulin she needed to take twice daily for her diabetes might become unaffordable or be denied her at the pharmacy.

She cut her dosage by half.

We learned later that because of the reduction of insulin, she sometimes went into shock. When she collapsed in the hallway, the other residents merely stepped over her.

My parents sent her money each month, but my father's salary was reduced so drastically that he was unable to help her as much as she needed. One month his money arrived late and Grandmother worried more. She reduced her insulin intake further. Her health deteriorated rapidly.

One summer afternoon in 1967, she lay down on her granite bed and again went into insulin shock. She was unnoticed and unattended for several hours. That evening she died alone, wrapped in a blanket on a granite bed bearing the names of her ancestors, in a house her family once owned. Among the names engraved on the stone beneath her body were those of her grandfather and the great-grandfather of her cousin Jiang Zemin, the future president of China.

Papa received a telegram notifying him of her death. He applied for leave to go to Yangzhou. By the time he was given approval, his cousin had already held a memorial service for Grandmother. Papa arrived just in time to attend the burial. He remained in the city, which he'd left in 1937, to visit places and people he remembered from his childhood. When he came home he told Mama about the burial and about his thoughts while wandering the streets of Yangzhou. He remembered that Grandmother had lived a lonely life as a widow for ten years before he'd returned to China. She'd come to live with him and expected the last years of her life to be peaceful.

Mama asked if he'd cried at his mother's burial.

"No, I have no more tears for the dead," Papa said. "I only have tears for the living."

21

The Red Guards broke into factions in late 1967. Armed with everything from swords to automatic rifles and grenades, they went to war with one another. Each faction in Hefei initially referred to itself as the Good Faction and to the other group as the Fart Faction. Both were dominated by university and high school students. Some members were children scarcely older than me. A brutal element was added to the mix when factory workers joined the fight. Industry in Hefei and other cities came to a stop. The streets became a battleground.

Soon after the factional fighting commenced, armed Red Guards stormed our school shouting, "NO MORE SCHOOL, GET OUT!" They waved weapons over their heads as they ran from room to room. The students and teachers fled in terror, leaving behind books and papers. Within hours the Red Guards had transformed the building into a fortress. The faction that occupied my school called itself the Jinggangshan Red Guards, after the mountain range where Chairman Mao had lived during the civil war. They assigned lookouts and snipers to the second-floor windows and the roof.

Day and night we heard explosions and the clatter of gunfire.

When prisoners were taken or arrests made, immediate public executions followed. Boys and girls were hanged from trees or from buildings with signs around their necks describing their crimes. Photographs of the dead appeared in newspapers as did flyers with detailed reports of the fighting and lists of "revolutionary martyrs." Food became increasingly expensive. Meat disappeared from the public markets. Vegetables and flour were available in small amounts from a few daring vendors who appeared and disappeared on an irregular basis. Public transportation came to a halt. Anyone might be seized, arrested, shot, stabbed or hanged if he ventured into the street.

In the midst of the brutality and chaos, I was surprised one morning to hear the milkman call from outside. I had not heard him in several weeks. I hurried down the stairs. The milkman was nowhere in sight. I saw his bicycle lying on its side. Broken bottles lay scattered around a puddle of milk. A short distance away a dozen Red Guards squatted in a circle on the sidewalk, each drinking from a bottle of milk. Two of them had rifles slung over their shoulders, and beside another was a long iron pipe.

Where the milkman customarily parked his bicycle, the sidewalk was spattered with blood. A Red Guard spotted me. His eyes narrowed and he glared venomously at me and said something to the others, who turned in my direction. "Get out of here before we break your neck!" one of them yelled.

I dropped my pot and bolted up the stairs. Once I was inside our apartment I tiptoed to the window to look down at the Red Guards. They were flinging empty milk bottles high into the air and laughing when the glass broke in the street. One of them pulled up the milkman's bicycle and pedaled away. The others ran behind him, laughing, trying to jump on.

I went outside to retrieve my pot and look for the milkman. I found a trail of blood and followed it around the corner, where it ended in a large dark pool. I called for the milkman. There was no answer.

In the face of the escalating violence, political meetings and confession sessions were suspended. Many university students and staff fled Hefei and sought safety with relatives or friends in other places. My mother's family was in Tianjin and my parents wondered if that distant city might be safer for us. The trains were running, although they were always packed with Red Guards rushing around the country making revolution. My parents were not sure how difficult it might be to put us all on a train. One afternoon they walked to the train station. They found thousands of people crowded around the terminal and lined up along the tracks.

Each train that pulled into the station was rushed by a frantic mob. People crammed so tightly into the cars that many were forced to lean far out the windows; there was room for only the lower half of their bodies inside. Others climbed to precarious positions atop the cars. Papa and Mama came home that night nearly in tears. They said it was more dangerous to leave Hefei than to stay. Escape was impossible.

We learned later that when the crowded trains entered a narrow tunnel outside Hefei, those atop the cars and hanging out the windows were knocked from the trains, cut in half or decapitated.

22

One of my chores was gathering kindling for our coal-burning stove. After school was suspended, I wandered around the campus each day looking for broken tree branches or bits of wood. I tried to be inconspicuous. I avoided soldiers, Red Guards, groups of students and other children. Most trees in the city had already been chopped down and carted away for fuel. Those that remained had been stripped of bark and branches. Anything made of wood and left outside unguarded was likely to disappear in a few hours.

I turned down a deserted alley behind a large building one afternoon. In an enclosure not visible from the street, I found a conspicuous mound covered with a tarpaulin. The only sound was the steady drone from loudspeakers. The mix of static with a voice passionately reciting revolutionary slogans bounced off the hulking nearby walls until it dissipated and died. The mysterious pile was nearly as tall as me and lay adjacent to the back door. I lifted the edge of the tarpaulin and discovered a disorderly mountain of books. They appeared to have been dumped there to await incineration. I picked up a volume and paged through it. I put it back on the pile and returned to the end of the alley and looked around. Reassured that nobody could see me, I returned to the books and uncovered more. I carefully pulled out several larger volumes and stacked them up to make a seat for myself. I sat down and resumed paging through the books.

I could not understand most of the words but I found the large glossy photographs utterly spellbinding. In a beautifully bound encyclopedia I discovered hundreds of astonishing pictures of snowcapped mountains and plains covered with trees or grass or ice, and of odd plants and animals. I could hardly believe they were real. There were pictures of tall clean buildings, and of strange-looking and strangely dressed people. There were pictures of the bluest lakes and seas and skies I'd ever seen, and of crowds of grinning, laughing children wearing bright colors, playing games and posing for the camera. In some of the pictures the children stood with their family and in some with other children. They smiled broadly. How wonderful, I thought. And how intriguing.

The pictures were a window to another world. I lost myself in them and in what I could read—all of it compelling and unfamiliar. I felt as if I were looking at scenes from dreams I'd not yet dreamed. I wondered how these children could be so carefree. Who were they? Where were they? How could I be one of them? I sat for hours, exploring this treasure.

I knew I could not take any of the books home. If I were caught carrying them, or if Red Guards found them in our house, the entire family would be punished. If anyone saw me here reading, I could flee or say I wanted to use the books for fuel or for toilet paper. That was an acceptable use of books. Yet since the books were shielded from the street, it was unlikely anyone could surprise me while I was reading. So I sat somewhat securely on my little throne and savored these forbidden fruits. When there was so little light that I could no longer read, I reluctantly put down the books, concealed the precious pile beneath the tarpaulin, and hurried home.

In the following days, I found my way back to the books. As I read

I shut out the world around me and I lived with the children in the pictures and the characters in the stories. I floated out of my own grim life to another I had barely imagined. I became excited as I turned each page and I never wanted the tales to end. I laughed out loud at many of the stories and felt deeply sad when characters experienced difficulties. Their lives became part of mine, and my life became part of theirs.

Not all of the stories were unknown to me. I recognized titles from my father's confiscated collection. I found *Gulliver's Travels* and journeyed with Jonathan Swift to strange countries with problems that seemed like the problems of China. I often thought of Papa while reading. I knew how he'd love the books, and I wished I could share them with him. For days I read the story of Edmund Dantes, locked away in his prison like Papa in his concentration camp. I read of Jean Valjean, who was not only sent to prison but was also tormented after his release—like Papa. But most of all, I loved Anne Frank, who lived with her family in a room hiding from cruel people. The similarity to my life and my family's was unmistakable. I felt she could be my sister.

Late one afternoon, after I had finished reading *The Count of Monte Cristo,* my eyes had grown tired. I lay the thick volume on the ground and repeated the last three words Dumas wrote: "Wait and hope." Mama and Papa had said that at our New Year's dinner. I wondered if they'd read the book and been as enthralled by it as I was. I stood and stretched my arms. I decided to see if there might be more books inside the adjacent building. During my weeks of solitary reading I'd never heard a sound from inside. No one came in or out of the door.

I tried the door. It was unlocked. I stepped into a long corridor that was illuminated only by a thin shaft of daylight that splayed through a broken window at the opposite end. The corridor reeked of old plaster and mildew. The sole sound was the shuffle of my shoes on the gritty floor. I made my way to the end of the corridor and turned the corner and noticed a sign over a door reading BROADCAST ROOM. I touched the door. It was heavily padded, like a quilt. I put my ear to it and heard a muffled voice inside. It sounded familiar.

I was curious. I pushed the door open a crack. I saw a man seated at a table speaking into a microphone. He was wearing large headphones. A small panel of glowing red and green lights covered part of the wall over his table, and the floor was crisscrossed with wires. The man was reading aloud from the *Quotations of Chairman Mao.* I recognized his voice. It was the one I heard each day over the loudspeakers throughout the campus, a voice modulated and paced perfectly to the familiar frequency of hate.

He was fascinating to watch. He made wild dramatic gestures with his hands and rocked back and forth in his chair as if addressing a live audience. His gesticulations and melodramatic intonations reminded me of a Chinese opera performed without masks or costumes or plot. I gingerly closed the door and continued my inspection of the building. I went into four other rooms and found them dark and empty. One room was lined with empty bookshelves. I thought I might take one of the shelves home as kindling. I attempted to pry it loose and found it was nailed solidly in place.

I made my way toward the back door. As I passed the broadcast room, I noticed that the wall had begun to deteriorate. The plaster had crumbled and fallen to the floor, exposing narrow vertical strips of wood beneath. I examined a strip. It seemed to be loose and might easily be removed. I gripped it and pulled gently, hoping to extract it without making a sound. But it held tight. I considered leaving the strip where it was and returning to my books. On the other hand, Mama would be delighted if I brought home a bundle of wood strips.

I grasped a strip with both hands, braced my feet and gave several quick jerks. The wood bent but neither broke nor came free. I looked more closely and saw it was held in place by small nails. I tried to loosen them. One popped out and dropped to the floor followed by another. I gave one last pull. There was a sudden explosion. Pieces of plaster and wood cascaded down and buffeted my head and shoulders. I thrust my hands over my head to shield myself. I was stunned by the blows, stumbled and fell to the floor. I was enveloped in a blinding and suffocating cloud. I gasped for air and tried to see. Suddenly, a bright light appeared before me. A face took shape near the middle of the light.

It was the broadcaster. A section of the wall between the studio and the corridor had collapsed, leaving a large jagged hole. The broadcaster was inside his studio, wearing headphones, holding a microphone. He was covered with plaster dust. His mouth was moving, but all I could hear was a loud ringing in my ears. We gawked at each other, trying to make sense of what had just happened. As my hearing returned, the voice of the broadcaster boomed out, "WHAT THE HELL IS GOING ON?"

I bolted for the door.

The broadcaster lunged for me through the hole, tripped and crashed through it, somersaulting into the debris on the floor. More sections of the ceiling and wall rained down on him. Howls of pain rang out, punctuated by a furious medley of profanity and threats. As I ran through the exit, I turned to see the flailing figure in the dust on his hands and knees being pelted by pieces of ceiling and wall. He brandished his microphone like a club, waving it at me. The frayed cord whipped back and forth above his head as he disappeared beneath the dust and debris.

I fled past my prized pile of books. *The Count of Monte Cristo* lay open on the ground, a few pages fluttering in the breeze. I hesitated for one final look before sprinting down the alley, around the corner, and onto the sidewalk. The speakers on the posts and trees up and down the street sizzled and snapped with static. Pedestrians pointed at them in astonishment and chattered excitedly. I kept running. Throughout the evening I was haunted by dread that the broadcaster had recognized me, that there would be a knock on the door and Red Guards would barge in and take me away.

The next morning I heard an impassioned announcement over the loudspeakers: REVOLUTIONARY COMRADES, WE HAVE UNCOVERED A CLEVERLY CONCEALED CLASS ENEMY. THERE WILL BE A

PUBLIC CRITICISM MEETING AT THE ATHLETIC GROUNDS AT SEVEN P.M. ALL REVOLUTIONARY TEACHERS, STUDENTS AND STAFF MUST ATTEND.

After dinner I walked to the athletic grounds to see the spectacle. I stood in the middle of the crowd. I recognized the man wearing a dunce cap standing on the stage. He was the broadcaster. His arms were bound behind him and Red Guards jerked up on his wrists so he was forced to bend forward at a painful angle. From where I was standing I could see his face was badly bruised and one of his eyes was swollen shut. A sign dangled from his neck with his name on it X'd out and the label: CURRENT COUNTERREVOLUTIONARY.

The Red Guard leader announced the crimes of the broadcaster: "Yesterday, on the Public Broadcast System, this current counter-revolutionary interrupted the words of the Great Helmsman, the reddest, reddest sun of our hearts, Chairman Mao, and began shouting profanities."

After every few words Red Guards slapped the broadcaster. "Confess your crimes," they chorused.

"I warn you," the Red Guard leader shouted, "you had better confess. Everyone here heard your counterrevolutionary filth."

A Red Guard held a microphone to the man's mouth but he was crying and could not speak.

The leader went on, "Not only did this class enemy try to escape revolutionary justice, when he left his studio, he led us to a cache of poisonous bourgeois books concealed behind the building. It was obvious he had been reading them before denouncing Chairman Mao."

"Confess! Confess! Confess!" the crowd chanted.

The leader raised his hand and the crowd quieted. A Red Guard held the microphone to the man's lips.

"I . . . I . . . I . . ." he stammered. "It was a girl. Or a boy. A child . . . broke down my studio wall . . ."

A Red Guard punched him in the mouth. The broadcaster's head jerked back for a moment before falling forward. Blood streamed from his nose and mouth to his bare chest. The dunce cap dangled to the side.

"Leniency to those who confess their crimes. Severity to those who refuse to," the Red Guards shouted in unison. The crowd repeated the chant.

Fear and regret filled my heart. I needed to get out of the crowd. I pushed my way past shouting adults and children and moved quickly away from the gathering. The crowd continued chanting, "Severity to those who refuse."

23

The administration of universities was placed in the hands of Mao Zedong Thought Propaganda Teams—an alliance of soldiers and industrial workers—in the spring of 1968. The Red Guards were forced to stop fighting one another and join forces with the Propaganda Teams. This coalition turned its attention to purging the country of its "undesirable elements." Cow demons and snake spirits became the primary focus of the campaign. The Propaganda Teams demonstrated a contempt for education and intellectuals equal to that of the Red Guards. The Propaganda Team at Anhui University organized the faculty and staff into military-like units.

My father was assigned to a group of a hundred men and women. They worked daily from dawn to dusk. Suspected thought-criminals and laggards were beaten and tortured. The professors were assembled to witness the brutality and to contribute condemnations demonstrating revolutionary zeal. In September the Propaganda Team decided to isolate the worst cow demons and snake spirits. Eighty men and women were sent to live in a student dormitory designated a "cowshed." They were divided into groups of eight and assigned to small rooms. Following a day of forced labor, the inmates were rigorously cross-examined by Propaganda Team members, and unsatisfactory answers to questions resulted in beatings.

One young teacher tried to run away. But where was he to go? All of China had become a prison. He was captured at the railway station, dragged back to the cowshed, strung up by his wrists and beaten throughout the night. The other prisoners were forced to witness the punishment and to chant quotations from Chairman Mao to drown out his cries.

News came to us regularly of a man or woman who had been beaten into insensibility. Many could not endure it. A math teacher drank a container of DDT and died in her kitchen. A history instructor and his wife hanged themselves side by side in their bedroom. A professor of French literature slit his wrists in the cowshed, and a chemist jumped out his second-story apartment window. Others were discovered dead in their beds and showed signs of beatings, but it was unclear if they had killed themselves or died as a result of mistreatment. Suicide was a crime against the Party and the people. Whenever victims were found, a public rally was held to denounce them. Afterward, their bodies were carted to a dump outside the city and left to be eaten by wild dogs. Those who died from beatings were cremated and their ashes thrown away.

On Saturday evenings, the cow demons were allowed a visit from a family member. When Papa spoke to Mama on her first visit, he asked her not to worry about him. He assured her he was emotionally and mentally strong. "My will to live," he said, "is unbreakable." He pointed out to her that most of those who killed themselves were young teachers and administrators. "The older ones," he said, "like me, have been through these things before. We know it will end someday. But the younger ones think this will go on forever. They see no reason to live. But I have you and the children. I have hope."

"I do, too," Mama assured him.

Yicun and I visited Papa on his birthday, during the second week of his incarceration. Mama prepared a gift for him—a bowl of dumplings. I watched as Mama made the dumplings, my mouth watering. I could hardly remember the last time we'd eaten meat. I was tempted to ask Mama for one—just one. But I decided not to. She placed the boiled dumplings in an aluminum lunch box, tightened the lid so nothing would spill, and wrapped it in a towel so they would stay warm. Yicun and I walked to the cowshed bearing the birthday present. At the entrance, we were stopped by a civilian sentry who snorted, "You kids go away! This is not a playground."

"We're here to see our papa, Wu Ningkun," I responded.

"What's that?" he asked, pointing to the container.

"It's a birthday present."

"Open it."

I removed the lid. He took the container and peered inside, held it to his nose, sniffed deeply, and looked at me suspiciously. He dipped his finger into the container and stirred the dumplings around. "Dumplings, huh? And for your father's birthday?"

"Yes," I replied. "And you are making them cold."

He fished out a dumpling, stuffed it into his mouth, chewed and swallowed it.

"Those are for my papa," I protested. He plucked out another.

I grabbed for his hand and screamed, "Stop it!"

He caught my wrist and twisted it hard. I let out a cry of pain.

"You little shit," he shouted.

Yicun began screaming.

"Damn you," the sentry bellowed. "Shut up! I am trying to see if you've put anti-revolutionary messages in the dumplings."

There was a commotion inside. Several voices cried, "What's the matter? What's going on?"

The sentry released me and handed me the container. "Go in," he ordered and waved his hand toward the door.

Inside stood a circle of several men and women, staring wide-eyed at us.

Papa rushed to us and lifted Yicun in his arms. "Are you all right?" he asked.

"No, Papa," Yicun whimpered.

I handed him the bundled dumplings. "From Mama," I said through my tears. "Happy birthday, Papa."

The others stood silently, staring hungrily at the dumplings.

We had been with Papa less than five minutes when the sentry shouted, "Time's up!"

I took my brother's hand and we left.

On the way home I saw a new poster on a wall near our apartment. It read DOWN WITH LIANG NAN THE ACTIVE COUNTERREVOLUTIONARY.

Liang Nan—Auntie Liang—was Xiaolan's mother. I'd just seen Xiaolan's father in the cowshed with Papa. I read the poster and learned that Auntie Liang had been caught sitting on a copy of the *Anhui Daily*. The paper carried a front-page photo of Chairman Mao. Sitting on the picture of Chairman Mao made Auntie Liang an "active counterrevolutionary."

24

The Cultural Revolution took yet another twist in the autumn of 1968, when a new Party directive was issued called "Cleansing Class Enemies." It was designed to identify and reeducate or remove class enemies from the ranks of the revolutionary masses. Mama was summoned to a mass meeting, where the new policy was articulated.

"The capitalist intellectuals of our nation live in large buildings in the cities, and many of them live capitalist lives," a Propaganda Team leader proclaimed. "Your lavish life is supported by the backbreaking labor of the poor and lower-middle peasants. Because of this division, it is impossible for intellectuals to understand the real cost of the lives you live. And it is impossible for you to reform your thoughts since thoughts grow from experience. If you are incapable of reforming your own thoughts," he concluded, "you are unqualified to teach students. Teachers and students of all institutions of higher learning will move to the countryside to live with the peasants, share their labor, their food, their huts and their daily routine and learn from them by doing what they do. From this experience and this experience alone can genuine thought reform and a real revolution emerge."

The faculty and students of Anhui University, he said, would be sent to live among peasants at the Wujiang People's Commune in Hexian County, a hundred miles east of Hefei. Children were exempt from the directive. Two rooms in the university child care center would be transformed into a special holding facility for them. The cost of maintaining children was to be deducted from their parents' salaries.

Mama came home deeply worried. "You will remain here," she told us. "But Papa and I have to go away."

"When?" I asked nervously.

"How long?" Yiding added.

"I don't know," she replied.

When Yicun began to whimper, Mama put him on her lap and comforted him. "Yimao and Yiding will take care of you. Papa and I will write to you."

Mama told me that I was old enough to watch over my brothers and to make sure they had enough to eat and were cared for if they became ill.

I became a parent to my five-year-old brother and a guardian of my twelve-year-old brother. What remained of my childhood was over. I was ten years old.

Many meetings were held during the next week to explain the logistics of the move and the routine of life in the countryside. Apartments were to be locked after the residents departed. When someone was properly reeducated and sent home, they could reoccupy the same apartment. Until that day the campus would be a ghost town, with only the child care center operational. On December 20, one day before the scheduled departure, Papa was released from the cowshed. Yicun clung to him throughout the day.

In the afternoon our mother took the bus downtown and bought bread and sweets for us to take to the child care center. She meticulously packed a bag of clothing for each of us and rolled up straw mats, blankets and sheets for our bedding. After dinner Mama tied a key to the door on a string around my neck. She told me if any of us needed more clothing, I should return home to get it. When it was time for Yiding and me to leave, we slung our bedrolls over our shoulders and picked up our bags. Yiding's parting words were "Don't worry, Mama and Papa."

"Mama, I'll take care of everything," I affirmed. I strained to keep my voice from breaking. I wanted to cry, to go to my own bed, to stay at home. I looked up into Mama's eyes and saw that she, too, was forcing back tears. I waved goodbye.

In the center, I found that six girls had been assigned to one room and fifteen boys to another. Children six and under were housed in three other rooms. When I went to my room, I found Xiaolan lying on her bedroll on the floor, staring at the ceiling.

"Xiaolan!" I squealed in delight.

"Maomao!" she said and jumped up.

We unrolled my bedding next to hers and sat together for the next hour, talking about and guessing at what life might be like in this facility.

My parents had prepared wooden placards that they were required to carry as they marched out of the city. Papa wrote on his placard, "It is hard for any person to avoid mistakes, but one should make as few as possible. When a mistake is made one should correct it, and the more quickly and thoroughly the better."

Mama told Yicun it was time to take him to the center. She held him, and Papa picked up his bedroll and a bag of clothing. They walked out into the starless winter night. Yicun wrapped his arms around Mama's neck. Along the way he began to cry. "I want to stay with you and Papa," he whined. "I'm afraid."

"Yiding and Yimao will be at the center, darling," Mama reminded him. "They'll take care of you."

"I don't want you to go," he sobbed.

They stopped. Papa put down the bags and took Yicun from Mama. Yicun buried his face against Papa's shoulder.

Inside the center, the woman in charge—Comrade Pan—

demanded, "Why are you so late?" She was one of the teachers who daily placed Yicun on the potty chair and refused to allow him to play with others. She was a chubby woman with a tiny nose, narrow eyes and big protruding teeth. She was a Party member and an enthusiastic speaker at rallies. When she was angry, her eyes seemed to close completely and she leaned close to the object of her anger as if she were going to bite. The children were terrified of her wrath.

"I'm sorry," Mama responded contritely. "We had many things to take care of."

"*We* have many things to take care of *here*," Comrade Pan snapped. "Now hurry!"

"Where will he stay?" Mama asked.

"The two- to four-year-olds are there," Comrade Pan answered, pointing to a large room where a dozen youngsters had already put down their mats and blankets.

Mama knelt and carefully unrolled Yicun's mat and blanket. Yicun watched from my father's arms. Papa put him down and gently pulled his hands free of his neck. Yicun grabbed Papa's leg, locked his fingers together and began to wail. Other children sat up to watch. Comrade Pan became agitated and scolded Yicun and my parents.

When Yicun was quieted, Mama and Papa turned to leave. Yicun rolled over and lay on his stomach and rested his chin on his pillow. He looked at his parents, pleading silently through his tears. Outside, Mama and Papa walked for a few steps, shuffling their feet. They stared at the ground. Suddenly, Mama turned and hurried to a window. Papa followed. They watched Yicun, still lying on the floor. His woeful gaze pierced Mama's heart. She covered her face with both hands. Papa started to cry.

I had been hiding in the hallway, hoping to get a last look at them. I watched as they trudged away, passing between row upon row of darkened dormitories and classroom buildings that lined the route like the ghostly ruins of a dead civilization.

They embraced before Papa returned to the cowshed.

25

The children of the child care center were awakened early by supervisors. There was no breakfast. We were marched to a special spot on the street. Each of us was handed a small paper banner with a quotation from Chairman Mao scribbled on it and instructed to wave it over our head as the marchers approached. Our supervisors reminded us to pay attention and to shout slogans together as loud as we could when they gave the signal.

Three thousand adults gathered at the athletic grounds. In the front ranks were the revolutionary faculty, staff and students. Behind them were the cow demons and the rest of the university's political menagerie. They stood four abreast in long columns. A leader of the Propaganda Team addressed them. "Our journey will be a hundred miles. We will cover the distance in six days. Now let us begin *our* Long March." He gave a signal, and everyone cheered and waved Little Red Books in the air. The columns turned and the journey began.

I heard a sound like thunder a few blocks away. I stepped out from the other children and saw a mass of men and women approaching. Those in the front ranks held Little Red Books and waved them over their heads while pounding the sky with their fists. As the marchers came closer, the throng lining the street five and six deep joined in shouting slogans. One earsplitting blast of phrases followed another. Hundreds of spectators—those selected to remain on campus along with the general population of Hefei—thumped drums and thrashed cymbals. With each fresh outburst from the crowd, the marchers responded with slogans. Yicun held both hands over his ears as he looked up at me curiously, wondering what this madness was all about. I tried to tell him but I could not even hear my own voice. When the first marchers were a few feet from us, our supervisors began jumping in the air, waving their signs and screaming for the children to chant with them. The smaller children began to cry. I held up Yicun so he could see over the heads of the others.

"Long Live the Great Leader Chairman Mao!" a teacher howled, and we responded in a screeching salvo, "Long Live the Great Leader Chairman Mao!"

"Long Live the Revolutionary Road of Chairman Mao," the marchers shouted back, and the teachers answered, "Long Live the Revolutionary Road of Chairman Mao." At a signal from the teachers the children intoned in their little voices, "Long Live the Revolutionary Road of Chairman Mao."

Comrade Pan was leaping up and down, waving both arms in the air and screaming slogans. She snapped her head from side to side like a dog chasing a fly and sprayed everyone near her with her spit. She sprang high into the air and came down on the foot of another supervisor. Both women screamed. Comrade Pan lost her footing and sprawled on all fours in the middle of the street. She lay there awkwardly as the marchers stepped around her. No one offered assistance. She rose slowly and limped to the side of the street. She seemed momentarily dazed. Another supervisor leaned in to her face and shrieked out a slogan. Comrade Pan once more took up the cry. But she was less energetic, and she no longer made revolutionary leaps.

I saw Mama and, a short distance behind her, Papa. They were both bent beneath the weight of their packs. "There's Mama and Papa!" I said to Yicun.

I put him down and took his hand and ran to Mama. She broke ranks and approached us.

"Mama," I cried. She embraced Yicun. She examined his face and pulled out a handkerchief and wiped his runny nose; he'd caught a cold. She squeezed his hands and said, "Be a good boy, Yicun. Bye-bye." She hurried back to her place in the column.

I turned to look for my father. I waved and pointed him out to Yicun. Papa looked at us forlornly. He forced a smile but I saw his eyes were shining with tears. "Goodbye, Papa," I called and raised my hand. In an instant he, too, was gone.

At the end of Papa's group was a big four-wheeled cart. It was pulled by several men harnessed to it. Among them were the president and the Party secretary of the university. On the cart were the bedrolls and the bags of the Red Guards and the Propaganda Team members. At the end of the parade was a bus with only a driver in it. The bus was there in case any marchers collapsed and could not be revived. But later, they were sure to be subject to accusations and criticism for anti-revolutionary exhaustion.

After six days, the marchers arrived at their destination and were assigned to several villages. Mama was sent to live with a family in Liushan Village. A young Red Guard was chosen to live with her and report on her labor and behavior to supervising officials. Papa was assigned to a room with eleven other cow demons in a peasant's hut in nearby Nan Village. The men worked during the day, attended criticism meetings in the evening and slept on the dirt floor at night as they learned from the peasants.

Mama agonized over the three of us in Hefei. She had never been away from my brothers. Yet she could not betray her feelings to the young woman watching her for fear of being accused of bourgeois sentimentality. She was so preoccupied with our condition that there were times she feared she was losing her mind. She worried that she might become ill and incapable of caring for us when we were reunited. After the migrants were settled, the Propaganda Team leader announced an "Iron Rule." "Under no circumstance," he said, "will anyone be allowed to return to Hefei. If someone dies in this village, he will be buried here." This, Mama concluded, was to discourage suicide among the cow demons and snake spirits. There was no hope of ever going home, dead or alive.

The Iron Rule, however, did not apply to the Propaganda Team members. The ruling elite went back to Hefei whenever they wished and returned to the village with warm clothes and food for themselves and their comrades.

26

The three of us adjusted to life in the child care center. At mealtime, one of the supervisors made an announcement, and we walked to the classrooms to eat with the younger children. The food—usually a bowl of rice porridge—was put before each of us. All children, regardless of age, were given the same portion. Each child was provided with a tin cup, and large thermoses of boiled water were placed in the room each morning for drinking.

A single latrine that consisted of a room with several stalls and holes in a concrete floor was divided into boys' and girls' sections. Iron water pipes with faucets projected from the wall over a drain in the floor. That was where we brushed our teeth and washed ourselves and our clothing. There was no hot water. Soap was rationed at one cake per family per month. Toothpaste was a concoction that looked and tasted like white glue and was also rationed.

The cook was a middle-aged man we called Uncle Liu. He had been a peasant and worked in the countryside most of his life. He had dark leathery skin and a mustache, the only one I'd ever seen. Shortly after we arrived at the center Yiding became Uncle Liu's assistant. After dinner each evening, Yiding sneaked food to Yicun, Xiaolan and me in his pockets. Some days he brought a fistful of rice he'd scraped from a pot and sometimes small pieces of meat or vegetables Uncle Liu had given him as a reward for his hard work. We had to go outside to eat the extra food so that the other children wouldn't report us.

We were allowed to write one letter each month to our parents. Everything we wrote had to be preceded and followed by effusive praise for Chairman Mao. I managed to get a little news in my letters to Mama. But my words made her sadder and she missed us even more. Classes resumed several months later, when fighting between the Red Guard factions ceased. Xiaolan and I walked to our school together after breakfast. We returned to the center for lunch. At the end of each day we did our homework while sitting on our bedding. I did the laundry for my brothers, washing their bedding and clothing by hand. I also mended their shirts and trousers and socks.

Divisions between red and black families persisted among the younger children. One afternoon I found Yicun standing with his face pressed to the cold windowpane while the other children played nearby.

"Yicun!" I called to him. "Let's go outside."

I bundled him up and took him to the playground. He loved to ride the merry-go-round. It was a little hand-pushed wheel with wooden animals mounted on it. I helped him climb onto a horse and pushed it around and ran beside him. He came out of his grim mood and began laughing and shouting, "Faster! Faster!" I recalled how delighted he had been when our parents had brought him here on weekends in the past.

As the weeks passed, the amount of food we were given each day decreased. Some days the vegetables were skipped, and some weeks there was no meat. Sometimes they served us all baby food for several days in a row. We licked our bowls clean. Mama sent ration coupons, and on the way to the center from school, I'd look for a black market. When I found food, I gave almost all of it to my brothers, just as

Grandma once had done for me. Mama sent us a bag of peanuts. Yiding was in charge of the peanut distribution. He gave them to us one per person per day until they ran out. Xiaolan and I talked about food constantly. We remembered and described the meals our mothers prepared. We dreamed of food. I awakened in the middle of the night aching with hunger. As everyone else slept, I opened my bag, squeezed several beads of toothpaste into my mouth and chewed on it as long as possible before swallowing it.

I went to Yicun's room each night, covered him and sat on his mat, and told him stories to lull him to sleep. The stories he liked best were those Papa told him, the ones I'd heard from my hiding place. The older boys and girls gathered in one room and told stories; we took turns. Xiaolan told wonderful tales from Chinese folklore. I tried to reconstruct *The Count of Monte Cristo* but found I'd forgotten long parts of the story. I sometimes confused my attentive listeners, so I improvised. I remembered well, however, the final words, "Wait and hope," and whispered them as a magical conclusion.

Yiding was the best storyteller among us. We gathered around him when he launched his colorful epics. One night he told so many stories that we were up until dawn. We could not be roused for breakfast. The supervisors asked us why we were exhausted and one of the boys confessed, "Because we were listening to Yiding tell stories last night." The supervisors were angry and ordered Yiding to stop telling stories. During the next few nights, Comrade Pan stuck her head in the door to make sure no one was talking.

The weather became colder. Our clothes were threadbare, and I kept them together through constant sewing, letting out hems, and stitching on patches. Yiding and I returned to our apartment and retrieved more clothing. The building was empty. We discovered the glass in the apartment door had been broken but everything appeared to be the way Mama had left it. We pulled shards of broken glass from the pane and nailed a board over it. We picked up winter clothing and returned to the center. In order to stay warm, we put on all of our clothing. I huddled on my mat beneath a pile of blankets with Xiaolan. We lay together shivering and listening to the wind and the sleet thrash the windows.

Yicun complained that he was so cold he could not sleep. I worried about him constantly. Each week he became increasingly withdrawn. At night he was afraid to go alone through the unlit hall to the latrine. He began wetting his bed. The supervisors were incensed. They forced him to sleep on his damp bedding. One night he had a bowel movement in bed. Comrade Pan was furious. She threatened to throw him out. Yicun burst into tears and called for Mama.

Comrade Pan and the other supervisors concluded the only way to prevent a recurrence was to deprive him of dinner. During the dinner hour he sat on his mat and watched the other children eat. When I saw him that night, he whispered, "Big Sister, I want to go home. I am hungry." I was about to say, "I'm hungry too," but stopped myself. I went to my room and squirted toothpaste onto my palm. I returned to Yicun and told him I had candy for him. "Close your eyes," I said. I rubbed the toothpaste on his tongue. He tasted it, chewed it, and asked, "Are you sure this is candy?"

"Yes," I said. "Xiaolan gave it to me."

He smiled and licked his lips and asked for more. I told him that Papa and Mama would return soon and then we could all live at home and eat all we wanted.

27

With the approach of the Lunar New Year in the second week of February, the Red Guards, factory workers and soldiers began preparing to return home for the week-long holiday. The Year of the Rooster began on Monday, February 17, 1969. It was believed that since the rooster's crow precedes the light of day at the end of a dark night, so, too, the Year of the Rooster might bring light at the end of a dark period of time. Mama was hopeful that the New Year would bring an end to her separation from her husband and children.

One week before the holiday, the Propaganda Team leader in Liushan Village made an unexpected public announcement. The Communist Party leadership had decided that female teachers with young children would be allowed to return home to celebrate the holiday. Details would be given later, he said. Mama became giddy with excitement. She cautiously anticipated a subsequent directive giving the exact day and hour she could depart. The women were summoned to the village canteen. The Propaganda Team leader read a list of names of those mothers authorized to leave. Mama's name was missing. She approached the Propaganda Team leader and asked why her name had been omitted. "I have three small children in Hefei," she reminded him.

"Li Yikai, you know very well your husband is in the cowshed with the other cow demons," he replied. "He is a bad element. We cannot allow you to go home."

At midnight she stood alone at her window and tried to find strength in memories of the few past holidays we had spent together as a family.

———————

Children were retrieved from the center by relatives who carried them home to celebrate the Lunar New Year. I hoped for a surprise when I returned to the center from school each day and imagined Mama or Papa waiting for us. Finally, Xiaolan and I were the only ones left in the girls' bedroom. We were sitting on our mats reading one afternoon when a familiar voice cried, "Xiaolan!"

"Mama!" Xiaolan shouted and leaped to her feet. Auntie Liang appeared in the doorway and Xiaolan ran to her. She had come to take Xiaolan home.

"Are my mama and papa coming home, too, Auntie Liang?" I asked.

"I don't think so, Maomao," she said. "I'm so sorry."

My heart sank. Auntie Liang told me she hoped Mama would come home within a few weeks.

The staff went home later that afternoon. Uncle Liu departed for his village. No dinner was served. Yiding came for me and we went to Yicun's room. Only the three of us remained in the building. As night fell, we heard muffled laughter and the intermittent pop of firecrackers.

It was New Year's Eve.

We wrapped ourselves in our blankets and stood at the gate to watch the festivities. We laughed at the bright flashes and explosions up and down the street, and moments later, jumped at the bang of the firecrackers. Little clouds of shredded paper drifted like snowflakes from buildings where people lit strings of firecrackers and flung them out the windows and shouted for good luck. We listened and looked and wondered what life was like for those people. None of us spoke except for a momentary "oh" or "ah." We remained there until we were shivering with cold. We went inside to Yicun's room and lay down and covered ourselves with three blankets.

I could not sleep. I was cold and hungry. I went to the window and peered out into the blackness. It was as silent as a cemetery. I lay my forehead against the icy glass and cried. I decided that I would take my brothers home, if only for one day. Nobody was going to check to see where we were. Nobody cared. I had a few food coupons for flour and meat, and I had two yuan hidden under my mat. I rose early and went outside to search for street vendors. I was able to find one and bought a bit of meat, cabbage and flour. I returned and told my brothers my plan. They were delighted. On the way home I promised I'd make dumplings for our holiday.

In our apartment we found a few coal briquettes for the stove. I tried repeatedly to light them by igniting pieces of paper. I failed. The paper burned and the smoke lingered in the apartment, and before long, we were coughing and teary-eyed. I ran out of matches and had no coupons to purchase more.

I remembered Xiaolan was at home with her mother. I went to their apartment and knocked. Auntie Liang didn't have matches or kindling to share with me but she told me to fetch my brothers and we could have our holiday meal together. I retrieved my brothers and my food supply, and we hurried to Auntie Liang's apartment.

Auntie Liang prepared a real feast. With no electricity in the building, she lit a kerosene lamp as night fell. We gathered around a small table when the meal was ready. Yicun scooped up the dumplings and soup without lifting his eyes from his bowl. Xiaolan and I nudged each other and pointed at him and giggled. Auntie Liang prepared two servings for each of us. I was full for the first time in weeks. After dinner we told Auntie Liang how we had little to do but study in the center and how we told stories to quiet the little ones and entertain one another. I described how Yiding's tales fascinated the other children and how he kept us awake. We were unusually talkative, and even Yicun emerged from his shell and haltingly told Auntie Liang about riding the merry-go-round and learning revolutionary songs.

After listening and laughing with us, Auntie Liang announced that she needed to take us back to the center because she was required to return in the morning to the village where she'd been assigned. I thought this odd since I knew other parents came home for the whole week. As we buttoned our padded jackets and tied our scarves Auntie Liang rummaged through some boxes in her bedroom. When she returned, she said, "Look what I found!" and held her hand near the lantern. There was a jade ring on her little finger. Jewelry had been denounced by the Red Guards as bourgeois, and could be confiscated. We gazed at the ring, enchanted, and reached out to feel it. "This belonged to my great-grandmother," she whispered wistfully.

"It's beautiful," I exclaimed, and everyone agreed.

After showing us the ring, Auntie Liang tried to remove it. She twisted and pulled, but it stayed on her finger. "It's all right," she said. "I'll take it off later. We must go now."

She tied a long red scarf around her neck and led us outside. It was snowing. The campus was white and the air was filled with snowflakes that danced around us. Auntie Liang turned her face to the sky and stuck out her tongue to catch snowflakes. We ran the short distance to the sports grounds, which were buried beneath untouched snow.

"Look at me," Auntie Liang called. "I'm a butterfly." She lay on her back in the snow and spread her arms and legs wide and moved them back and forth and got to her feet and showed us her impression in the snow. It looked like a white butterfly. "Make your own butterflies," she said, and we did. We looked like the happy children in the picture books outside the broadcast studio. At last I knew how the children in those pictures felt and why they smiled so broadly.

In the amber halo of the streetlamps I saw how truly beautiful Auntie Liang was. Her skin had a lovely sheen. Her hair was black and radiant, and her eyes shone like silver. I stopped making my butterfly and watched her run around, throwing snow at Xiaolan and my brothers. She was a little girl. She darted between us and hugged us and twirled us around until she fell and then she hugged us again. She lifted Xiaolan into the air and kissed her and twirled her until Xiaolan screamed with joy. We all collapsed in gales of laughter.

I watched Auntie Liang and Xiaolan and felt a pang of envy. I wanted to play with my parents and hear their laughter. I longed to be held by my mother. We lost track of time. Eventually, Auntie Liang pulled each of us to our feet and brushed the snow off our clothing. We held hands and danced our way toward the center.

One supervisor and a few children had already returned. We put Yicun to bed. Yiding said good night and went to his room. Auntie Liang followed Xiaolan and me to our room, and we crawled together under our two blankets and lay down. Auntie Liang pulled the covers up to our chins. She tenderly kissed me on the cheek. I wrapped my arms around her and pulled her to me and choked back my tears. She moved to the other side of the mat, held Xiaolan in her arms, kissed her and slowly pulled away. She breathed a brief ragged sigh. She stood for a moment before switching off the light and backing away. I watched her silhouette and saw her glistening eyes. Her footsteps faded in the hall. The outside door opened and closed and she was gone.

Xiaolan cried and we wrapped our arms around each other.

The following morning Comrade Pan poked me awake with her foot. In a brusque voice, she called, "Wake up, Wu Yimao! Your little brother shit his bed. You fed him last night. You had better take care of it now!"

I rubbed my eyes and sat up.

"Do you want me to come with you?" Xiaolan asked.

"No," I replied. "Go back to sleep."

I went to Yicun's room. He sat on a stool beside his mat crying. His soiled underwear, trousers and sheet lay in a pile on the floor. I comforted him and led him to the washroom to clean him up. The water pipe had frozen and a long stalactite of ice hung from the mouth of the faucet. I returned to Yicun's room, poured a cup of hot water from a thermos and carried it back to the washroom. I wet a towel with it and washed Yicun.

Comrade Pan watched. "The water pipe is frozen," I told her. "I can't wash anything today."

"Go to the pond," she barked.

I borrowed a large bamboo basket and a wooden laundry paddle from Uncle Liu and put the soiled laundry in the basket. Outside the snow had stopped falling. I trudged down the winding path to the pond. No one else was around.

The surface of the frozen pond was covered with snow. I raised the paddle high over my head and slammed it down on the ice. With a loud crack, the ice broke, and water bubbled up. I pushed aside the shards of ice to create a hole large enough to do my washing. I pulled the soiled blanket from the basket, the new snow beneath my shoes shifted, and I slid and tumbled backward into the hole. The icy water had hundreds of tiny teeth that bit my hands and arms. I let out a loud gasp and thrust out my hands to break my fall, then turned and pushed myself back up the bank of the pond. My jacket was soaked and I was shivering. I started to work fast. My teeth chattered as I pounded the laundry with the paddle. Each time I plunged the blanket and clothing into the water, it seemed to take another bite from my flesh. I wrung out the sheet and blanket and dropped them into my basket and hurriedly washed and paddled the underwear and trousers.

When I was finished, I had difficulty standing because my clothing was sheathed in ice. Icicles hung from my hair and the sleeves of my jacket. Sharp little needles of ice in my trousers and jacket pricked my skin when I moved. I struggled unsteadily to my feet. I could not lift the loaded basket. I had to drag it behind me.

A light snow had begun to come down. Gusts of wind blew flakes in my face, and I shielded my eyes with my hand as I plodded along.

After I had struggled a short distance, an unusual flash of color caught my eye. I peered hard through the screen of white, trying to make it out. I released the basket, moved several steps in the direction of the color and strained to see what it was. Part of it was a streak of scarlet but the shape was a blur. I went closer. When I was a few feet away it became clear. The color was one end of a scarf tied around the branch of a tree. The other end was knotted around the neck of a naked body.

I was stunned. The body twisted slowly above me. The face was swollen. The flesh was alabaster, but the head, hands and feet were the color of a bruise.

There was something eerily familiar in the features. I forced myself to look. It was Auntie Liang. A finger on her left hand where her jade ring had been was chopped off. The blood from her wound had congealed in a splatter of black ice beneath her body.

I let out a deep harrowing howl. I sobbed and scratched at my eyes, trying to make everything go away.

I backed away while keeping my eyes fixed on Auntie Liang. Then I turned and ran. I raced into the center, screaming hysterically. Two supervisors appeared and asked, "What is the screaming about? Have you seen a ghost?"

The sound that erupted from somewhere inside me was a pathetic frightening "ahhhhhhhhhhhhhhhhhh" as I pointed in the direction from which I'd just come. One supervisor took my face in her hands and demanded, "What is wrong?" When I continued screaming, she slapped me hard.

I found my voice. "Help," I sobbed. "She's hanging from the tree." I broke loose and ran out the door with the supervisors following me. As we neared Auntie Liang, I slowed and pointed.

The supervisors halted and looked. They cautiously approached and circled the body, mumbling to each other. I stood at a distance and noticed dozens of footprints and several bricks piled in the snow.

"Someone else was here—look at these footprints," one supervisor said.

"Several people have been here," the other said.

"They stood on these to steal her clothes," the first said, pointing to the bricks.

"I'll get help," the other one said and trotted away.

The supervisor asked what I'd seen. She asked if I'd noticed anyone near the body.

"No. Just Auntie Liang."

"You know this woman?"

"Yes."

"Are you sure?"

"She is Xiaolan's mother," I said.

The first supervisor looked up at the body once more and walked under it, looking in the snow, examining the footprints. "I think those damned shit stealers were here before you," she said. "They stole her clothes."

The shit stealers were peasants from villages surrounding the city who sneaked onto the campus every night. They were an army of shadows that glided silently through the dark. They stole sewage from the university toilets to use and sell as fertilizer. They also stole anything else that might be found unguarded.

The first supervisor returned with Uncle Liu and two security men. Uncle Liu asked, "Yimao, are you all right?"

"No," I said.

He joined the others around the body. They found dark stains where the shit stealers had put down their buckets while they tore away Auntie Liang's clothing and cut off her finger.

Uncle Liu climbed the tree, pulled out a small knife, and sliced through the red scarf. Auntie Liang's rigid body fell to the snow. I was embarrassed for her when the supervisors and the other men stood staring at her naked body. She lay on her back, arms and legs outstretched, as if she intended to make a butterfly. The scarf was still knotted around her neck. Uncle Liu untied it and used it to cover her private parts.

"They took everything," one of the security men said.

"Even her underwear," the second added and nudged the first.

"She was a fine one," the first one said in a low voice, and both men chuckled.

I watched the fluttering snowflakes gently powder Auntie Liang's body with a chaste veneer. I turned and began walking away, but the supervisors shouted for me to stay.

One of the security men approached and asked me how I'd discovered the body and if I'd seen anyone else lurking around.

A supervisor volunteered that Auntie Liang was a counterrevolutionary.

Another said she'd heard that Auntie Liang had several lovers. A security man mumbled something about having heard this, too. "No loss," the other security man nodded. All of them except Uncle Liu nodded agreement. Uncle Liu gave me a concerned glance and then looked away as if ashamed.

A sudden gust sent a piece of Auntie Liang's scarf skittering over the snow. The man questioning me snatched it up. He held it out for me to see. "This was hers?" he asked. "Are you sure?"

I looked at it. I had not noticed the subtle pattern in the scarf before. Embroidered in the silk were hundreds of little red butterflies of a slightly different hue than the rest of the scarf. Held to the light, they were clear and appeared to shimmer.

"Let the child go," Uncle Liu said. "She's told you all she knows."

"Okay. You can go," the security man said.

I hurried to the center and sat on the floor and felt sick. I realized only then that I'd left the laundry basket outside. I retrieved it.

The full consequence of everything I'd just seen slowly dawned on me. Not only was Auntie Liang dead, but she had committed a crime in taking her own life.

Later that morning her body was removed. No one said how it was disposed of. But I knew that the bodies of those who killed themselves were hauled outside the city to be devoured by wild dogs.

Xiaolan found me sitting in the hallway crying. She asked what was wrong. I told her I'd fallen through the ice. She helped me out of my wet clothing and we slipped under our blankets together. She lay next to me to keep me warm. I didn't know how to tell her what had happened. I wondered if I should tell her before the supervisors did. I decided not to.

When I closed my eyes that night, I dreamed of Auntie Liang's scarf. It was caught high in the branches of the tree where I'd found her, waving like a long flag in the wind. I approached the tree, looking up. As I watched, the scarf unraveled and the butterflies embroidered in the silk came free and floated up on the air. The first ones free flapped their tiny wings and circled the tree while the others worked their way out of the fabric and the scarf became smaller and smaller. As the last threads of the scarf came undone, the butterflies rose in the sky and began flying away. They grew smaller and smaller and finally disappeared in the white winter world. I was left standing alone beneath the skeletal branches of the tree. I awakened with a start, tears pouring from my eyes. Xiaolan was resting on her elbow, looking at me. I buried my face in the blanket to hide my tears. Xiaolan laid her hand on my shoulder and cried out, "Mama, I want mama." She had been told the news.

She turned away. I held her tightly and felt her shudder. Her skin was cold. She moaned and said words I did not understand.

"Xiaolan?" I whispered. "I had a dream about your mama. If I tell it to you then you can have the same dream."

She calmed in my arms.

"Xiaolan, I saw Auntie Liang's scarf outside. And guess what? While I watched it turned into little butterflies that danced in the air and flew over my head. And then they flew away, all of them, together."

"Where is my mama?" Xiaolan whimpered.

"Auntie Liang was there, Xiaolan. But it wasn't really her anymore. Instead, she was the last beautiful red butterfly to come out of the scarf. And the butterfly fluttered around my face. It spoke to me in Auntie Liang's voice."

I could see the shine of Xiaolan's eyes as she turned to me. "What did she say?" she asked.

"She told me to tell you that she was a butterfly. And she said that we should watch for her in . . . in the spring. And she told me to tell you that she would visit us often."

It was quiet for a moment as Xiaolan thought about what I'd said.

"Is that all? Did she say my name?"

I don't know where my words came from. It was as if Auntie Liang were in my heart and her words were tumbling from my mouth into Xiaolan's ear.

"Yes," I said. "She told me to tell you that she was watching over you. And she said you should wait and hope."

28

Shortly after the holiday, my mother was summoned by the Propaganda Team leader.

"We have decided to send your husband back to the countryside near his birthplace of Yangzhou, Jiangsu Province," he said.

Mama nodded. She concealed her trembling and stared at the frozen earth.

"But the question is, where precisely to send him? It is difficult to send criminals like him anyplace. Nobody wants them."

Mama waited until the next morning to tell Papa the dreadful news. She found, however, that he'd been told earlier and withheld it so as not to upset her.

"There is nothing we can do," he said. "Let's see where they send me before we despair any more."

Mama wondered how he could survive by himself. When he was sent to the concentration camp in 1958, he was only thirty-eight. Now he was nearly fifty. Could he bear it again, emotionally and physically?

In early May the Propaganda Team leader held a meeting with the migrants from the university. He announced that the Propaganda Team was giving certain selected comrades "permission to volunteer to settle down in the countryside." These volunteers were to establish permanent homes among the peasants, according to Chairman Mao's directive. Their residency permits and food and oil quotas would be transferred. Their dependents would be moved with them but they were all to be stripped of the right to free public health care.

The purpose of this program, he said, was to provide a lifetime of reeducation for bourgeois intellectuals and their families among the peasants. He read from a list of names. This time my mother's name was first.

"The day after tomorrow," he continued, "trucks will return you to Hefei. You will have one week to prepare to leave for your new homes."

My mother felt as if the sky had suddenly fallen on her. It's the end of the world, she thought.

She asked the leader, "What about my husband?"

"He is still under our control as a cow demon," he said. "But we may consider sending him to the village where you reside. Party policy is full of compassion for families."

The next morning Mama was given permission to visit Papa. They discussed the problem of relocating. She doubted her younger children could survive in the countryside. They decided she should take my older brother with her and that my younger brother and I would remain in the center.

A meeting of the Communist Party Politburo was scheduled to take place in Beijing in April. Schoolchildren around the country spent many hours in the classroom preparing for the celebration. We were taught a special song and dance as we waved paper sunflowers above our heads:

The Yangtze River flows to the east,
All the sunflowers bloom toward the sun,
We are waiting excitedly for the Ninth Party Congress,
And we all sing and praise
Our great, glorious and correct Party.

Day after day we practiced. I danced beside Xiaolan and watched her. Sometimes she just mouthed the words and went through the dance steps, without her previous energy and grace. Finally our teachers pronounced us ready. We went into the streets to dance and celebrate for pedestrians. After the Ninth Party Congress song and dance, we practiced a new one. For this performance, we sang, "All the cadres are going down to the countryside to be reeducated by the peasants, it is a good chance for the cadres to learn." We had no idea what this meant. We nonetheless performed it daily in the streets. I noticed that few passersby seemed amused or stopped for longer than a moment to listen to us.

Shortly after we began performing the new number, Xiaolan's father arrived at the center. He had been assigned to a village in the countryside, and he and Xiaolan were moving there in a few days. Quietly, Xiaolan packed. "Goodbye, Xiaolan," I said as she left. There was no response. The next day we were organized by the supervisors to welcome our parents—now referred to as "settle-down cadres"—home. When I saw Mama climb out of the truck, I released Yicun's hand and he ran to her. He leaped into her arms and asked, "Where's Papa?"

"He'll be here soon," she said. "He misses you."

Yiding and I picked up Mama's bags and we walked home together. We were excited and animated. I noticed that Mama walked slowly and seemed exhausted.

In our apartment we told Mama everything that had happened, each of us stammering to share our stories. When we were washing the dishes, I told Mama about how I'd found Auntie Liang. She listened without saying a word. As my story unfolded, she bowed her head and hid her face with her hands and cried. She motioned for me to come to her and held her face next to mine. "Poor Auntie Liang," she choked. "Poor Xiaolan."

I wept with her.

29

That evening Mama said nothing about our impending separation. The night was unusually quiet. There was none of the customary noise—no tramp of marching feet and no chorus of hate. In the morning Mama explained what was about to happen. "I will be going away," she said. "Yiding will come with me. Yimao and Yicun will stay in the center. But I will come back for you soon." Yicun moped. I looked at my mother's sad, tired eyes and fought back my tears.

She tried to cheer us up but our spirits would not be lifted. After breakfast we began packing.

A woman came to our apartment and notified Mama of a meeting at which officials would announce where she was to be sent. Mama said it didn't matter whether she attended the meeting. Everything had been decided. She sent me in her place. I listened to the reading of names and villages. I wrote the information in my notebook and ran home. "Mama, they are sending you to Hexian County, Xiaohe Village," I announced. "They said this village is far from the county headquarters. They said there will be one room for you but no electricity."

Mama listened in shock. She asked, "Are you sure?" I showed her my notes. The color drained from her face. "How can this be?" she asked. "How can we live there?"

She started talking as if speaking to my father. "Ningkun," she said, "what ever happened to the Five Haves they promised us? They said we'd have a house, have a stove, have a water jar, have food, have a salary." Her voice rose and broke. After a momentary silence, she left. She found others who had been at the meeting and asked about their assigned villages. As she suspected, her village was the most remote and primitive.

She went to the headquarters of the Propaganda Team and asked to see the leader. "Please allow me to trade my village for another," she begged, "at least a village with accessible transportation. I have three small children to care for." He listened but said nothing. After she had her say, he went back to his work as if she were not present. She stood in front of him silently for several minutes. When she realized he did not intend to respond, she came home.

That afternoon a Red Guard came to our apartment and announced, "Li Yikai, we have decided to allow you to exchange your assignment with another teacher. You will be sent to Xipu District, Sunbao Commune, Xinjian Work Brigade, Gaozhuang Production Team. This village is not in the mountains. It is on the plain. And it is only ten miles from the Hexian County headquarters and near a main road. You will be given one and one half rooms, and you will have electricity."

Mama beamed and said, "Thank you."

She was increasingly anxious as the deadline for departure neared. We all worked hard packing. I boxed coal briquettes for the stove. Mama filled bags with kitchen utensils, dishes, and other supplies along with clothing. We disassembled the beds and tied them up.

Two days before the move, I became ill. Mama put me to bed and monitored my temperature. Around ten o'clock that night, my condition worsened and she decided to carry me to the clinic. She trudged down the middle of the abandoned street, taking short, quick steps, panting heavily. She held me so tightly I could feel the pounding of her heart. She called my name to make sure I was conscious. "Maomao," she'd whisper, "are you okay?" and I'd reply, "I'm okay, Mama." After we'd gone several blocks, I found I could no longer speak. The door of the clinic was locked. Mama knocked, but there was no response. She pounded desperately on the door, crying, "Help me. My child is ill."

I drifted in and out of consciousness. Mama's voice faded and rose. Her plea sounded as if it came from a great distance. The night air was cold and I was drenched in sweat and shivering.

A light came on. The bolt clicked and the door opened a crack. A short, stout, frowning woman appeared in night clothing. "Are you mad?" she sputtered. "What is wrong with you?"

"My little girl is very ill," Mama said.

The woman peered around the door and looked at me. "And what do you want me to do?" she asked.

"Get her a doctor."

"Impossible!" the woman said. "There is no doctor on duty at this hour." She started to close the door.

Mama stuck her foot inside and prevented her from shutting it. She asked, "Who is the doctor on duty during the day?"

"It is Dr. Tang."

"Where does she live? I'll take my child there."

The woman stared at her in astonishment.

"Please," Mama cried. "Where does she live?"

The woman hesitated before saying, "Building one-twenty-seven, number nine, third floor. But you didn't hear it from me."

"Thank you," Mama said.

The door slammed and the lock clicked and the light went out. Mama hurried down the street with me.

I heard no sound but Mama's labored breathing. Suddenly a dog rushed out of the dark and began growling and snapping at Mama's ankles. I smelled and heard the animal beside us. Mama wove her way down the street as the dog repeatedly lunged at her. Several times it nipped at her heels, and when she kicked back, it raced around us. Other dogs began to bark in the distance. I feared the racket came from wild dogs that slunk into the city each night to eat garbage and the bodies of dead counterrevolutionaries.

I was petrified. The snarls of the animal chasing us became ferocious. Mama slowed and stood still. The dog raced from side to side, its head kept low, its eyes glaring as it approached. With my remaining strength I put my arms around Mama's neck and tried to pull myself up. The dog hesitated, ceased barking and warily approached Mama, smelled her feet and legs, then raised its head and sniffed the bundle she was carrying. When it was finished, it sat and looked at us. Mama cautiously resumed her journey. She didn't dare run and provoke the animal. The dog acted as if it sensed the urgency in Mama's actions. It no longer sought to intimidate her but rather to accompany her through the street.

Mama arrived at building 127 and carried me up to the third floor. She strained to read the numbers on the doors. When she found number nine, she kicked at the door softly. There was no response. She yelled, her voice more desperate and plaintive with each word. "Dr. Tang! Is Dr. Tang at home? This is an emergency. Please help me."

A light came on inside. The scratch of slippers across the floor was followed by a voice, harsh and unhappy. "Who the hell is making such a noise in the middle of the night?"

"My daughter is very ill," Mama said.

"What does she have?"

"I don't know. But I am afraid she is near death."

"How do you know?"

"She has a high fever. She has no energy. She cannot move."

"Can she open her eyes?"

I opened my eyes when I heard this. "Yes," Mama said. "She just opened her eyes."

"Can she speak?"

"Say something," Mama whispered.

"I am here, Mama," I murmured.

The voice inside said, "She doesn't sound sick to me. Go away."

Mama begged Dr. Tang to look at me, but the physician refused to open the door. "Wait till tomorrow. I'll see her then," Dr. Tang advised. The light went out and we were left alone.

Mama concluded that if she persisted in pleading, the doctor might refuse to see me in the morning. She carefully carried me down the dark stairs and out of the building. The dog was waiting for us and started barking and jumping around. Other dogs joined in a distant howling chorus. A moment later, a pack of them, all snapping and barking ferociously, ran at us. In a tremulous but defiant voice, Mama began talking while flicking her foot to keep them at bay. "Go ahead," she dared. "Take a bite of my leg. See how it tastes. Then nobody can send me to the countryside."

The barking ceased. The animals quieted and withdrew. Mama stood still as the dogs circled us, sniffing the air. The biggest dog in the pack approached warily and smelled Mama's feet and her burden. The others watched him. The lead dog sidled up to Mama, lifted his hind leg and relieved himself on her feet. When he was done, he trotted away and the others approached. Two more dogs paused to pee. Then, as suddenly as they appeared, as if on a signal, they were gone. Mama let out a long sigh and laughed. "At least it's warm," she said. She shook her feet and resumed her way home.

Later, Mama laid cool wet towels over my forehead, arms and legs to control my temperature. She was there throughout the night, bathing me, stroking my hair, whispering encouragement.

In the morning she carried me to the clinic. Dr. Tang saw us immediately. She said nothing about the previous night. She examined me, pronounced me not seriously ill, and prescribed a potion. After I'd taken the medicine Mama ran to the office of the leader of the Propaganda Team to ask for more time to prepare to leave. "My daughter is very sick," she told him. "I have been up all night and was unable to finish packing. I am requesting permission for my husband to come home and help me."

He looked at her in astonishment and burst out laughing. "You actually expect me to do that?" he said. "Li Yikai, you are even more stupid than I imagined. Go home. I'll send someone to help you."

That afternoon a university instructor—a notorious and outspoken ultra-leftist—arrived to "assist" us in packing. The unusually short woman, who always seemed to be squinting at the world through her thick wire-rimmed glasses, was celebrated for her ability to root out enemies of the people. She was childless and had a distaste for children.

Instead of assisting us, she unpacked some bags and examined every item inside. She was particularly interested in the books. When she started to page through them, Mama said, "Toilet paper!"

"Yes," she responded. "That is all they are good for."

She abruptly departed at dinnertime.

"Thank you for your help," Mama said as she left.

"This house is a mess," she shot back.

Yiding worked throughout the day. He rolled up the blankets and tied them in neat bundles. Mama saw his work and smiled and recalled how poorly she had tied her pack for the first journey into the countryside. "We could travel around the world," she said, "and these would never come loose. Such a good job."

The day of departure was May 16. A big ceremony commemorating the exodus was planned. Two hundred families were to leave the campus that morning. The night before, two hundred trucks had arrived to transport them. They lined up bumper-to-bumper along the university campus. The truck designated for our family parked near the front door to our building. We stacked our belongings on the bed of the truck and Yiding tied them down.

We completed our work just before midnight. When everything was set, we went back to our apartment. As we prepared to sleep on the bare floor, we saw a flash of lightning outside, followed by a roll of thunder. Minutes later, a heavy downpour began. All of our belongings on the truck were exposed to the rain. Mama saw that the beds on all of the other trucks had been secured and covered with large heavy tarpaulins. There was none for our truck. Mama ordered us all inside and hurried to a driver's apartment. He answered, angry at having been awakened.

"Why are you here?" he growled. "I have to drive all day tomorrow and I need my rest."

"Everyone's truck is covered but ours. I want ours covered," she said.

"I'm a driver," he shot back. "What in the hell can I do about it?"

Mama ran home. She and Yiding began unloading the truck, carrying the belongings inside and stacking them in the hall. Yiding never complained. I felt so sorry for him. He crawled onto the truck and untied the ropes he'd lashed across our things, threw them aside and handed the bags and boards to Mama.

Mama wrung out the blankets and laid them flat on the floor. We did not finish unpacking and sorting and drying until dawn. The rain stopped an hour later. Mama and Yiding moved our belongings back onto the truck. They finished tying everything down minutes before an announcement on the loudspeakers that it was time for everyone to assemble at the sports grounds. The drivers crawled into the cabs of their trucks and drove there. We walked to the assembly point with throngs of others. By the time we arrived, thousands of people were already gathered. Each of the departees was given a red paper flower to pin over his heart. A small ribbon with the slogan TO SETTLE DOWN IS GLORIOUS was attached.

The "Supreme Ruler" of the province, a PLA commander, took the stage. "Congratulations!" he shouted. "You are all answering Chairman Mao's call. You are settling down in the villages to learn from the peasants. Become one with them. Through physical labor you will transform your bourgeois views. We salute you. We congratulate you."

The commander was not leaving Hefei, yet he celebrated the heroism of those who were. He concluded by waving a Little Red Book over his head and shouting, "Victory on Chairman Mao's revolutionary road!" The crowd repeated the phrase. When the commander was done, other party dignitaries followed him to the platform and repeated word for word what he'd already said.

Everyone cheered.

Yicun fell asleep in Mama's arms. I glanced at Yiding and noticed he was struggling to stay awake. A command blared over the loudspeakers for the departees to get into their trucks. The moment of our separation had come. Mama turned to me and said, "Yimao, your little brother is in your care. When I'm settled I'll come back for you. Go to school and study hard!" She gave me a dreary look. She hugged Yicun and put him down. He grasped my hand. Mama and Yiding climbed into the truck beside the driver, who smoked and stared into space. I noticed LIBERATION MODEL printed in metallic characters along the side of the truck's hood. At a signal, the drivers started their engines and honked their horns. There was a tremendous roar and the air was filled with blue fumes.

I waved my hand in front of my face to clear the air and Yicun buried his face in my shirt. I watched Mama as she leaned out the window and waved at us. I wished she would open the door and run back to us. The streets were lined with people singing and dancing and waving Little Red Books. The scene brought back the memory of my parents marching away earlier. This time Mama was going with my older brother and leaving me in charge. The trucks rumbled past, and Yicun and I waved and yelled, "Goodbye, Mama, goodbye, Yiding."

Shortly after four P.M., Mama's truck arrived at Gao Village. The driver jumped out. Mama watched as people approached the truck from nearby hovels. A short man wearing soiled clothing and no shoes strutted in front of the others. He held a cymbal the size of a large plate in one hand and a stick in the other. As he neared the truck, he lifted the cymbal and began pounding on it with the stick. The cymbal had a hole in it. It made a pathetic bang like an old tin can. Nonetheless, he struck it vigorously.

He had a swollen face. His hair was unkempt, his teeth were stained amber. One of his eyes rolled around, seemingly independent of the other. He reeked of alcohol and was unsteady on his legs. From the corner of his mouth drooped the stub of a cigarette.

"I'm Li Tinghai," he slurred. His accent was so heavy my mother had difficulty understanding. "I'm the head of this village."

"This is your settle-down cadre," the driver volunteered.

"Oh, shit!" Li Tinghai muttered and gave my mother a sullen glare.

A woman in the group cackled, "Don't call him Li Tinghai. Just call him Lao Panghai—Old Crab."

The man exploded, "You shut up, you filthy slut!" He extracted a crumpled piece of paper from his pocket and waved it menacingly at her. "See this? Six Articles of Public Security! Any of you"—he waved it at the others—"will fall into the Six Articles as a counterrevolutionary if you make trouble. Then you'll be shot."

"You old fart," a young man said. "You can't read that."

Everyone burst out laughing.

Old Crab turned to my mother. "What's your name?" he snapped.

"I'm Li Yikai."

"And that?" he said, nodding toward my brother cowering in the truck.

"My son Yiding."

"Two more mouths to feed!" He spat out his cigarette stub and circled the truck, examining our belongings. "I don't suppose you brought any cigarettes, did you?" he asked.

"No, I'm sorry," my mother replied.

Old Crab approached the driver and asked for a cigarette. The driver grudgingly handed him one. He asked for another. "For my brother," he explained. The driver gave him another. He put it in his pocket, and the two men stood smoking and chatting.

The driver told my mother and Yiding to unload their belongings. "And hurry," he said. "I have to get back to Hefei tonight."

Old Crab shouted, "Put that stuff on the ground and I'll decide later what to do with it." Mama and Yiding began unloading as the others watched.

30

I returned to the center with Yicun. Although school was in session, nothing much was taught. Students spent almost all the time singing revolutionary songs and reciting Chairman Mao's quotations. We bowed to the bust of Mao and read the Little Red Book and the Three Old Articles, "Serve the People," "In Memory of Dr. Norman Bethune" and "The Foolish Man Who Moved a Mountain." We read them every day until we could recite them perfectly, line by line. That was our education.

I was solely responsible for my little brother. Yiding was gone and all of the older children had departed with their parents. One morning I went shopping with my ration coupons and tried to buy candy for Yicun. I searched for nearly an hour but could find none. I decided instead to get him a toy. All of the available toys were political. So I paid four fen and bought him a small paper portrait of Chairman Mao standing on Tiananmen, waving to Red Guards. I had heard in school that holding a portrait or icon of Chairman Mao was energizing. "It will give you ten thousand pounds of energy" was one of the things our teachers taught us. In return, you had to be very respectful toward it.

On the way back to the center I became exhausted. I rested on the steps of a building. I didn't feel well. So I took out the picture of Mao and prayed for him to give me energy, make me strong and well.

Nothing happened.

I started to think about everything I'd been taught to believe about Chairman Mao and the Party. It dawned on me that it was all lies. I felt ridiculous holding a piece of paper and praying to it.

I looked around at children with their Little Red Books, the Red Guards chanting, the soldiers offering to serve the people. I looked at all of the drab clothing and the blank stares and the short haircuts of young women in shapeless slacks and soiled shirts, posters praising or condemning this or that person. I sensed the deep sadness of people buried beneath all the shouting and slogans. I sensed the true sadness of Grandmother, Auntie Liang, Xiaolan, Mama and Papa. I saw the unhappiness of everything and everybody. My ears had been filled with the ecstatic noise of the teachers and the crowds at parades as our parents left us behind, of the weeping of families broken apart, of the pleas of innocent people punished for being born into the wrong family, of the cries from people being beaten and dragged away. Could I be the only one who saw this for what it was? Everyone was pretending and everyone was afraid and everyone was wearing a mask.

I felt more alone than ever.

I wondered if this was what Auntie Liang knew the night she left Xiaolan at the center. I wondered what might happen to me, alone in this vast sea of liars.

———

Mama sent me a letter saying she had arranged to bring my little brother to the village. I was to stay in Hefei. Since the PLA was still in charge of the university, a PLA soldier would bring Yicun to her. She enclosed money and ration coupons. I went shopping and bought Yicun a new pair of shoes and candy and cookies.

A few days later the soldier arrived. I was uneasy when I saw the young man. I didn't trust soldiers. I scrutinized this one carefully, looked into his eyes to see if I might see anything frightening. I listened to his voice for the tone I'd heard from the soldier who had hurt me. This soldier was young and seemed to be honest and trustworthy. I gave him fifty fen and four ounces of rice coupons so he could buy a bowl of rice for Yicun on the journey. I explained to Yicun that he was going to join Mama and Yiding. He left without a word. I watched him leave the center with the soldier carrying a box of cookies.

I no longer had anyone to care for. There was no one to talk to when school was not in session. I sat on the floor and read or stared out the window. Days passed. Each one seemed the same.

I developed a fever. When I tried to eat, I vomited. I drank warm water and ate nothing. Soon I had throbbing headaches that felt like there was a stone rolling around inside my head. I skipped school and stayed in my room. The supervisors forgot me. One night my head hurt so much that I cried out for help but no one answered. I cried for Mama. Finally, I drifted into a hazy delirium.

After a sleepless night, I decided it was time to stop living. I knew I was near death but I wasn't afraid. I remembered Grandma and Auntie Liang and I knew they would take care of me. I waited for death. I had visions of my brothers and Mama and Papa eating together at a table in the village. They didn't miss me.

I breathed a cheerless lonely soliloquy to the bare walls and the cold floor. I called to Auntie Liang. At last she heard me and replied. I saw her face in the window. I opened my eyes wide and smiled. I whispered her name and she nodded. I told her I wanted to go outside and make snow butterflies. She held out her hand and beckoned me to come with her. Her skin was radiant. Her eyes sparkled like stars in a black winter sky.

"I am coming, Auntie Liang," I said. I raised my arms to embrace her.

PART II

TEMPORARY PEOPLE

The Things that never can come back, are several—
Childhood—some forms of Hope—the Dead—

—EMILY DICKINSON (1830–1886)

31

I did not take flight with Auntie Liang that night. Even as I reached up to her she changed into a cloud of tiny butterflies that dissolved in the night. I wanted to cry but I was too weak. Sometime later—I'd lost count of the days and nights—the door opened and someone gasped, "What is going on here?"

I managed to open my eyes, and as my vision cleared, I recognized the familiar face of one of Papa's close colleagues, Professor Wang Yichuan. I'd last seen him imprisoned in the cowshed with Papa. He hurried from the room and returned a few minutes later with Comrade Pan. "Why was this child left alone?" Professor Wang asked angrily.

"We had no idea she was sick," Comrade Pan answered.

"We know her father is a rightist, Comrade Pan. But what crime has this little girl committed?" Professor Wang demanded. "Why are you letting her die on your floor? Where is your heart?"

Comrade Pan's voice was suddenly soft and solicitous. "We will take her to the hospital," she said and left the room.

Professor Wang knelt beside me. He took my hand in his and whispered, "It's going to be all right, Yimao."

Comrade Pan returned and said, "Army Representative Zhang Xing has given us permission to use his car, Professor Wang. It's here now. Let's go."

Professor Wang pulled away my soiled sheet and picked me up and carried me outside to the car. After laying me across the backseat, he said, "I have to go now, Yimao, I'm sorry." Comrade Pan climbed into the front seat next to the driver. As the car pulled into the street, I felt as if my insides were being shredded. The road was in disrepair, and as the car bounced up and down, I wanted to tell the driver it was killing me. Yet my lips could form no words; my tongue lay dry as paper in my mouth.

We stopped outside the city hospital. The driver carried me inside. We passed through a thick confusion of stretchers and beds and crying children, of IV bottles and people lying on the floor moaning or sitting against the walls smoking or walking up and down the halls looking dazed and lost. I was carried into a room where a doctor examined me.

"She is as good as dead," he said and stepped back. "There is nothing I can do. Anything I might try would just be a waste of my time."

"No, you must do *something*," Comrade Pan protested.

"Listen," the doctor responded impatiently, "stop this! Tell her family to prepare for her burial."

"No," Comrade Pan answered. The doctor walked away. Comrade Pan told the driver to carry me back to the car. Half an hour later we stopped outside a building. Comrade Pan went inside and returned with a man. "Is this her?" he asked. His voice was deep and rich.

"Yes, it is, Representative Zhang," Comrade Pan said. "They would not admit her to the city hospital. They said she was beyond hope. Will you help her?"

The representative leaned over me, touched my forehead for a moment, pulled back my eyelid to see my eye, felt my pulse. He withdrew and stood outside the car for several seconds, saying nothing.

"Well?" Comrade Pan asked imploringly.

"The PLA hospital is better than the city hospital," the representative said. "But it is restricted to officers and their immediate relatives and soldiers."

"What is to be done?" Comrade Pan asked.

"I could tell them I'm her father," the representative said.

"Wonderful." Comrade Pan sighed. "I knew I could count on you." With that, she crawled into the backseat with me and shut the door. The representative got into the front seat. He gave directions to the driver. "When we get there," he said, "let me do the talking."

At PLA Hospital 105, the representative filled out admission forms affirming that he was my father and Comrade Pan was my mother. Attendants immediately wheeled me to an intensive care ward. As a doctor and nurse examined me, I opened my eyes. In the bright light, I could see the representative's face. He was a tall man, middle-aged, slim, confident in his manner. When he noticed me looking at him, he smiled and whispered, "It will be all right now. No need to worry." I forced a hint of a smile and blinked once to let him know I had heard him. Like so much else in my life, this man's kindness was as inexplicable to me as the wickedness of so many others. The last time I had been this close to a soldier, he had hurt me. Now another soldier was posing as my father in order to save my life. Why? I understood neither. And Comrade Pan, who had never said a single kind word to me—who despised me because of my family background—was pretending to be my mother. I no longer had any idea what she might actually be thinking. So many adults around me seemed to be playing roles that changed dramatically in a moment. Their behavior was utterly unpredictable.

"I think it's spinal meningitis," the doctor said to the representative. "I'm going to have to isolate your daughter from the other patients."

"Will she survive?" Comrade Pan asked anxiously.

"I can't say," the doctor answered.

I watched the doctor take out a long needle. The nurse pulled me into a sitting position and lifted my shirt. The doctor inserted the needle and drew spinal fluid. He administered no anesthetic. The pain was excruciating. I let out a little squeak and struggled for a moment, but I was weak and easily restrained by the nurse.

I was taken to a private room. The doctor prescribed several Chinese medicines and acupuncture to bring down my fever. Hour by hour I wasted away. Nothing seemed to work. Comrade Pan visited every day and sat silently beside my bed.

One night I awakened with a start and sat up in bed. My pain had vanished and I seemed to have recovered my strength. The moon shone brightly through the window bathing the room in a blue haze. I slipped to the floor and walked to the window. The courtyard below was empty. There was no sound and no movement. The world was like a dreamy still-life painting.

As I gazed around, I felt my feet leave the floor. I rose through the air to the ceiling and floated there facedown, looking at the room below me. In the bed beneath me, eyes closed, I saw a wasted little girl. In each of her arms was a needle attached to an IV. She was as pale as the sheet covering her. Her breath was barely perceptible. I thought, Poor little girl. I felt so sorry for her. I wanted to ease her suffering. I remembered something I'd learned in school. I began to speak to her. But the gentle voice from deep inside was not my own. It was the voice of Auntie Liang. It said, "Your life has not been a long one, little Yimao. But now it is over. There is nothing more for you in this world. You may leave it now. Come with me."

The little girl didn't move. Did she hear me?

I began to cry for her. I reached down but could not quite touch her. I cried for her and my tears fell like raindrops, splashing one after another on her face and hair. Her eyelids fluttered like butterfly wings. She blinked and stared up at me hovering above her. Her hand moved toward mine and our fingertips drew closer. At that moment I descended like a feather toward her. Her arms encircled me. When our faces were nearly touching, we looked into each other's eyes and she smiled. Our eyes blended. Our fingers, hands and arms flowed into each other. Our faces became one. Everything darkened.

A few days earlier Mama had set out to enroll Yiding in a school eight miles from Gao Village. As she and my brothers neared the school, a stranger shouted behind them, "Li Yikai! Wait!"

"What is it?" Mama asked.

"I was sent here by the leaders of Anhui University to find you," he said. "Because of the flood, I couldn't get in touch with you. Your daughter is very sick. And you have to go back to Hefei immediately."

The temperature that summer day was well over 100 degrees. Mama and my brothers were exhausted by the humidity and heat when the messenger found them. Mama braced herself against her bicycle. "What is her illness?" she asked.

"I don't know. I have not seen her," the messenger replied. He climbed onto his bicycle and rode away.

Mama decided to drop Yiding off at school as planned. When she was satisfied that he would be cared for there, she said goodbye to him.

On the way back to Gao Village with Yicun she pondered the problem of getting to Hefei quickly. A major flood occurred in the region in the previous week. Most of the roads were closed, and the train and bus systems were disrupted.

She was not feeling well, so she first proceeded to the commune clinic. As soon as she walked into the facility, she heard someone wailing. It was the cry that comes from deep within the soul, the sound of suffering that cannot be contained. The doctor in charge told Mama that an eleven-year-old girl had just died of a lung infection. "She didn't arrive in time to get effective treatment," he said.

Mama looked through the open door at the three forlorn figures standing around a table on which lay the body of a little girl. The dead child was dressed in rags. The mother and father were holding each of her hands. A brother, about the age of my younger brother, clung to his mother, sobbing. Mama immediately thought of me in Hefei. She imagined at that moment I might be lying dead on a hospital table, just like this, but with no one beside me. She became both sad and desperate and began praying under her breath. She prayed that God would hear her and that He would save me and that I would not suffer the fate of this poor little girl.

She returned to Gao Village and received permission from Old Crab to leave after giving him a pack of cigarettes. The following morning she put Yicun on her back and set out for Hefei. She waded across a shallow stream where the flood had washed out a bridge, passed an abandoned bus stop, and walked twelve miles to another stop to catch another bus. In the adjacent county she caught a train to Hefei and arrived at the child care center after midnight.

Mama pounded on the door until Comrade Pan responded.

"Where is my daughter?" she demanded. "What disease does she have?"

"She's not here," Comrade Pan answered. "I took her to PLA Hospital 105 a week ago. The doctors don't know what her problem is."

"Why is she in the PLA Hospital?" Mama asked.

"The city hospital refused to admit her. The PLA representative for the university took her there. He said he was her father. I said I was her mother," Comrade Pan said. "That's how she got in."

Mama was speechless at this revelation of compassion. The top university administrator had lied to get me admitted to the best hospital in the city. And Comrade Pan had assisted him.

Comrade Pan led Mama to my room. Mama saw my mat on the floor. She saw books and papers from school and my shoes beside it. She concluded that I had been carried from the room because I was too sick to walk. She burst into tears. "I need to see her right now," she sobbed.

"Impossible," Comrade Pan said. "You'll have to wait until the morning. You can stay here tonight."

Early the next morning Mama left Yicun with Comrade Pan and hurried to the hospital. At the western gate of the university she ran into a colleague who was surprised to see her. "Your daughter is very sick," the colleague said. "We didn't think you'd make it here because of the flood."

"What is her illness?"

"You didn't know?" the woman asked. "Well . . ." Then she stopped and averted her eyes and hurried away. Mama concluded that she knew but would not say because it was so serious. Her anxiety intensified. Mama ran the rest of the way to Hospital 105. She burst in the door and hurried down the hall. A soldier stopped her and demanded to know who she was. "My daughter is here," she answered. "She is very sick. I am from the countryside and I don't know where she is."

"Go to the registration desk," he told her. "Find out what room she is in."

At the registration desk the receptionist went down the list of patients. "There is no one here with that name," she said.

Mama went to the children's ward. She asked an attending nurse for me. "No one here by that name," the nurse said.

She searched through the other departments, more desperate by the moment. Finally she found her way to the contagious diseases wing of the hospital. She went from room to room until at last, on the third story, she found me alone in a room at the end of the hall.

"Maomao," she sobbed, "please do not die," and rushed to my bedside.

———

"Mama?" I whispered. "Is it really you?"

"Yes," she said. She laid her face against mine and sobbed.

A doctor came into the room and asked, "Who are you? No visitors are allowed at this hour. Please leave!"

"I am her mother," Mama replied. "I traveled all night to get here from the countryside."

"If you are her mother," the doctor said, "then who is the other woman who claims to be her mother? Does this child have two mothers?"

"That is Comrade Pan. She cared for my daughter until I could get here."

"And her father? The representative?"

Mama just shook her head. The doctor not only seemed to understand, he also seemed to sympathize. He walked to my bedside and began examining me. Mama stepped back to make room for him.

"What is the problem with my daughter?" Mama asked.

"I did a spinal tap and ordered blood tests. The original diagnosis was meningitis," the doctor said, his voice gentle and empathetic. "Now I am no longer sure what she has. I suspect she may have contracted typhoid fever. I treated her for it and she stabilized. But she still has a high temperature. Now I believe she does not have typhoid fever. I am still watching her and testing her. But I really can't yet give an accurate diagnosis."

"How serious is it now?" Mama asked the doctor.

"She was fortunate they brought her here. She had a high fever for at least ten days. She has not responded to treatment. To be honest with you, it's still touch and go," he said. "But she has a chance now. I promise you, I'll do everything I can." He gave me a concerned look and left the room.

Mama closed the door and returned to my side. After several minutes, she said, "Maomao, there is something I must do for you."

"What?"

"You can never tell anyone," she said. "Never! No matter what happens, you have to keep this a secret. If anyone found out"—her voice choked with emotion—"they would hurt us. Do you understand me?"

"Yes," I said. "I won't tell anyone. What are you going to do?"

"I am going to baptize you."

"Baptize?"

"Yes, Maomao. Your mama is a Christian. Your aunties and uncles in Tianjin are Christians, too."

I had never heard the word "Christian" before. I had no idea what she was telling me.

"If I do this, whatever happens to you from this morning on, someone will always be watching over you. You will never be alone."

"Are you going away, Mama?"

"No, but I'm afraid you might, Maomao. And I want someone to care for you and love you until I am with you again."

"I won't go away, Mama."

"I know," she said. "I know."

She dipped her fingertips in the basin of water beside my bed and touched them to my forehead. She whispered something about mother and father and blessings, all the while crying. I watched and listened in wonder as she said in a low voice, " 'Hail Mary, full of grace, the Lord is with thee. Blessed art thou among women, and blessed is the fruit of thy womb, Jesus—' "

"Mama?" I asked. "Who are those people?"

" 'Holy Mary, Mother of God,' " she continued, " 'pray for us sinners, now and at the hour of our death . . . Amen.' "

32

My mother stayed with me in the hospital. My brother remained with Comrade Pan in the child care center. My fever continued for three days after she baptized me. On the morning of the fourth day, the fever finally broke. My desire for food returned. I told Mama I was hungry.

"If I bring you some watermelon, do you think you can eat it?" she asked.

"Yes," I responded. "I'd like that."

Mama asked the doctor if she could give me watermelon and he agreed it was a good idea.

Mama found a nearby street market and bought a small watermelon. She cut it open and spooned out the juice and fed it to me. I was able to swallow several spoonfuls.

On her fifth day in Hefei, Mama went to the university offices to make a request that my father be given permission to visit me in the hospital.

Her request was denied.

The doctor was delighted by my sudden dramatic improvement and announced I could leave the hospital.

Mama borrowed a two-wheeled cart and brought it to the hospital. A nurse helped her carry me outside and placed me on the wooden bed of the cart. Mama then wheeled me to our new quarters, a room in a dingy hostel provided to us by the university. The room was without a kitchen, bathroom or running water. It had beds fashioned from unfinished wooden planks. In a room next to ours resided one of Mama's old colleagues, who had been in the cowshed with Papa. He took pity on us and gave a few cooking utensils and a small coal-burning stove.

Mama brought Yicun from the child care center to live with us. A few days later, Yiding arrived from the countryside. His school semester had been canceled because of the extensive flooding. The four of us lived in the dark hostel room for the next three months while I gradually recovered my strength. The conditions were crude, I heard Mama tell her colleague, yet they were superior to Gao Village. During those days, Mama had to carry me to the bathroom. For a long time I was so weak I could not stand.

At the end of September 1969, the four of us went to Gao Village. Mama found a truck going that way and secured a ride for us. Mama and I rode in the cab with the driver, and my brothers rode in the back with some of our belongings. The ride was long and grueling and the country roads deeply furrowed by the recent wet weather. Exhaust fumes flowed freely into the cab of the truck and the driver smoked constantly. In a short time I became sick to my stomach. I vomited in the cab and the driver became angry and swore at me. After that he drove with both windows down and often stuck his head out for fresh air.

When we arrived near the village, I was weak and sick and sore. All my muscles ached. Carrying our bags, we walked across the countryside for a quarter of a mile. I was stunned by my first look at Gao Village. Filthy women and children adorned in rags approached us. The women helped my mother carry our luggage. The children stood around gaping at me.

I had never before seen children as dirty as these. None of them wore shoes. Everyone came with us as we proceeded through the village to a dilapidated shed. "This is your new home," Mama said, opening the door and stepping inside. I followed her in. The crowd pushed from behind and many of them entered the rickety structure with us.

I was unpleasantly surprised. The walls were mud and the floor was dirt. Wood beams crossed overhead, and on them was piled straw for the roof. The ceiling was low. It was especially low for my mother who was tall for a Chinese woman. At five feet seven, she was about six inches taller than most men in the village. The structure, Mama explained, was previously the village warehouse, used to store rice, seed and tools for the production team. Villagers had built a four-foot-high mud wall down the middle to separate our living quarters from the storage area.

In our quarters was one double bed. There was a clay stove just inside the door and a chamber pot in a corner of the room. In another corner was a large clay water jar. Our trunks were stacked against the wall. There was no electricity and no window. The only light came from the doorway.

"Where will I sleep?" I asked Mama.

"On the bed," she answered, pointing to the double bed. "We all sleep on this bed."

The shed was filled with wide-eyed villagers watching our every move and listening to us as though we were a performing troupe.

After looking over the room, I told Mama, "I think I need to go to the bathroom. Where is it?"

"I'll show you where to go," she said. She tore two pages from a notebook next to the stove and led me outside. A dozen steps away was a large open depression in the ground. As we approached it I noticed that it seemed to be seething as if it were alive, and was making a loud buzzing sound, something like a dull persistent stringed instrument. As we stepped closer, the entire surface began to rise, quickly, like black steam from a pot. I realized that the cloud ascending into the air was millions of blackflies that fed on the surface of this sewage hole. Whenever anyone approached, they buzzed around overhead, then resettled when one left.

Around the pool was a mud wall, about a foot high, but it had eroded in parts. The sewage pool itself was a circle of about six feet in diameter. At the edge were two bricks wedged in the dirt. Between them at a sharp sloping angle were several other bricks that formed a trough into the black pool. Mama said, "You stand on these, turn your backside to the pool, squat and relieve yourself. Put one foot on each outside brick. Be sure to relieve yourself on the middle bricks. If you relieve yourself directly into the pool, it will splash on you and the flies will follow you back inside."

Mama helped me position myself. I was about to untie and lower my trousers when I realized that a dozen children and adults had followed us to the open latrine and were watching me with fascination. Mama asked the audience to leave, and when they had gone, she handed me the notebook pages. "We don't have a toilet paper ration here," she said. "This is how you do it. You crumple it up in your hand, then open it and crumple it again. Do this several times to soften it, and then it is comfortable to use."

When I got back to the hut, I told Mama I needed to wash my hands. "The water is in the jar," she said, pointing to the large container in the corner. I lifted the wooden cover from it and stuck my hands in the water.

Mama blurted out a plaintive "*No!*" She startled me, and I pulled my hands from the jar immediately. "That's our water supply," she said. Too late. She showed me the gourd ladle I was supposed to use to draw water from the jar, pour it into a basin and wash my hands there. My carelessness had just contaminated our water.

33

Early the next morning Yicun told me, "I want to take you to see a pet dog."

I'd never seen one before. Dogs were not allowed as pets in the city. Wild dogs ran in packs and came into the city at night. Officials often hunted them down and trapped them and beat them to death. I was intrigued by the idea of a pet dog. This was to be my first adventure in the countryside. We skipped out of the shed and ran along the path between the village huts. As we ran, a big black dog lunged at me, seemingly out of nowhere. He caught me from behind, growling ferociously and bit hard on my right calf. I fell to the ground screaming. The dog released me and ran away. I was bleeding and in terrible pain. Villagers came running from every direction when they heard my cries. One old woman approached waving a large cleaver over her head, cursing the dog. She examined my injured leg and announced, "This is very serious."

A crowd hovered around me, all of them shouting advice or asking what had happened. Because the local dialect was new to me, I could not understand most of what they said. It sounded like hysterical clatter and heightened my anxiety. The old woman quickly took charge and told one of the men to carry me home. The woman had a weathered, wrinkled face and walked with a pronounced stoop that diminished her slight stature. She was the shortest of the village women but appeared to have unquestioned authority in this matter. The others instantly followed her orders without question.

Hearing my cries, Mama was shocked to see a man carrying me. Yicun was also crying from fright. "What happened?" she asked.

The old woman responded sharply, "Don't just stand there. Hurry up and get some rice water."

"Rice water?" Mama asked. "What is it?"

"You city people!" the woman shot back impatiently. "Just put rice in water and stir it with your fingertips and give it to me when the water colors."

Mama grabbed a fistful of rice and stirred it in a bowl with water and then handed it to the woman, who dipped her hands in it and washed my wound with the water. When it was clean she sprinkled the rice water on my head.

A moment later her eyes rolled back in their sockets and she turned her face toward the ceiling and broke into a shrill haunting incantation. "Child, come home, child, come home, child, come home." The women who had followed her into our shed joined with her immediately and their chorus became a drone that grew louder each time they repeated the stanza. They closed their eyes and began waving their hands back and forth over their head, like long leaves of grass bending in some invisible wind.

Mama was bewildered by all of this. She stood aside, shifting her gaze back and forth from the women to me, wide-eyed. I was silent, mesmerized by the whole thing. I momentarily forgot the pain and fright from the dog bite. Quickly the chant spread from dwelling to dwelling as villagers emerged and stood in front of their huts, raising their hands to the heavens and joining in. Peasants from the nearby fields heard and came running, chanting as they approached.

After a while the old woman stopped and everyone else quieted. She listened for something in the air. She looked at my mother and said, "The dog that bit this girl scared her soul from her body. We are calling her soul home. If we don't, her soul will be wandering far away and she will lose it forever."

At a signal one of the women grabbed our broom and a young woman put me on her back. Another filled a small bowl with dry rice. Then everyone left our shed and began parading in a long column through the village. The woman with the bowl of rice headed the procession. The woman carrying me followed close behind. The other women, along with my mother, came after them. Children brought up the rear and joined in the chanting. They proceeded up and down the path through the village. The woman holding the broom waved it back and forth in a wide arc "to sweep away bad luck."

The woman at the head of the parade threw rice in a circular motion as if planting. She kept repeating, "Child, come alive. Child, come alive." When she threw the rice, chickens came running to snatch it.

Eventually the procession returned to the place where the dog had bitten me. At that point a new chant began. It continued until the woman directing this ritual paused, closed her eyes, listened for something and then relaxed. She made several silent circles around the spot and pronounced that my soul had returned. The crowd slowly dispersed.

Mama carried me home. As she approached our shed, I remembered what had happened after she found me in the hospital in Hefei and asked, "Mama, are they Christians? Did they baptize me?"

I felt her stiffen at my words. She slowed and turned a complete circle to make sure no one else could hear us. "No," she said. "I'll explain it to you when you grow up. Keep it a secret between the two of us for now."

The nearest elementary school was a twenty-minute walk from Gao Village. It consisted of three dirt-floor rooms in a straw-roofed mud building. One room served as living quarters for the teacher, and the other two were classrooms. Students were required to bring their own stools and desks. I had a crude little three-legged stool about a foot tall. I had no desk. The elementary school system had recently shifted from six to five grades. Chairman Mao had issued a directive to revolutionize the system and shorten the amount of time children spent in class. Grades one through three were instructed in one room and grades four and five in the other. I was in the fourth grade.

In the countryside girls attended school, if at all, only through the third grade. After that they worked in the fields. The peasants considered girls to be "giveaways," meaning they would someday live with the family of their men. Consequently, educating them was a waste. I was the only girl in my classroom. There were half a dozen girls in the other room. Because I was the oldest girl in the school, it became my duty to cook for the teacher, who lived at school. There was a large clay stove in the center of our classroom, and the teacher taught while I sat on my stool and tended the stove.

The teacher himself had only an elementary school education. Yet this distinguished him from the illiterate villagers. He was once a peddler, walking from village to village beating on a little drum to attract people when he approached. He sold toys and candy. When the villagers needed a teacher for their children, they asked him to stay on. He had a son who was in my class. The teacher and his boy were unusual to us because they were members of the Uighur minority of western China and they were Muslims. They no longer prayed openly each day—that was forbidden after the Communist takeover—but they did not eat pork, and during part of each year, they did not eat during the day. When he spoke privately with his son, none of us could understand a word.

Some of the teacher's clothing was unusually colorful, as was the small rug he kept on the dirt floor of his living quarters. But perhaps most unusual was his practice of wearing shoes every day. Only in the dead of winter or during special celebrations like weddings did the peasants or their children wear shoes. But the teacher was never without his. When school was not in session, the teacher and his son did not mix with other villagers, nor did they join the groups working in the fields during planting and harvest. They kept to themselves and no one in the village seemed to mind.

In Gao Village there was a curious absence of other girls my age. There were many girls three and four years older than me and some two or three years younger. But I was the only one born in 1958. Late one morning while the other children were playing outside and the teacher was sitting at his desk smoking, I brought him his lunch and asked, "Teacher Lu, why am I the only girl in the upper grade in this school? Where are the other girls my age? I don't even see them working in the fields."

He responded, thoughtfully and somberly, "Once there were many little girls your age here. I remember passing through the villages in those years and seeing them." He paused wistfully and looked out the window at the sky.

"Where are they now, Teacher Lu?"

"They're all dead."

"Did they get sick?"

"No," he said. "There was no sickness." He looked away and thought for a moment and sighed. "You're too young to understand, Yimao."

He drew on his cigarette, held in the smoke for a time, then turned his face up and slowly exhaled, studying the blue spiral that floated on the air, as if trying to read meaning into it. He whispered, "They died because there was no food. There was no food in any of these villages during that time. There was a famine. You don't know what that means, do you?"

"I do, Teacher Lu. My grandma in Tianjin starved herself to save me during a famine." I felt a sudden urge to cry.

"Maybe we shouldn't talk about this," he said sympathetically.

I held back my tears and asked, "What happened here?"

"My wife . . . did the same thing," he said. "She saved all of her food for our children. She died first." His voice broke and he paused for a moment. "After she was gone, there was still not enough food. My daughter was five. My son was two. You remind me of my daughter."

"What happened to her?"

"My daughter," he answered softly. "Her name was Xiaobao—Little Treasure. I took my Little Treasure to Nanjing. I couldn't watch her starve. I told her I had a big surprise for her in the city. I took her to a Muslim restaurant near the Drum Tower. I can even remember the name of the restaurant—Ma Xiang Xing. I ordered her a plate of squirrel fish and a cup of tea. It cost two yuan, sixty fen, all the money I had. Her eyes lit up when she saw the food. She smiled for the first time in months and began eating. I watched her for a few minutes. I said, 'Papa has to go to the latrine. You wait right here for me.'

"She just nodded. She was too busy eating even to look at me. I walked to the door of the restaurant, turned and watched her eating at the table. Then I left. I never saw her again. That is how I remember her. Sitting at a small table, alone, eating eagerly. She was happy." Teacher Lu looked up at me, his eyes moist. "I think she must look like you today."

He continued eating and I sat quietly across from him. When he was done, he stared at his empty bowl until I lifted it from his hands and carried it outside to wash it.

34

After school each day the children immediately went to work. Their principal task was collecting animal droppings for fertilizer. I learned how to do this and soon was working beside them. This was my first real job. I wanted to be like the other children. I carried a small basket and a rake and prowled the edge of the village looking for animal droppings. For every ten kilograms I delivered to the production team's sewage pool, the accountant recorded one work point for me, which was worth two fen.

The first time I joined in the work I wore a pair of "liberation sneakers." The other children saw me and pointed and laughed. "Look at the city girl," they said, "collecting shit with shoes on." I went home and put my shoes away. As long as we lived in the village, I went barefoot most of the time. It hurt at first. But soon the soles of my feet hardened with calluses and I could go anywhere painlessly. I was even able to walk across hot stones in the summer or climb on sharp-edged rocks.

Some afternoons I was accompanied on my searches by a neighbor girl named Little Rabbit. She was only five but very intelligent for her age. She had a baby brother who was bound to her back every morning. Carrying him, she trudged along beside me as I did my work. I began to spend most of my spare time with Little Rabbit. Slowly she took the place in my life that Xiaolan once filled.

She reminded me of myself when I was five, doing the household chores and caring for a younger brother. I taught her some of the games I'd played when I was her age. I made a length of rope from straw and tied one end to a post and turned the other and taught her how to jump rope. She was delighted. I also showed her how to make bird nests out of grass roots.

Little Rabbit taught me how to catch fish in the irrigation ditch. The water ran swiftly from the pond to the rice fields when the dikes were open. She knelt at the water's edge, leaned down and blocked a section of the ditch with a bamboo basket to snag fish. Within minutes she pulled up half a dozen fish. We called them *can tiao*, little white fish. They were only about three inches long. We cleaned them and cooked them and made a feast for ourselves.

Little Rabbit was not healthy. She tired easily. On our shopping trips to the brigade store, she often had to stop and rest and complained that she had a headache. Sometimes I tried to help her and had her transfer her baby brother to my back. She behaved like an old woman rather than a child. I did everything I could to cheer her up. I remembered how I had become ill and my energy had drained away. But I'd eventually been taken to the hospital. Someone had cared for me and wanted me to live. Little Rabbit appeared to have no one like that. Her parents and grandmother were indifferent. She liked me to tell her stories. When we sat together making straw fuel bundles for the stove, I'd tell her stories and sometimes she'd tip toward me and rest her head against my shoulder.

I talked with Mama about her and she said Little Rabbit should go to the clinic at the commune headquarters. She suggested this to Little Rabbit's mother, who told her there was nothing wrong with the child and that she had always been listless and quiet. One morning Little

Rabbit came to our shed and asked me to walk with her to the brigade store. Her grandmother wanted her to buy soy sauce. I also had to go to the store to buy salt. I scooped up a few fen and joined her. But when we had walked only a short distance, she stopped and said she wasn't feeling well. She appeared unusually pale. She also had the burden of her little brother strapped to her back. I touched her forehead and told her, "Your skin is hot, Little Rabbit. Go home. I'll get your soy sauce." She handed me her money.

I hurried to the store and bought the supplies and saved a single fen. The store had yam candy for sale, one fen each. I bought a piece for Little Rabbit. I ran most of the way home, imagining the broad smile that would bloom on her face when I handed her the treat. As I entered her front yard, I saw her lying in the straw with her little brother tied to her back, sleeping soundly. Little Rabbit was on her side with her legs drawn up, clutching an unknotted thatch of straw.

I called to her, "Little Rabbit. I have a surprise for you."

She didn't move. I thought she must be asleep. I sat down next to her on the straw, unwrapped the candy and held it out to her. Only then did I notice that her eyes were half open. I touched her face and found she was cold.

I cried out and ran to the door of her shed and summoned her grandmother. She hurried outside and saw Little Rabbit and scooped her up in her arms and began calling to her and stroking her forehead. The baby boy tied to Little Rabbit's back began crying. I loosened the cloth that bound him to Little Rabbit and held him. Little Rabbit lay as limp as a rag doll in her grandmother's arms. The old woman began wailing. Other women heard the commotion and came running. When they saw Little Rabbit in her grandmother's arms, they, too, began screaming and crying. I continued staring at Little Rabbit in disbelief, still clutching the candy I'd bought for her.

That evening several men dug a grave outside the village. They wrapped Little Rabbit in a blanket and lay her in the grave and covered her. There was no marker. There was no ceremony.

During the next weeks I walked to her gravesite every day. Once I found that animals had scratched away at the surface. I piled more dirt on the grave and stomped it down. When I was finished, I sat down and talked to Little Rabbit.

35

The twenty-five families of Gao Village were a "production team" that was part of a "brigade" composed of several village production teams. The brigades were organized further into communes. The commune headquarters had a general store, a middle school, a clinic and a meetinghouse for Party officials. It was a thirty-minute walk from Gao Village.

Old Crab, the team leader, was the only Communist Party member in Gao Village. He dressed in a tattered green uniform that was always caked with dried mud and bits of food. With his Party membership and his appointment by the brigade as team leader, he acquired absolute power over the villagers. Although the peasants sometimes made fun of him, they also feared him. They carefully courted his favor and never pushed their barbed jibes too far. If he felt anyone was challenging his authority he threatened them and waved a copy of the Party rules in their faces. "I can have you shot!" was his common warning. And everyone knew he could. If he passed our house and smelled food, he invited himself inside for a meal, always helping himself to the largest portion.

Mama had brought two beds from Hefei to Gao Village but there was space for only one in the quarters assigned to us. She kept the second bed with the farming equipment in the storage section adjoining our living space in the shed. One afternoon I heard someone rummaging clumsily in the storage area. I peered over the low wall dividing the space from ours and saw Old Crab. He looked at me and mumbled, "I saw an extra bed here. My nephew is going to be married and he needs it. I am borrowing yours."

Of course Old Crab never *borrowed* anything. He *took* what he wanted or needed, and it never reappeared. If he took our second bed, I knew we would never see it again. As he pulled it from a stack of our belongings, I blurted out, "You can't have that."

He eyed me and was highly annoyed by my objection. "Shut up," he spat at me. "Why don't you go collect some shit?"

As he turned to leave with the bed, I scrambled over the wall and grabbed a corner of the frame. "This is my bed," I yelled. "And you cannot have it."

He attempted to jerk it away from me, but I hung on and screamed, "Don't you dare steal my bed."

He tried to pull and kick me at the same time. We moved out the door to the area in front of the shed, each hanging on to an end of the frame, Old Crab kicking and trying not to lose his balance. "Damn you, let go. This is mine now. I'm the boss," he shouted. Although he was accustomed to intimidating adults, I don't think he'd ever been challenged by a child, especially not a determined eleven-year-old girl.

He planted his feet to make a final pull on the frame to force it from my hands. As he did, I released my grip. He stumbled backward and fell flat on the ground. He let go of the bed and jumped up with his fists clenched to beat me. I ran inside the house, closed the door and blocked it. He pounded on the door, unable to force it open, and threatened to kill me. After a string of obscenities, he left me alone, picked up the bed and stumbled away. As he did, I opened the door a crack and shook my fist at him and yelled, "You can't keep my bed, Old Crab! I'm going to come and get it back!"

At my words, he dropped the frame and rushed the door. I

slammed it shut and blocked it. After hitting it twice and threatening me, he resumed his theft.

Old Crab exempted himself from common labor. He declared that it was his official duty to make sure everyone else worked. Each morning, just after sunrise, he marched through the village blowing a whistle and banging on his broken gong, shouting, "The sun is shining in your asshole! Get up! Go to work! Go to work!" As the villagers emerged from their dwellings, he told them that their daily assignment was to go to this or that field and do this or that.

Once the villagers had begun their daily tasks, he walked to the brigade headquarters or the store where he might find Party officials from other villages and confer with them. After a few drinks and a few cigarettes he made a circuit of the fields, checking to see that everyone else was working. After that he returned to the village and searched for men who might be shirking their duties or women who were alone.

One autumn morning I overslept and departed for school late. As I passed one of the small huts near the edge of the village, I saw a shadowy figure crawling next to the back wall and then disappearing around a corner. I became curious. I left the main path and padded to another hut and peeked around the corner. I saw Old Crab on his hands and knees, looking around the corner of the next hut. I suspected at first that he was about to steal something from one of the villagers, but it was unusual for him to do it so secretively. His normal tactic was merely to walk in and take whatever he wanted. I followed him and saw him approaching a young woman who was nursing her baby. She was seated on a pile of straw facing the morning sun. Old Crab approached her stealthily from behind and bent down and wrapped his arms around her. She struggled for a moment but stopped when she saw it was Old Crab. She put her baby down on a blanket and turned to him. Her full breasts swung lose from her open blouse.

"Don't worry," Old Crab slurred. He covered her breasts with his open hands. "I won't squeeze them hard enough to steal your milk. I just want to have some fun."

He circled her waist with one arm while he loosened his trousers. She lay down on the straw beside her baby and said, in mock protest, "No, no, no, no, you shameless old man." At the same time she was smiling. "And what do you have for me?"

"How would you like . . . ten work points today?" he said as he kneaded her breasts. She loosened the waist of her trousers, and when she lifted her hips to pull them down, she began to turn her head in my direction. I jumped back before she could see me and hurried to school.

Old Crab was both the law and the chief law enforcement officer of the village. He dictated reports to brigade officials about the villagers who behaved suspiciously in his eyes or who were not sufficiently revolutionary. These people were called in for questioning and Old Crab's complaints became part of their record. He brought news of Party policy and rules back to the village. The illiterate villagers knew only what he told them about dictates and commands from Party headquarters in Beijing. Several women whispered to Mama that Old Crab had become a Party member because "he was the cruelest man in the village, and local Party officials were looking for a cruel leader during the famine years."

Party officials at the brigade level appointed him team leader and gave him control over the distribution of food in the village. He decided who received food and who did not. He determined whose children lived or died. Food was kept in a central storage facility, and anyone caught trying to steal was shot in the head on the spot. No one forgot those years. Half the villagers starved to death during the famine. All members of Old Crab's family survived. When the famine ended he was granted Party membership in a lavish ceremony at brigade headquarters and praised for his selfless service to the nation, the Party and the people of Gao Village.

36

Papa unexpectedly arrived in Gao Village one spring day. He had taken the bus to the nearest main road junction and walked the final few miles.

He told us that before releasing him from Nan Village, Communist Party authorities had one final humiliation in store for him. His work contract with the university was canceled. Not only was he deprived of income, but he also was denied access to the national medical care system. In the eyes of the state he had become a non-person.

At the same time university officials discovered the deception that had allowed me to stay in the PLA Hospital in Hefei. They billed my mother for the cost of my medical care. The charge was two months of her salary. We never learned if Comrade Pan and the kind PLA representative had also been disciplined for their role in saving my life.

Father had been in our hut only a few minutes when Old Crab arrived with a number of villagers trailing behind him. Father presented his release papers to Old Crab, who scanned them but could not read them. After pretending to examine them, he crushed them in his hand contemptuously. "The most important thing for you to remember," he spat at Papa, "is that I am in charge here. You do what I tell you. You obey me."

"Of course," Papa responded deferentially.

Old Crab studied him and added loudly enough for everyone outside the hut to hear, "You are a piece of meat on my chopping block. I can slice you. I can dice you. I can cut you any way I want. And I will when I feel like it."

"I understand," Papa replied, and the rest of us stood around close-lipped, listening to Old Crab's tirade.

"And one more thing," Old Crab added. "Do you have any cigarettes?"

Papa withdrew a pack of Big Iron Bridge cigarettes from his pocket. As he was about to pull one out, Old Crab snatched the entire pack, shook out a cigarette and stuffed the rest in his own pocket. "Match?" he asked.

Papa lit the cigarette with a wooden match, and Old Crab turned and left. The others followed.

During the next days Old Crab spoke with Papa at length about his background. He was delighted that Papa could read, write and do math and was also completely under his thumb. Old Crab needed someone literate to help him, he said. "I've always hated depending on a man from the brigade level to do our numbers. They don't appreciate our local problems. Now I have you."

He put Papa in charge of recording work points that he assigned to every individual in the village. Papa was given the account book, which Old Crab retrieved from brigade headquarters, and told how the work points were to be distributed. Each male was given ten work points for a day's labor. Women were paid seven, and children were paid three. Ten work points were worth twenty fen. Old Crab assigned himself ten work points a day. He told Papa that his work for the Party and supervising others was the most important job in the village.

After only one month in the village Papa became so sick that he could not walk to Old Crab's hut to fill out the account book. He'd contracted malaria. So Old Crab brought the book to him each evening. There was always a lot of illness in the village. People washed their clothing in the same pond where they drew their drinking water. On the opposite side of the pond, villagers washed their night soil buckets. We poured alum in our water before boiling it. Mud and other solids collected at the bottom of our water jar. We used only the top portion before emptying it and drawing fresh water.

After that, Papa ran a high fever once a month and often became delirious. He tossed and turned in the bed and was drenched with sweat. During these lapses, he repeatedly shouted in English, "Long Live Chairman Mao," then laughed hysterically at his own words.

I understood a little English and recognized what he was saying. Mother worried that he might shout something in Chinese and someone might hear and report him. He could get into serious trouble because of the tone of his laugh. He might be labeled a current counterrevolutionary. As long as he stuck to English, the villagers thought he was speaking nonsense and he was safe.

I was the sickliest child in our family. Every few weeks, I became so ill that villagers had to carry me to the commune clinic on a bamboo pallet. On my first stay at the clinic I found, when I went to use the latrine, that a copy of *David Copperfield* was about to be used as toilet paper. As I squatted over the concrete platform, I picked up the book and read the first page. I realized how much I missed the written word and remembered my excitement at discovering the little hill of books outside the building in Hefei. I kept reading until I heard someone coming. I then stood up and tucked the book into the front of my underwear and pulled my shirt over it. Another woman entered, saw me, looked around for the toilet paper, found nothing, and left. As I went out the door, she reentered the latrine carrying another large volume.

I kept the book under my pillow. In the following days I was able to rescue parts of *Anna Karenina* and *A Tale of Two Cities*. I brought them home with me when I was well. Each time I stayed in the clinic for one illness or another, I stole several volumes of "toilet paper."

Not long after Papa arrived, Old Crab received funds from the Commune Settle-Down Cadre Office to build our family a new dwelling. He pocketed the money and ordered the villagers to construct a hut. It consisted of mud walls and a dirt floor and was partitioned into three rooms. Old Crab did not want to build our home on good rice land. The area where they built our shed, we learned, was the old Gao family cemetery. The villagers were superstitious about this plot of land and Old Crab ordered that no one was to tell us that we were living over the bodies of the Gaos.

Gao was the name of the family who had founded the village hundreds of years earlier. Many of them fled during the Taiping Rebellion a century before. Still more fled during the war against the Japanese, and some of those who stayed behind were murdered. Some fled during the civil war. With the victory of the Communists, those who remained were arrested, charged with exploiting peasants and executed. Others were sent to prison camps. During the great famine, we learned, the last Gaos had starved to death, deprived of food by a decision of Old Crab. By the time we arrived, there were no more Gaos in Gao Village. The dominant family names now were Li, Sun, Zhang and Chen. Not far from our newly constructed shed was a narrow drainage ditch that was part of the irrigation system. It carried water from a pond to the rice paddies. A tall gravestone with the names of Gao family members etched on it lay on its side and served as a bridge over the ditch.

Other huts in the village were built more sturdily than ours. The villagers had used real fired bricks for their own structures and mud for ours. They had not bothered to create a window, so the only light entered through the open front door. This was what Old Crab had ordered to save both time and money, and we could not object. Once the workers were done, Papa had a neighbor help him punch a small hole through the wall at each end of the house, a rudimentary window for additional light and ventilation. Mama hung material over the holes to provide privacy and protection from the elements.

The door remained open throughout the day. If we closed our door, villagers whispered that we were doing something secretive and suspicious. Before long Old Crab would come along and kick the door in to make sure nothing was happening that he didn't know about. My parents never complained openly about our treatment or our living conditions. We tried to live like the peasants. We worked in the fields, attended every village meeting and did as we were told by Old Crab.

The allotment of food we received in exchange for our work was never enough. So we augmented our diet, as many of the villagers did, by raising chickens. We started out with ten chicks Mama bought at commune headquarters. They matured and laid eggs and hatched more chicks. They lived with us in our quarters. My older brother and I shared responsibility for raising the chickens. We kept them in a coop that he made. Just before dark, when I called to them, "Coo, coo, coo," they came running to the house to be fed and kept beside his bed. They were healthy and became legendary in the village for their number and size.

Within a year we had more than a hundred chickens. The secret of our success was that we raised them scientifically. Papa had discussed raising chickens with a doctor whom he befriended at the clinic during one of his visits to me. The doctor told him about antibiotics that could be given to our flock. The doctor provided him with some. I injected them into the chickens. But our success made some villagers jealous. They wanted to raise chickens in large numbers, too, but failed. So they turned to stealing ours. Old Crab didn't have to steal. Whenever he wanted a fat chicken for his pot, he merely stopped by and took one of ours.

The village collectively owned four water buffalo. The animals were highly valued because they were the only real labor-saving device available to the peasants. During the famine, villagers ate the water buffalo, and men yoked themselves to plows. Families with teenage girls were assigned the care of the buffalo. In exchange, they were given work points. The girls tended the animals when they grazed, took them to streams to drink, fed them hand-tied bundles of rice and straw and fenced them in their yards at night.

Our neighbors, the Chen family, were assigned the care of one of the village animals. Chen Chunying, who was fifteen—three years older than me—led the buffalo into a pasture every afternoon. Soon after meeting her, I began to accompany her. We rode together on the back of the buffalo and steered into a grazing area near the river. Then we sat on the ground and talked and sang while he foraged nearby.

One afternoon Chunying began making a pair of shoes. Peasants wore shoes only on special occasions or during the winter, and they always made their own.

"Where did you learn to make shoes?" I asked, fascinated by her deft cutting and sewing.

"My grandmother taught me," she said. "Didn't anyone teach you yet?"

"My grandmother died. And my mother doesn't know how."

"Then I'll teach you," she said. "You can watch me, and after you learn, you can make shoes for yourself."

So I watched and listened to her instructions. She made the shoes from old clothing. Shirts and trousers that were too ragged and patched to be used anymore were cut up into small flat pieces of material. Chunying meticulously glued them into thin layers with paste made from a mixture of flour and water and laid them out in the sun to dry into a hard material. Then she made hundreds of tight little stitches in them to hold the pieces together. I watched as the sole and the top of the shoe slowly took shape. The work took several weeks. I was fascinated by her patience and artistry.

One night I asked my mother for rags so I could make my own pair of shoes. "Making shoes?" she asked. "What in the world is that good for? Read books. That will give you a future."

I told Chunying I was not allowed to make shoes. She thought for a while and said, "How about this? I'll make you a pair of shoes and you read to me while I'm working."

"Really? You will do that?" I asked excitedly.

"Yes, I will," she answered. "Read me beautiful stories and I'll make you beautiful shoes."

We had brought a few books from Hefei—Papa's prized copy of *Jean-Christophe* and *Les Misérables*—and I had stolen some from the latrine at the commune clinic. Mama kept our books in a pile beside the stove and told any inquiring visitors that these were for fuel. I carried a copy of *Les Misérables* with me the next afternoon. We sat on the grass and Chunying sewed and I read aloud to her. She loved the passages describing the life of Cosette. She often asked me to repeat the words slowly, and she closed her eyes and listened to me. One warm lazy afternoon, she said, "I admire you for being able to read, Yimao. How can you do that? And such fat books."

I told her, "If you come to school with me, Chunying, you can learn to read, too. It's not as hard as making shoes!"

"My parents tell me it's a waste of time," she replied. "I have wanted to go, but they refuse. I've always been curious, though."

"That's funny," I said. "My parents say making shoes is a waste of time."

"What do you think? Do you think we're both wasting our time, Yimao?"

"No, I don't," I told her.

She smiled at me and said, "But you will be unless you keep reading."

"Where are my shoes?" I asked, and we both laughed.

Each day that summer we took the water buffalo to the pasture and I read *Les Misérables* to Chunying. When my eyes tired, I sang her the songs I learned in school. She was so easily amused. It was as if I were an opera performer and she was my only audience. I had been taught the songs from Madame Mao's approved operas, and I sang them to her and told her the stories. She listened and smiled.

When summer vacation was almost over, she completed making my shoes. They were exquisite. The soles were white and the tops were embroidered with tiny colorful flowers.

"How beautiful," I gasped when she handed them to me. I could hardly believe they were mine. I ran my fingers over the little flowers and admired the elegant stitching on the white soles.

"You must wear them only on special occasions," she said. "On New Year's Day or for a visit to relatives in other villages."

That night, before I went to bed, I washed my feet in a basin. Then I put on the shoes. I didn't want to soil them on the floor, so I lay on my bed and held my feet over my head and walked through the air with them, as if I were on a cloud.

The next morning I asked Mama to take me to visit our relatives in Tianjin. She told me it was too far away. I said, "But I want to go. I have to show them my new shoes. Mama, I'd be happy to walk barefoot just to put on my shoes when I get there."

"Those shoes have made you silly," she said. "Put them away."

I knew of no place to wear them in the countryside. So they became a special unused treasure. I took them out every night and put them on and walked in the air. They never touched the ground.

Ten months later there was a special occasion for me to wear my shoes. As we sat in a field tending the buffalo, Chunying began to sob.

"What's wrong?" I asked. I'd never seen her so sad.

"I'm going to be married," she said.

"Then why are you crying?"

"Because I have to move to another village. Because I'll never see you again. Because I've never even seen my man."

"I'll visit you," I said. "No matter where you go, Chunying, I'll visit you."

Her marriage had been arranged by her parents, as was the custom in the countryside. According to village tradition, a bride and groom were not supposed to see each other before they wed. Their first glimpse of each other came on the wedding day.

Because Chunying's family was poor, they had worked out a special exchange of weddings with a family in nearby Bao Village. They agreed that Chunying would marry the son of the other family, and the daughter of that family would marry Chunying's brother. No dowry was involved. The arrangement was considered balanced and fair. Chunying worried because she knew nothing of her future husband or his family, only the name of their village. She hoped that he would not be cruel or ugly. She hoped he would not beat her.

I was sad. Chunying was my closest friend. Her marriage meant there would be no more stories or songs or shoes. We would never again ride on the back of a water buffalo together and watch the sun set over the flooded rice paddies. Chunying's mother, Auntie Chen, asked me to be the special assistant for her daughter and accompany her to the groom's village. I was delighted.

On the morning of the wedding I put on my best clothes, a clean white shirt with a small green-flowered pattern and my least patched pair of dark trousers. I combed my long hair carefully and braided two perfect plaits. Finally, I took out the shoes Chunying had made for me. I tried to pull them on but they no longer fit. I put them away sadly. "No more Chunying. No more shoes," I whispered to myself, on the verge of tears. I set out barefoot for Chunying's nearby hut.

Many people had already gathered at the dwelling. Red paper squares had been pasted onto the door with golden double-happiness cutouts.

"Congratulations, Auntie Chen," I greeted Chunying's mother.

"Ah, look at you," she said. She touched my hair. "Your braids are so wonderful. They are as thick as a baby's arm. When you get married, you will make a very pretty bride."

I was embarrassed by the mention of my own marriage. I blushed and asked where Chunying was.

"She is inside getting her face opened for her marriage," Auntie Chen told me.

"What is that?" I asked.

She invited me inside to find out. Three old women huddled around Chunying, who sat on a stool next to the window. Auntie Sun held a thread between her teeth and wrapped the other end around her middle finger. The thread was taut. She slowly rolled it over Chunying's forehead to scrape off the wisp of tiny hairs. Chunying's eyelids fluttered as the thread was drawn over her skin. She saw me and smiled without moving her head.

"Are you opening her face, Auntie Sun?" I asked.

"Yes," she replied, "because she is no longer a girl. She is now a woman. When you get married, you will have this done, too."

"Does it hurt, Chunying?" I asked.

"No," she said. "It tickles."

"Don't talk!" Auntie Sun reprimanded.

One of the women combed Chunying's hair and tied it into a bun at the nape of her neck. "This means," another woman told her, "that from this day on, you are a woman and no longer a girl." The others nodded assent.

Chunying stood and the women disrobed her. Once she was naked, they dressed her in red undergarments, red trousers, red shirt and a red head covering. A red veil was pulled over her face. One of them brought in a pair of elegant red shoes. I recognized them immediately. For weeks Chunying had worked on them as I read to her. On the toe of one shoe, she had embroidered a green dragon, and on the other, a golden phoenix. These were the symbols for happiness and a good marriage. Chunying sat down and lifted her feet, and the women put the shoes on her. But to prevent them from touching the earth floor, they put another pair of slippers over the new shoes—an older pair.

Chunying's brother announced breathlessly, "They are coming! They are coming!"

I ran from the bedroom to watch. There was a flurry of activity, and someone shouted, "Quick, close and bar the door!" It slammed shut.

Auntie Chen barred it from inside. In the distance we heard gongs and drums approaching. We sat silently as they drew near. When they were outside the door, there was a series of explosions from strings of firecrackers. As the noise died away, someone began pounding on the door. "Open up!" he shouted. "Open up!" others in the crowd repeated. Their chant became a song, and soon everyone outside was singing together,

> *Open the door.*
> *Open the door.*
> *We're here for the bride.*
> *Let us in.*

For a moment I was frightened and ran back to Chunying. She was sitting on her stool, trembling, her hands folded in her lap.

People in the next room responded to the men outside:

> *It is not so easy,*
> *It is not so easy,*
> *Not so quick for a girl from this family.*
> *You have to give us the red bag first.*

A woman opened the door slightly and a red bag was pushed inside. The door was closed and barred again. Auntie Chen put the bag in her pocket.

Another song came from outside:

> *Open the door,*
> *Open the door,*
> *Time to take the bride.*
> *We must hurry home.*

The people inside sang back:

Go away,
Go away,
It is not enough.
Go away.

And so the lyric went back and forth until the door was opened and the groom's people came inside. As they entered, the women inside began crying and moaning. I watched in wide-eyed fascination. Auntie Chen cried, "She does not want to leave, you cannot take my daughter. You cannot."

She was so convincing I thought a struggle might break out. Yet this was merely another village tradition. The women pretended to be sad.

Soon everyone in the hut was crying. An old woman turned to me and said, "You are supposed to cry. Cry! Cry!"

I couldn't squeeze out any tears, so I rubbed my eyes to make them red.

Another woman whispered in my ear, "It is time to assist Chunying through the door." She led me to Chunying, who remained seated within a circle of crying women. The older woman showed me how to extend my hand. Chunying raised her head. I could not see through her veil but I saw a dark spot on the material—from her tears, I thought. She took my hand and stood. The old woman cleared a path for us and I led Chunying toward the door. It was difficult for her to walk and she teetered back and forth as if she might lose her balance at any moment. I didn't know who was more frightened between the two of us. We were both shaking like leaves.

Just after Chunying crossed the threshold, she paused, and one of the women removed her old slippers and set them down inside the door. Every eye was fixed on Chunying. I led her out onto the path that passed through our village and into the countryside. As we walked, I heard her mother and father burst into tears behind us. At that moment the gravity and finality of this ceremony finally sank in, and I began to cry. Chunying heard me and gently squeezed my hand.

The groom walked at the front of the procession. He seemed as nervous and self-conscious as I was. He was a common-looking man, nearly indistinguishable from all of the other young men who lived out their lives in the countryside. His face was round and ruddy, his eyes narrow. He was about the same height as Chunying. He was not good-looking, but he was not ugly.

We marched in a long line through several villages. In each village people came out to greet us with singing and chanting. They good-naturedly teased the bride and the groom. The bride was supposed to be shy and say nothing. As the villagers laughed and shouted, Chunying gripped my hand even tighter. Neither of us spoke during the two-hour walk to her new home.

Just outside Bao Village a delegation met us and led us to the home of the groom. Children came running to gape at the bride. A dozen tables were set up in front of the groom's hut for a feast that included everyone in the village and all of those who arrived from Gao Village. Chunying was seated at a table beside her husband. The villagers had killed and cooked a pig, so there was pork and vegetables for everyone. It was the best meal I'd had in months. I stuffed myself. I was seated next to Chunying, who was so nervous she could not eat a thing. In the midst of such a festive occasion, I felt so sorry for my dearest friend.

Everyone drank the village's special brand of liquor, a milky white concoction distilled from rice for special occasions. It was so powerful, many of the people from Gao Village observed, that drinking it was like consuming liquid fire. In fact, one of the men touched a match to a glass of the liquor and it burned. The more people drank, the more they sang and the happier they became. There were scores of toasts, each one ending with people emptying their glasses and shouting, "Bottoms up."

Old Crab was seated with his son at our table. He wore a clean white shirt that contrasted sharply with his ruddy face. As the time passed and he consumed more and more liquor, his face began to glow. He stood and offered half a dozen drunken toasts to the bride and groom, collapsing onto the bench after each one.

When the feasting was finished, it was time for the wedding ceremony. The parents of the bride and groom and local dignitaries were assembled. But Old Crab was nowhere to be found. A search party was organized, led by his concerned son. They found the team leader sprawled out unconscious next to a latrine. He had carelessly dropped a half-extinguished cigarette into his pocket and burned a large hole in the front of his shirt. His face was smeared with vomit. His son revived him with a bucket of cold water, cleaned him up and led him to join the other dignitaries. But he could not stand on his own; his son had to put Old Crab's arm around his shoulder and prop him up during the ceremony. Everyone noticed the large brown-rimmed hole in Old Crab's shirt and said how lucky he was not to have set himself on fire.

The bride and groom stood before a portrait of Chairman Mao that was held high in the air by two men. They wished for a long life for the Great Helmsman and bowed three times. The bride and groom bowed three times to each set of parents. Then they bowed to each other. With that the marriage was sealed.

One of the young men shouted, "Now it is time to make havoc in the bedroom." The bride and groom were escorted into the bedroom. Villagers played games with the couple, making them sing a popular revolutionary song to each other, then making them dance or stand on a stool on one foot. Some put dates under the sheets of the wedding bed. These were supposed to have the power to induce the bride and groom to have a son soon. Others made the new couple sip lotus seed soup, which was thought to make them have one son after another. "Big strong sons are more valuable than gold," one of the village elders reminded everyone.

As night fell, people began to file back to their own villages or huts. I was invited to remain in Bao Village overnight. All night long I thought about my friendship with Chunying. The following morning I quietly let myself out. As I was leaving the village, I saw Chunying outside, fetching water for her new family. I ran to her and she turned and smiled weakly at me. We held each other's hands, as we often did in the past. I blurted out, "Did you like sleeping with your husband last night, Chunying?"

I'd listened to all the joking the previous evening about what the couple would do at night. Chunying and I had talked about it just before she was married, but neither of us knew much about what went on between a man and a woman in bed. It was a secretive and forbidden subject.

She blushed and looked at the ground. "You'll know when you are married," she responded.

"But I want to know now, Chunying," I insisted.

"What happened is that he hurt me. He hurt me a lot."

That was all she said. It made me feel very bad. She had been hurt on her wedding night by her husband. After that I had mixed feelings about marriage. All the ceremony and the feasting and the fun, and it all ended when the husband hurt his wife. I was going to tell Chunying that I wanted her to be my attendant when I married. But now, seeing her and hearing her sad words, I said only, "I'll come back and visit you soon, Chunying." She nodded and trudged back toward her new home, carrying water.

37

I spent my afternoons alone after that. I missed Chunying so much. One day I saw two little girls on the back of a water buffalo going out to graze, and I remembered Chunying and was sad. I went to visit her during the next Chinese New Year, when it was customary to visit relatives and friends. By that time she had given birth to her first child, a girl. The baby was cute, very fat with a round face. She was wrapped in a new blanket and wore a red padded shirt and green pants. She looked well fed and healthy. When Chunying and I talked, I felt as if we did not have much to say to each other. There were long silences and awkward pauses as never before in our conversations. She responded to my questions with a single word or a nod. She seemed distracted and melancholy. We held hands for a moment before we parted, but she looked away from me, as if embarrassed or disappointed.

Chunying's mother and father visited us the following year on New Year's Day. I asked about Chunying. "How is she? Is she visiting you this year?"

"Oh, no, Yimao," her mother said. "She has given birth again."

"Was it a boy this time?" I asked, knowing how much the in-laws wanted a grandson.

"No," her mother said. "She had twin girls."

I giggled with delight. "Twin girls! I'll go see them."

Two days later, I went to see Chunying. I grabbed a handful of special candy that had been sent to us from relatives in Tianjin. I wanted to give it to Chunying. Snow had fallen throughout the night. As I passed out of Gao Village and the road rose into the hills, I paused to catch my breath and look back. Everything was buried beneath a thin blanket of fresh snow. But the landscape around Gao Village had changed since Chunying's wedding. There were no trees. The previous autumn Old Crab had ordered every tree around the village cut down. He called this "chopping off the capitalist tail." He wanted to prevent villagers from cutting the trees for their own use, so he eliminated the forests in the name of socialism. He sold the lumber and pocketed the profits.

In the middle of the village stood a wooden pole made from what had once been the tallest tree in the surrounding forest. It was topped with a loudspeaker that blared announcements, news, and patriotic songs from commune headquarters. Plumes of frost rose from my nose and mouth. The cold air on my face was razor sharp. I sang to myself as I crossed the countryside. Chunying was fortunate to have twins, I thought. I wondered what names she had chosen for them. What did they look like? What would their smiles look like?

As I approached the village, I saw smoke rising from the chimneys. No one was outside and there were no footprints in the snow. Everything seemed tranquil and I imagined the happy families celebrating the festival together.

Just outside the village I crossed a narrow bridge over a rapidly rushing stream. It was constructed of three logs lashed together. The water was filled with chunks of ice. I remembered that when Chunying's wedding party had crossed the bridge, she had lifted her veil momentarily and stared down fearfully at the water before she was pulled across by villagers. On this morning I was alone and afraid. If I slipped and fell, there was no one to save me. I summoned my courage and sidestepped slowly across the logs.

I pushed open the door to Chunying's shed. "It's me, Yimao," I announced. "I'm here to see the new babies!"

My greeting was met by silence. I blinked several times to adjust my eyes to the darkness in the room. As my vision cleared I saw Chunying's husband and father-in-law squatting in front of the stove, smoking. Neither looked up. I noticed movement in the middle of the room and was able to make out Chunying's daughter, in padded clothing, staring at me. Her nose was running and there were bits of food on her chin and jacket. A hand touched my arm. I jumped and turned to see Chunying's mother-in-law standing beside me.

"Where are Chunying and her babies?" I asked. She motioned to the next room.

I stepped into the bedroom. The only light came from a small window. "Chunying," I said. "It is me, Yimao. I am here to see your babies. And I brought you candy from Tianjin."

I moved to the side of her bed and looked for the babies. Chunying's hair was matted, and a soiled white cloth was knotted around her head. She was thin and haggard. Her dark sad hollow eyes followed me. She watched me as if she'd never seen me before. "What is wrong, Chunying?" I asked. "Where are your baby girls?"

She didn't reply. She just continued staring at me blankly.

A single tear rolled down Chunying's cheek. I leaned down to her. Her lips moved slightly but I could not hear her. I put my face close to hers. In a weak little girl's voice, she said, "Xiao Mao. Xiao Mao . . . you are here." When we played together in the past, she called me Xiao Mao or Little Mao.

"Yes, it is Xiao Mao," I said. "I came through the snow to see you and your new babies."

"My new babies," she said. She paused as if the words didn't register. Then she said again, "Xiao Mao, you are here."

"Where are your babies, Chunying?"

She turned her eyes to the wall and responded with a low broken moan. Her mother-in-law came into the room. "Chunying needs her rest," she said. She pulled the blanket up to Chunying's chin. I laid the candy on the blanket and left the room with the older woman. "I'm leaving now, Chunying," I said. "But I'll be back."

When we were in the next room, I asked, "Where are the babies, and why is Chunying so sad? She should be so happy."

"Oh," the mother-in-law began and paused to breathe a long sigh. "It is such a pity. It is just her fate. She has a bitter life. And now she brings bitterness to us. She already had a thing that we are destined to give away." She pointed to the little girl on the floor when she said "a thing." "We are poor. We cannot afford any more debt collectors." By "debt collectors" she referred to girls, who cost a family money to raise and then married and left to join another family. "Those new ones were real debt collectors because they came on New Year's Eve, the traditional time for collecting debts."

I felt a chill as she spoke. A premonition of what she was about to reveal wormed its way into my mind. I wanted to cover my ears, to run, to put my hand over her mouth so she could not tell me. Instead, I stood before her and tried to wish away the awful truth.

"We let Chunying keep them on New Year's Day for good luck. It was a difficult delivery. She held one in each arm. But she knew . . . she *knew*."

"Chunying knew what?" I asked, trying to control my voice.

"Whatever one does on New Year's Day determines what will happen the rest of the year. So we kept them for one day."

The men listened, but neither looked up. The only move they made was to lift a cigarette to their mouths and then withdraw it. The rest of the time they seemed like statues made of mud.

"Where are the girls now?"

"Where are they? On the second day of the New Year . . . we took them from Chunying's arms when she was sleeping and we threw them in the river."

A sickness erupted in my stomach. I doubled over and my heart fluttered wildly. I covered my mouth, braced myself against the wall for a moment and then rushed from the shed. I began screaming. The door slammed shut behind me. I fell to my knees sobbing.

Finally I stood and walked straight to the bridge leading out of the village. I hurried to the middle, no longer afraid of falling. I dropped to my knees and peered down into the freezing water and wondered if Chunying's husband or father-in-law or both had thrown the babies in the stream. "Did they wrap you in a blanket?" I wailed. "What did you feel?" I asked, looking down. "Were you asleep when they took you from Chunying's arms? Did you cry from the shock of the cold? Did you make a sound?"

I choked on the words. I wondered if the cold had killed the girls before they drowned. What were these men thinking? Had they regrets? Had they any feelings about this at all? Was it merely something they did, like throwing out the trash, with the same lack of thought or consequence? Did they feel bad because they had killed the little girls? Or did they feel bad because Chunying had given them little girls? There must be some guilt, I thought. Some regret. There had to be some little spark of human compassion, some warmth, some sympathy.

I began answering my own questions. "Not enough sympathy to keep you alive. Not enough sympathy to give you away. Not enough. This world of monsters."

I wondered how many hundreds of thousands of other baby girls had been flung from a bridge like this. Some often met an even worse fate. Sometimes, I'd heard, peasants didn't even bother to go to a river. They placed the naked baby outside and let her die of exposure. Or they held her upside down in a bucket of water or urine.

I whispered to the twins, "At least you died a clean death, maybe even a quick death. Maybe it was so fast you hardly felt it."

That was the best thought I could conjure up as I knelt on the bridge looking down at the icy black water. I headed down the path toward home and wept. The tears froze to my face. I wondered what might happen if I ever married someone from this village, if I had a baby girl. Could my husband do this? Kill my child? I decided at that moment that I would never marry in the countryside. I'd die first.

It started to snow. I looked into the thick white veil of snowflakes and tried to find an image of the girls, together now, playing, in a better life, in a better world. I was soon talking out loud to the twins again, in a nearly hysterical singsong voice, thinking and questioning and answering and clenching my fists and wiping away tears with my sleeve. I stumbled several times, blinded by my tears. Once I slipped and fell off the road. I got up without brushing myself off and continued on. When I got home I was cold and covered with dirt and snow.

As I walked in the door, Mama called to me, "How are the babies, Yimao?"

"Dead," I said and burst into tears. "They killed them, Mama."

My father was sitting at the table and looked up at me but said nothing.

"Oh, dear God in heaven!" Mama cried. She stepped in front of me and asked, "Are you going to be all right?"

"No," I told her. "I am not." I took off my jacket and trousers and crawled into my bed and cried for the rest of the day.

Mama never brought up Chunying's babies again. Nobody did. This was not an uncommon practice. But it harrowed up my heart and left the deep furrow of a memory that would haunt me to the end of my life. Before that morning I'd heard stories, but they were just stories. Now I knew it was all real.

My father (leaning, far left) with school friends in a posed studio shot, Yangzhou, 1932.

In Tianjin, 1956: my mother standing, center, flanked on the left by my maternal great aunt and, right, my maternal grandmother. Seated, center, is my maternal great-grandmother at 102, holding my older brother, Yiding, with my cousin on the left. Note the bound feet.

Mama holding me, flanked, left, by Grandma (maternal) and by Grandmother Jiang Zhongjie (paternal) in a Beijing studio shot, 1958. This photograph was taken to be sent to my father in prison.

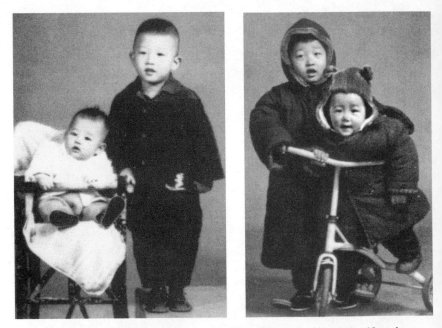

left: My brother Yiding, almost three years old, and me, five months old, in Beijing, November 1958. This was the last picture taken before we went with Mama to Hefei.

right: Yiding and me in Tianjin, 1960, taken at Wondrous Peak Photos just before Mama left me behind to live with Grandma (maternal).

At the sports grounds in Hefei where the professors would be denounced, before the start of the Cultural Revolution in 1965: my younger brother, Yicun, front with cap, and Yiding, to his left. I am partially hidden in the back.

I am flanked by my brothers, Hefei, 1966. Taken at a studio a few days after Uncle PLA gave me the Mao badge I am wearing. My shirt was buttoned up to hide the bruises left from our encounter.

Posing in front of a studio backdrop of Tiananmen Square with my father and my brothers, Chinese New Year 1970, in Wujiang, where Papa was being kept in the "cowshed."

Nanjing, 1971, where father and I had been visiting relatives. It is the only picture taken of him during the years we lived in Gao Village.

Graduation picture of the Communist Youth League members from middle school in Gao Village, November 1973. I am in the front row, left.

With Yicun in Wuhu, 1974, in front of the truck that had brought us from Gao Village.

above: With Xu Yuqing the Communist Youth League leader and student supervisor, in the factory in Wuhu, 1975; note both of us are wearing Red Guard badges.

left: Washing laundry in front of the converted church where we lived with seven other families in Wuhu, 1976. We all shared the one water faucet on the left.

The high school graduating class members of the Communist Youth League posing in front of its flag and the slogan "We once fought together," January 21, 1976; I am in the second row, second from right.

above: Hiking in the mountains in the rain, 1976. I have a stick to scare away the many poisonous snakes.

right: In one of the streams, when I was teaching in the mountains, summer 1976.

On the Bund in Shanghai during a break from teaching in the mountains, months before going off to college, 1977.

我们的教育方针，应该使
受教育者在德育、智育、体育
几方面都得到发展，成为有社
会主义觉悟的有文化的劳动
者。

毛泽东

姓名　巫一毛
性别　女　　年龄　19
籍贯　江苏省扬州县市
专业　英语
入学年月　1978·2

学号　7702052
证号　770232
发证日期　1978·3

Student I.D. from Anhui Teachers University, which I entered in February 1978. The quotation from Chairman Mao to the left of the picture says, "Our educational policy must enable everyone who receives an education to develop morally, intellectually, and physically and become a worker with both socialist consciousness and culture."

38

I met the village idiot early one morning while I was searching for manure. As I scooped up a pile of dog excrement, a voice behind me screamed, "Stop! That's my dog shit! Don't you dare touch it!"

I turned to see an unusually tall, heavyset young man. His hair was long and uncombed and his face was filthy. He looked like one of the wild animals I'd seen in the zoo in Hefei. Before I could respond, he approached, his eyes narrowed menacingly, and he shouted, "I saw you. I know what you are doing."

"All right," I said. "This shit is yours. I don't want it." I picked up my basket and fled.

When I got home, I was out of breath. My mother asked what was wrong, and I said, "A screaming guy said I was stealing his dog poop, but it was just dog poop that didn't belong to anybody but some dog. Why is an adult collecting this? They are supposed to let the children do it."

Mama smiled and said, "Oh, you just met Sun Jigui. He's the village idiot. He's a good boy. He's big and loud, but he's harmless."

"Why is he called the village idiot?"

"I don't know why," she said. "But everyone in this village refers to him that way."

A few days later a middle-aged woman came to our shed.

"Have you eaten, Sun Breast?" Mama greeted her.

I was startled to hear my mother use the Gao Village expression. The peasants referred to married women as "breasts." In the city the common term for such women was "Auntie."

"Sun Breast is Jigui's mother," she explained to me.

As they talked, I sat beside the stove and listened. Mama asked her, "Do you mind if I ask how Jigui became the way he is? What happened?"

Sun Breast took a deep breath and sighed. "It is difficult for me to tell you this. He is such a heartache for us. He is fifteen years old. He eats, he sleeps, he collects manure. Other than that, he doesn't do anything but cause trouble. He was three when the famine began. His sister was five. In those days all of us ate in a public kitchen. There was a set portion of food for each person. We told everyone that his sister was sick and brought her portion home. Then we fed it to Jigui.

"She cried and tried to run out of the house. My man tied her to the bed and gagged her.

"When she died two weeks later, I dared not cry for fear that people might realize what we had done. We kept her body inside so we could still get her food ration. Eventually she started to rot and smell, and we had to bury her.

"It was difficult for us, but only in that way could we save Jigui.

"If we knew then how he would turn out, of course, we would have fed her instead. How much easier our lives would be if we had made that decision.

"The doctor said maybe he is the way he is because of those years. Maybe we still did not give him enough food."

"Sometimes he seems normal," Mama said. "Why don't you take him to a different doctor?"

"Oh, we barely have enough to eat," Sun Breast replied. "How could we afford a doctor? When we eat our breakfast, we do not know where dinner will come from. We have never had enough money to see another doctor."

After that I knew what to expect from Jigui. One day I was in front of our shed with my brothers playing hide-and-seek. He watched and asked if he could play. "Sure," I said. "Turn your back and count to ten and then try to find us. You must say, 'I am going to find you. I am going to find you.' When you find us, touch us and shout, 'You're it!' And then you get to hide."

He didn't understand. He thought you just ran around and hit people, and he loved that. So he ran wildly around the yard chasing us and hitting us so hard it hurt, shouting, "You're it! You're it!" He had a wonderful time.

While we were playing, Old Crab happened to pass by. Jigui dashed over to him and slapped him hard on the back of the head and shouted, "You're it!" Old Crab stumbled and whirled around and bellowed, "You damned idiot! How dare you? How dare you lay a hand on a Communist Party member?"

He grabbed Jigui by the wrist and began beating him. Jigui fell down and Old Crab grabbed a rake and jabbed him with it. Jigui managed to get away, and Old Crab couldn't catch him. As he disappeared in the distance, Jigui was yelling, "You're it, Old Crab. You're it."

Old Crab went to the boy's house and summoned his parents. "Your son tried to kill a Communist Party member," he told them. "This is a crime against the state. Your boy is an anti-revolutionary. According to the Six Articles of Public Security, I can send him to jail."

Jigui's father was shaken by Old Crab's words. "I am so sorry," he cried. He begged Old Crab to spare the life of his boy. Sun Breast pushed a new package of cigarettes into Old Crab's hand. "Please come back later for dinner, Team Leader. I'll kill a chicken for you. I'll beat Jigui. And we'll make him kowtow to you."

Old Crab hesitated before replying, "I'll forgive him this one time. But no more."

"Thank you," Jigui's father said. "He'll pay for this, believe me."

Three days later Jigui came to our hut. His face was swollen and bruised. "Old Crab said that I cannot come into your house," he said.

"Why did he say that, Jigui?" Mama asked.

"Because you are bad people. You walk on the capitalist road."

"I see," Mama said.

"Old Crab said if I come into your house, he will break my legs."

"In that case, you'd better not come in, Jigui," Mama said.

"I kowtowed to Old Crab," he said.

"Is that so?" Mama asked. "And did he forgive you for what you did?"

"No. He kicked me in the head," Jigui said. "Is Old Crab a good man or a bad man, Teacher Li?"

Mama pretended that she hadn't heard the question.

Suddenly, Jigui blurted out, "Teacher Li, Papa beat me because he is not my real papa."

"I know your mama and papa, Jigui. They are good people."

"No, you don't. My real papa is Chairman Mao," he said, his voice rising.

"What do you mean?" Mama asked.

"Chairman Mao is my papa," Jigui said. "I have his Red Book. I have his picture. I love him."

"How did you learn this?" Mama asked.

"I heard people say Chairman Mao is dearer than any mama or papa. They said Chairman Mao loves me. So Chairman Mao is my real papa."

"That's good," Mama said. "Go play now."

"Okay," he said and smiled. "I'm going to find some shit and make my real papa proud of me."

39

In the autumn the entire village participated in harvesting rice. Classes were canceled so children could join their parents in the paddies. Even the smallest children worked in the fields. After the harvest, the fields were plowed and the smallest children went through them and stomped down the roots of the previous crop.

At dawn Old Crab awakened everyone with long shrill blasts on his whistle. After barking out the work assignments, he led the villagers in a long column into the fields. He marched at the head of the column, holding a huge picture of Chairman Mao on a wooden pole high in the air. On the march to the fields one morning I was accompanied by my friend Wang Jinlan. Jigui, the village idiot, who was not required to work in the fields, walked behind us. Jinlan was sixteen, and she had already blossomed into a strikingly beautiful young woman. The eyes of all of the young men followed her wherever she went. But her heart was spoken for.

"Old Crab came to our shed yesterday," she told me as we walked. "He brought a matchmaker with him. They talked to my parents about marrying me to Young Crab."

"Oh, no!" I protested. "You can't marry him. Everyone knows you are in love with Shuizi."

"Yes." She smiled and sighed. "Everyone knows that. But what can I do? I'm just a girl. I can't say anything about my marriage. It doesn't matter that I don't want to marry Young Crab. My papa and mama make that decision."

"And what does Shuizi say about that?" I asked.

"His family is no match for Old Crab's family," she said. "He's sad. But there is nothing we can do about it."

Shuizi and his father lived in a shed near Jinlan's family. Shuizi was the tallest and most handsome of all of the young men in the village. Ever since he and Jinlan were children, they'd played together. Villagers often saw them walking and talking together just beyond the perimeter of the village. Everyone expected that when they grew up, they'd marry.

Shuizi reminded me of the tenderhearted and melancholy poets of the Tang Dynasty whom I'd read about in Papa's books. He saw and related to the world differently from anyone I'd ever known. He smiled more and laughed more than the other boys. He seemed filled with a joy for life and he communicated that to others. Somehow he had taught himself to play the flute. He learned songs by listening to broadcasts of music over the public loudspeakers in the village. Some afternoons I saw him sitting at the base of the loudspeaker pole with his eyes closed as Peking operas or revolutionary anthems were broadcast. The next day he'd be sitting in another part of the village, playing the same tunes on his flute. Villagers stopped what they were doing when they heard him and many sat on the ground and listened to the music he made. The young women in the village adored his talent and his temperament and envied Jinlan.

As we neared the rice paddy, Jigui suddenly grabbed Jinlan's braids and gave them a jerk and shouted, "Look at the braids! Longer than cow tails! Thicker than my penis!" Jinlan turned and slapped at Jigui, who ducked and retreated a few steps. Before he could make another move, Young Crab appeared and swung a hoe at Jigui, striking him across the shoulder and knocking him to the ground. "Why are you harassing my breast, you damned idiot?" he shouted. "I will kill you right here!" The procession halted and everyone turned to see the commotion. Old Crab raced back and began hitting Jigui with the pole he carried with the picture of Chairman Mao on the end. Mao's beatific face rose and fell on Jigui's skull. Jigui cowered and shrieked, "Stop hitting me with my real papa! Stop! I am the good son of Chairman Mao."

The peasants gasped as the portrait tore upon hitting Jigui's upraised hand. "Shit!" Old Crab screamed. "Now look what you've done! You've punctured the face of the Great Helmsman. You are a current counterrevolutionary."

Realizing the seriousness of what had happened, Old Crab quickly raised the portrait high over his head. But it hung askew and there was a gaping hole under Chairman Mao's left eye.

"Look what *you* did," Jigui yelled. "You hurt me and you hurt my papa!"

Old Crab and his son kicked Jigui until he stopped shouting and rolled onto his side and groaned with pain.

"Okay," Old Crab proclaimed to the villagers. "Let's get to work!" Holding the damaged portrait of Chairman Mao, he led the procession into the fields. I looked back to see Jigui crawling away.

We stopped working early that afternoon as a powerful thunderstorm approached. The sky darkened, and a heavy rain was soon lashing the village. The wind increased throughout the evening. The roof of our shed groaned and shook with each new blast that night, and the door creaked on its hinges. I lay in bed listening apprehensively as the storm battered our shed. Shortly after midnight I saw a flash of lightning overhead and the rain hit my face. I sat up in bed looking at the ceiling. Everything was black. Then there was another flash, a boom of thunder, and more rain fell on me. I realized that the wind was lifting the corner of the roof off and exposing everything inside. I sat on the edge of my bed and called out, "Mama, the roof's flying away."

But before anyone could respond to my cry, another huge gust of wind caught the corner of the roof. It curled and twisted off the wall, rose into the night sky and in an instant disappeared. I was drenched by the rainfall, and several bright strings of lightning terrified me. I ran into my parents' room shouting, "The roof is gone, the roof is gone!" I huddled in bed with my parents and brothers. We listened to the rain sloshing onto the floor of my bedroom. As we clung together in the dark, I felt the rain once more splashing my back. I turned to see the east wall of our house dissolving, and what remained of the roof was beginning to tilt at a precarious angle. Afraid that the wall might collapse and bring the roof down on us, we fled into the middle section of the house.

In the morning we saw the part of the roof that formerly covered my room lying scattered over the nearby rice paddies. The wall in my parents' room was half its original height and the roof sloped at a 45-degree angle. We could hardly believe our eyes. Mama remarked, "Let's just count our blessings. At least we're all alive."

Old Crab examined the damage and concluded, "Well, I've seen worse. You'll have to take care of this yourself."

"We don't know how to repair this," Mama said. "We haven't the tools or the materials."

"What are you suggesting?" he asked.

Papa quickly rummaged through a box in the bedroom and emerged with two packs of cigarettes. "These are still dry," he said and handed them to Old Crab.

"That's more like it," the team leader said. "I'll see what I can do for you."

As Old Crab was leaving, Sun Breast came to our door. "Jigui is missing," she said. "He didn't come home last night. Have you seen him?"

"Good," Old Crab said. "He damaged the portrait of Chairman Mao yesterday. I hope the lightning killed him."

"We haven't seen him," Mama said.

"I'm worried," Sun Breast said. "Where can my poor idiot be?"

No one saw Jigui for the next two weeks. Many villagers concluded he had been caught in the storm and killed. People stopped asking about him. Even his mother stopped looking for him.

When the rice harvest was finished, Old Crab supervised a crew of village workers who patched our roof with new straw and replaced the fallen wall with mud bricks. While they were working, Mama took Yiding to enroll in the local high school, four miles from Gao Village. At the door to the school they were nearly run down by a gang of students chasing someone. She recognized the boy they were chasing: Jigui. He wore only his underwear and was caked with mud. The students were pelting him with stones.

"What's going on here?" Mama asked a teacher.

"That damned idiot came here from the leper colony," the teacher told her. "He's running around at all hours of the day and night, stealing food and hitting students and telling them, 'You're it! You're it!' We're all afraid of getting leprosy from him and some people want to hunt him down and kill him."

Mama was glad to learn that Jigui was alive, but deeply concerned to hear he'd been living among the lepers in their nearby isolated settlement. As soon as she'd gotten Yiding registered for school she hurried home and told the Suns what she'd seen.

"We can never bring him home now," Jigui's father said. "He'll give leprosy to his younger brother."

"We can't just leave him out there," Sun Breast pleaded. "We have to do something. He's our son."

"No, we don't have to do anything," the father said. "It would be a damned lot better if the lightning had struck him. This is just our luck. That idiot will never die."

That night Jigui quietly returned to Gao Village. He went into his shed and tried to crawl into his bed. His parents caught him, however, tied his hands, pushed him outside and bound him to a post in the yard. They left him there for the rest of the night.

In the morning Sun Breast doused him with several buckets of water and handed him clean clothing. She was careful not to touch him. "If you try to untie the rope," she warned him, "I know your father will beat you to death."

He understood the warning and sat obediently at the post through the next day and night. When I saw Jigui during the following days, he was sitting silently on the ground, playing with some pebbles he'd dug up. He glanced up at me and then, as if embarrassed, turned back to his pebbles.

Late one afternoon, Sun Breast burst into our shed crying, "Help! Old Crab and my man are killing Jigui! Maybe they'll listen to you, Teacher Li," she pleaded. "Don't let them kill my idiot."

Mama ran out with her. I followed. A crowd had gathered in front of the Suns' shed. From the midst of the crowd came the shouts of many people. I squeezed my way through until I could see Old Crab and Jigui's father standing over the cowering boy. They had bound him like a pig about to be slaughtered. He lay in the dirt. Each of the men held a manure-collecting rake and took turns clubbing Jigui with them. The boy was covered with blood.

"Stop it!" Mama shouted. I was astounded by both her courage and the volume of her voice. The two men holding the rakes turned to her, and I thought they might strike her. But they froze as if waiting to hear her next command. She strode up to them fearlessly and said, "Leave the boy alone."

Sun Breast threw herself over her son to shield him from further blows. She wailed, "Kill me. But don't hurt my son anymore. I gave birth to him. I made the mistake. Not him."

Old Crab and Jigui's father looked at each other. "Stupid bitch," Old Crab said to Sun Breast. "Get out of the way."

Mama knelt to untie Jigui. Sun Breast ignored Old Crab and helped Mama free the boy.

Jigui's father looked to Old Crab as if to ask, "What now?" But Old Crab merely stood there, perplexed. Jigui got to his feet between the two women and the three of them pushed their way through the crowd. The moment they had broken through the outer edge of the circle, Jigui ran. Old Crab was on his heels in a second, waving the rake over his head, cursing and commanding the boy to stop.

I followed behind with the crowd. Jigui was fast on his feet, despite the beating he'd taken. He crossed the nearby fields, ran up and down a slight rise, and was about to cross a road when a large truck approached.

The driver heard the noise and was looking toward the approaching crowd of people when Jigui darted in front of the truck. There was a loud bang as the truck slammed into Jigui. The boy flew into the air and landed on the other side of the road.

The driver leaped from the truck and ran to the boy. The crowd converged on the scene. Sun Breast cried, "My son! My son!"

Old Crab burst into a demonic cackle when he saw Jigui lying in the ditch. He turned to the driver and spat, "Damn it! You just killed my best team member! Which work unit do you belong to? You're going to pay for this!"

Meanwhile, the other villagers huddled around Jigui's body and Sun Breast wept, "My son! My son! Why did this happen?"

Suddenly, Jigui appeared to rise from the dead. His body convulsed, and a moment later he moaned.

"Oh, shit!" Old Crab mumbled. "The stupid idiot is alive!"

"That's good!" the shaken truck driver said. "That's good! Let's get him to the county hospital right now and discuss a payment later."

"Shit!" Old Crab repeated, ignoring the driver's words. "Oh, shit!"

Sun Breast and several men lifted Jigui onto the bed of the truck. Sun Breast climbed up beside him. But Old Crab seemed to come to his senses and grabbed her and pulled her down. "I'm in charge here," he said. "I'll take this idiot to the hospital to make sure he gets proper care."

Old Crab and Young Crab climbed into the cab of the truck. The driver looked at them in astonishment. "Someone has to ride in the back with the boy," he said, "or he'll fall off."

Old Crab turned to his son. "Get back there with that idiot," he said. "And if he dies, bang on the top of the cab."

Young Crab got out and climbed up beside Jigui and the truck turned around and pulled away. Mama put her arm around the sobbing Sun Breast and told her, "He'll be okay. Let's go home."

Ten days later the truck returned. Someone cried out, "Look!" and pointed to it. Everyone ran to the road. The truck stopped and the villagers gathered around it. Old Crab stumbled from the cab. He fell back against the door for an instant, steadied himself and tried to stand tall. He was drunk.

Young Crab jumped down from the truck bed. Jigui was sitting on the truck bed, his back against the cab. He slid to the side of the bed and Young Crab helped him down. Jigui turned and pulled two crutches from the truck. We were horrified to see that his right leg had been amputated above the knee. The leg of his trousers had been shortened and pinned shut around the stump.

Sun Breast began moaning, "Look what they did to my son!"

"What are you crying about," Old Crab said. "Your good fortune has finally arrived. The idiot is good for something. This driver, he's a good man. And his work unit compensated us for the medical expenses. And look here," he said, pulling a roll of cash from his pocket and holding it out for everyone to see. "They even gave us money for all the trouble they caused."

Jigui's father stepped forward and held out his hand to take the money. Old Crab peeled two hundred yuan from the wad and thrust it into his palm. "That's all?" Jigui's father protested. "My boy lost his leg. He's my idiot."

Old Crab stuffed the remaining money into his own pocket. "Hey," he said, snorting, "I got you this. You were trying to kill him when he ran away. He was worth nothing to you. But I lost a team member. This is mine!"

Jigui's behavior changed after he came home from the hospital. He sat alone outside the family shed on a bundle of straw for hours each day, paging through his Little Red Book. One might have guessed from watching him that he was literate. He hobbled around the village on crutches and none of the children teased him. Whenever someone asked what he was doing, Jigui smiled and said, "I'm waiting for my real papa to make my leg grow back."

His mother brought him his meals and sometimes squatted and talked with him. His father and Old Crab ignored him.

40

After completing fifth grade in the brigade elementary school, I moved on to the commune middle school. It was a forty-minute walk from home. That year Teacher Lu returned to being an itinerant peddler. He decided it was less trouble selling his wares than teaching children. In his place the brigade hired a young man who had finished middle school the previous spring. He was sixteen years old and had never taught before. Unlike Teacher Lu, who was patient with the children, he was a strict disciplinarian. He held a ruler tightly in his right hand, and whenever students spoke out of turn or answered his questions incorrectly, he struck them. When I heard Yicun complain about the new teacher, I was happy I'd moved on but was sorry for him and the other children. Yet there was nothing I could do.

The middle school was larger than the elementary school. It consisted of three structures rather than one, constructed of bricks and tile rather than mud. There were three teachers. Best of all, there were two other girls in my class. One of them—Li Bingzhi—was in class because she was crippled. When she was small she contracted polio and one of her legs withered. She walked with a crutch and was unable to work in the fields. Her family concluded that if she continued on in school, she might learn how to become an accountant and have a better chance of finding a husband. She was useless as a peasant and therefore not desirable to the village men.

The other girl in our class, Liu Chaoping, was the daughter of a settle-down family in a nearby village. Her father had been a colleague of my parents. Each of us was supposed to bring our own table or desk and a stool to school. Bingzhi brought a small square table. I brought my little stool and shared the table with her. Chaoping brought her own stool and shared the table with Bingzhi and me. Our table had shorter legs than the others, so the teacher had us sit in the front of the class. During recess the three of us played together.

It was difficult finding teachers for the country schools. Consequently, the commune leaders solved this problem by employing the educated youth to do the job. The educated youth were middle school and high school graduates sent to the countryside at Chairman Mao's order to be reeducated by the peasants. But instead of being reeducated by the peasants, they were employed to teach the children of the peasants.

Our English teacher was a young woman from Nanjing named Ying Zaizhou. She was chubby and soft-featured and looked like a city girl. She had pale skin and short curly hair, which was unusual in the countryside. When she smiled, her eyes became two lines across her face and almost closed. She spoke with a heavy Nanjing accent and we often had difficulty understanding her. Ying Zaizhou had only a high school education, but she did her best to teach us. As peasants, we wondered what use we might have for English. But it was a requirement.

Papa helped me with my English lessons. When I arrived home in the afternoon, he'd say, "Read me your English for today." And when I read it, he'd say, "No, no, no, not like that—like this." He'd read the sentences and words with a completely different pronunciation.

When I read English words aloud the way Papa pronounced them for me, the teacher ridiculed me. "Why do you think the word is pronounced like that?" she'd ask. I was frustrated. I hated English. Eventually Papa figured out what was wrong. Ying Zaizhou was pronouncing each English word as if it were derived from a Chinese character. She had never actually heard the proper English pronunciation. Papa laughed when I read to him and said, "I'm afraid you are learning a language that is spoken only by your teacher and her students. No one else in the world can understand a word you are saying!"

The temperature inside and outside our classrooms was always the same. In the winter, each class period began with warm-up exercises. We rubbed our hands together, did jumping jacks and patted ourselves on the arms and legs. In the summer, we sat at our desks and perspired until we were completely drenched.

After the first few weeks of class I was told that I was eligible to apply for membership in the Communist Youth League. In elementary school in Hefei, I had been ruled ineligible to join the Little Red Guards because of my family background. But in the countryside the ruthlessness of class consciousness was tempered. I had been classified as an "educable child of problematic parents" by the Communist Youth League members who examined my background. They invited me to apply. I was cautioned that I must prove I was truly qualified for membership. I had to demonstrate that I was a good student and a good Communist, and I had to try harder than everyone else because of my family background.

I wanted to join. The Communist Youth League represented a sort of liberation for me. I did not believe a word of the phrases I memorized or any of the lines from the *Quotations of Chairman Mao* that I recited. In fact, from my last days in Hefei, I knew it was all a lie—fairy tales and fantasies justifying cruelty and brutality. Yet I needed to join the believers to keep them from hurting me further. It was a way of insulating myself from the stain of my family's political past. I thought China would never change, that the Cultural Revolution would go on forever. Therefore the only way for me not to live exactly as my parents lived was to come to an accommodation with the ruling powers rather than hide and cower constantly.

I worked hard to qualify. I volunteered to sweep the floor of the school every afternoon. I cleaned the blackboard for the teachers after each class. I kept the classroom tidy. I assisted other students with their homework. At the end of each week, I was required to write a "thought report" to the CYL branch chapter. I wrote things like: "I read Chairman Mao's slogans again this week. These were the most relevant to me . . ." Then I'd repeat a dozen or so sayings. Of course all of this was very formal, even the commentaries I made on their relevance to my experience. I knew what I was expected to write, so I wrote it, robotically.

After several months of showing my sincerity and enthusiasm for membership, I was told that I had passed the test and could be admitted. A formal induction ceremony was scheduled. I was to be sworn in and to pledge my allegiance to the Party and to Chairman Mao in front of the other members. I was told the date and the time of the ceremony.

I was willing to work to become a member, but I refused to stand before the other students and swear allegiance to the organization that had persecuted us. I could not. When the day of the ceremony arrived, I pretended to be sick and stayed home. It was my way of maintaining some integrity. On the following day, when I returned to school, representatives of the CYL handed me my membership certificate and congratulated me. I was never required to be sworn in publicly. I told my parents that evening what I'd done. I emphasized that I hadn't sworn allegiance to the Party. They congratulated me.

I attended weekly CYL meetings after that. And I posed with other members for the CYL group picture. Everyone seemed convinced that I was a good Communist.

41

The age for marriage in the village was sixteen. Long before a child turned that age, however, the parents arranged for a marriage that might be advantageous to the family. Jinlan's father came to an agreement with Old Crab to marry his daughter to the team leader's son. After the announcement of the engagement, both Jinlan and Shuizi were very sad. Shuizi's father approached Jinlan's father and asked if there might be some way to break the other arrangement. "You know that everyone has always expected my son to marry your daughter. You've seen them together. You know how they look at each other. You've heard him sing for her."

But Shuizi's family was among the poorest in the village. Although Shuizi's father had attended school and done well and might have become a country scholar, he had gone into the army during the Korean War. In late 1953 he returned to the village a changed man. He was not interested in becoming a Communist Party member, even though, as a veteran, he was asked to join. And he was no longer interested in school or books. He was different, people said, from the bright young man who had marched away in 1950. He was quiet. He worked hard. He married a village girl and had Shuizi. He raised his son alone. He had no connections, no Party membership, and no prominent relatives in other villages or towns. He had nothing to offer Jinlan's father except an old tarnished medal for heroism and empty words. So Jinlan's father told Shuizi's father to find another girl for his son. But soon afterward people whispered that they'd seen Jinlan and Shuizi walking along paths near the village, laughing and talking as if they were betrothed.

The rumors and stories angered Old Crab. He went to Jinlan's father and demanded, "What's going on here? Do we have an arrangement or not?"

"Of course we do," Jinlan's father assured him. "The stories are not true. Jinlan is a good girl. She will marry your son."

Several days after that, Old Crab returned from brigade headquarters and went to the village warehouse. As he approached the building he heard a woman's voice. He slipped inside silently with a large lecherous grin. He peeked around the mud wall and spotted a pile of clothing on the floor. He inched closer until at last, atop several sacks of rice, he saw Jinlan and Shuizi. They were naked and entwined in each other's arms. Old Crab's lecherous grin turned into a grimace. He let out an ear-piercing bellow of rage. Shuizi and Jinlan leaped to their feet. Jinlan tried to cover her nakedness, and Shuizi grabbed for their clothing. Old Crab grabbed a hoe and yelled, "Shuizi, I'll kill both of you if you make another move." They clung together. Jinlan cried hysterically, and Shuizi tried to comfort her and protect her. Old Crab snatched up their clothing and flung it outside. He summoned a group of villagers working nearby to witness what he'd found. When they came running, he ordered them, "Go to the fields and get the others. Hurry!"

He went back inside the warehouse and stood over the mortified girl and her companion, waving his hoe menacingly and spitting out a long litany of choice obscenities and threats. Scores of peasants arrived from the fields and huts. Old Crab called the men into the warehouse but commanded the women and children to remain outside. When the men saw the naked youngsters, they were both embarrassed and appalled. They seemed unsure why Old Crab needed them.

"Tie them up!" he ordered and motioned toward several lengths of rope in the corner. Old Crab pulled Jinlan out of Shuizi's arms and pushed her into the hands of the men. He held the blade of his hoe against Shuizi's neck and said, "Now you'll get a dose of revolutionary justice, you sneaky bastard." Shuizi glared defiantly back at him as the men bound his arms. He looked at Jinlan as she frantically tried to cover herself, and he spat at Old Crab, "Let her go, you heartless old fart! I'm the one who did this! I am guilty. She's not."

Old Crab made a swipe with the hoe near Shuizi's mouth and hissed, "I'll cut your damned tongue out if you say another word."

He instructed the men to throw a rope over the beam in the ceiling and to bind Jinlan's hands over her head and pull her into a standing position exposing her private parts. She screamed and begged to be released and pleaded for the men to kill her instead. Old Crab pulled the rope taut himself until only her toes touched the floor. Jinlan squeezed her eyes shut and turned her face to the ground as the men stood around her.

"I caught them here," Old Crab said. "They were both shirking their work and coupling like rutting pigs."

He stepped in front of Jinlan and grabbed her between the legs. "And to think that this whore wanted to be my daughter-in-law!"

She let out a cry.

"Please forgive her, Team Leader," a voice rang out. It was Jinlan's father. He'd been the last to enter the warehouse. "She's not that kind of girl, Old Crab, and you know it. Shuizi must have lured her here with his music and his sweet words."

Old Crab's expression changed as Jinlan's father spoke. He appeared to find the words convincing.

"Let me take her home," Jinlan's father continued. "All she needs is a good beating."

This was followed by a hum of assent among the men.

Jinlan's father stepped outside and gathered up her clothes while some of the other men untied his daughter. She kept her eyes glued to the ground as her father covered her with her clothing and led her away.

Once they were gone, Old Crab turned to Shuizi and asked, "So what do we do with a rapist?"

There was no response. The silence appeared to anger Old Crab even more. "Let me show you what we do," he said. He raised the hoe above his head and brought it down hard on Shuizi's skull. The young man let out a moan and his eyes closed. Blood streamed down his face and shoulders and he slumped to the floor. Before Old Crab could strike him again with his hoe, several men stepped in front of him. "You'll kill him if you do that," one said. "He doesn't deserve to die." Old Crab threw the hoe aside and pushed past the men and kicked Shuizi again and again while the boy lay motionless on the ground. At last the other men pulled Old Crab back and said, "Enough! He's learned his lesson." Old Crab tried to shake them off at first but finally yielded to their restraint. He spat on Shuizi's body. "I'm not finished with you," he muttered. Old Crab pushed his way through the crowd and strode outside into the sunlight. Several men picked up Shuizi and carried him home.

Late that night Old Crab went outside to his family's latrine to relieve himself. As he squatted in the dark, he suddenly saw two bare feet planted in the earth in front of him. He looked up and was shocked to see Shuizi's father standing over him. At first he didn't recognize the man because of his attire. He was wearing his PLA tunic from the Korean War, with his medal for heroism pinned prominently over his heart.

Old Crab rose to his feet and asked, "What are you doing out so late?"

A hand shot out and grabbed him by the throat and jerked him forward. Old Crab's loosened trousers fell to his ankles. Shuizi's father pulled Old Crab's face close to his own. Old Crab struggled to breathe. Two wide, hate-filled eyes glowed like burning coals in the darkness only inches away. Old Crab felt the hot breath against his face. "You filthy piece of dog shit! I should drown you right here, right now," Shuizi's father growled.

Old Crab pawed wildly but ineffectually at his assailant. As he struggled, the fingers tightened around his throat like a steel trap. A final plea for mercy issued forth as a pathetic, barely perceptible squeak

"If you ever touch my boy again, I swear, Old Crab, I'll kill you. Just as sure as the sun rises in the east, I'll find you and I'll kill you. Do you understand?"

Old Crab nodded frantically. Shuizi's father flung him to the ground. Old Crab was paralyzed by fear as the other stood over him. He didn't move or speak. And then, as quietly as he'd appeared, Shuizi's father disappeared in the blackness.

42

During the next weeks Shuizi's father nursed him back to health. Jinlan was beaten by her father and warned not to see Shuizi again. Soon she was back at work in the fields.

I saw Jinlan one afternoon leading a water buffalo through a nearby rice paddy. I ran to join her and we both crawled onto the back of the animal. I sat behind her, my arms locked around her waist. Each of us was reluctant to say anything at first. After an uncomfortable silence, I told her, "I heard what happened, Jinlan. And I'm sorry. Shuizi is a good man."

She touched my clasped hands and said, "I know, Yimao."

We stopped beside a river and let the buffalo graze. We sat on the grass and put our feet in the water. I remembered sitting near the same place with Chunying a few years earlier and watching her make her wedding shoes.

"What do you think will happen?" I asked Jinlan.

"My father convinced Old Crab that Shuizi raped me. He insisted it was not my fault."

"You mean they believe it was Shuizi's fault?" I asked.

"Not Shuizi alone," she said. "Old Crab and my father concluded that what happened was caused by a fox spirit."

A fox spirit, according to local legend, was a crafty ghost that roamed the countryside in search of an unwary victim. When it found one, it possessed her and tempted her into sexual misbehavior. This superstition was contrary to the socialist thought of the Communist Party and Chairman Mao. Yet it was only one of many that continued to be a persuasive and powerful force in the countryside. The Communist Party's effort to destroy or discredit such provincial irrationalities had failed miserably.

"What are they going to do about it?" I asked.

"You don't believe this, do you, Yimao? Your parents are teachers. Surely you know better."

"Of course I don't believe it," I said. "But what is Old Crab going to do?"

"Old Crab took two bottles of good wine from my father and used them to induce Medium Zhang from Zhang Village to come here for an exorcism. He's going to chase the fox spirit out of me. And then they're going to marry me to Young Crab."

"Will you marry him?"

"Marry Young Crab? I'd rather die," she said.

She confided that she had visited Shuizi in his home late at night. She'd spoken to his father. "He said he'd help us. He said he'd take care of everything."

"Will he do that?"

"I don't know. But I hope so. You know the story of Shuizi's mother, don't you?"

"I've never seen her."

"She died giving birth to Shuizi," she said. "Shuizi's father never remarried. They say he still nurses a broken heart. He knows how Shuizi and I feel."

"I really hope you can marry Shuizi," I blurted out.

She took my hand and said, "So do I." And then we cried.

Several days later Old Crab went from shed to shed and explained that he had summoned a medium to Gao Village. He told us that we must close our doors and windows to keep the freed fox spirit from possessing us. Finding no new victim in our village, the fox spirit would flee to another.

The next day Medium Zhang arrived. Old Crab ran up and down the paths between the sheds, pounding on his cymbal, crying, "Stay in your shed. Close the window. Close the door. Don't come out until I tell you."

A few handpicked men were allowed to assist the exorcist. They had to be at least forty years old. The day was overcast and warm. Not long after Old Crab instructed everyone to stay inside, it started to rain.

Our hut was near the warehouse where it was believed the fox ghost first found Jinlan. The exorcism was to take place there. My parents followed orders and closed the door and windows. I went to my room and opened the window a slit and peeked out. I'd never seen anything like this before—catching a fox spirit.

I watched the rain and saw rivulets in the paths through the village turning into little streams. Finally I saw movement through the curtain of rain. Several forms materialized. They were eight men from the village—ghost catcher assistants—carrying a pallet over their heads. As they passed our shed, I saw that Jinlan was tied to the pallet. She stared straight up into the rain without blinking. She was like someone in a trance. Long acupuncture needles protruded from her forehead, breasts and thighs.

The exorcist was the last man in the procession. He held a pole that was nearly nine feet long. A bundle of rooster feathers dangled loosely from a leather thong affixed to the end of it. He slapped the feathers back and forth through the rain like a fan. In his other hand he carried a bundle of joss sticks. The rain had quenched most of them, but a few still sent trails of incense into the air. He repeatedly chanted a cryptic incantation. His voice rose to a near shriek and plummeted to a deep hoarse bass. The men somberly repeated the chants. Old Crab guided the procession through the heavy downpour.

"What are they going to do with Jinlan?" I asked myself. "And why did they take off her clothing?"

I sneaked out of the house and followed the procession at a safe distance, careful to stay out of sight. When the men entered the warehouse, I ran to the far side. I knew from living in the building that there was a slit between the wall and the roof on that side. I could see in if I stood on my tiptoes.

I peered inside. The men put down the pallet in the center of the room. Two kerosene lanterns had been lit. The village men stared at Jinlan's naked body as they stood around her. The exorcist circled the pallet and continued his chants. Old Crab stood in a corner of the room, his eyes glued to Jinlan, his face flushed. After several minutes the exorcist stood very still and closed his eyes as if listening for distant voices. No one made a sound. I could see Jinlan's bare breasts rise and fall slowly. Her unseeing eyes remained open. The only sounds were the steady drip and hiss of rain and the rapid pounding of my heart.

The exorcist opened his eyes and blinked. He announced it was time for the others to leave. The moment had come to expel the fox spirit. No one else should remain in the building because the spirit might take refuge in them.

The men were ushered out by Old Crab, who closed the door behind him. I heard the men splashing down the path on the opposite side of the building.

The exorcist waited several minutes without moving. At last he turned and opened the door a crack and peeked out to make sure the men had followed his instructions. Assured that they had, he closed the door tightly and locked it with a crossbar. He turned to Jinlan's supine figure. He lay down his feathered pole and the joss sticks and stood over her. Slowly he reached down with both hands and covered her small breasts. He caressed and pinched them, whispering something to her. She did not respond. He untied her quickly.

Then he did a little dance around her and sang a few phrases and touched parts of her body. Still she didn't move. He grasped her ankles and pulled her legs apart. He stepped back and untied his long black robe. He pulled off his trousers and underwear. He climbed onto the pallet and lay atop Jinlan. I covered my mouth to muffle a cry and hoped he wouldn't hurt her.

The exorcist made a strange sound, as if in pain. It was not another incantation but a long sighing "oh." His naked hips pressed down on Jinlan. His bright red face hung in the air above hers, a long thread of saliva dripping from his mouth onto Jinlan's frozen features.

The exorcist shuddered several times as if being tickled, made one long gasp and collapsed against Jinlan. He pushed himself off her body and stood beside the pallet. He pulled up his trousers and put on his robe. He withdrew a cloth from his bag and wiped off Jinlan's thighs, which had become wet during the exorcism.

There was a faint knock on the door. "Are you finished yet?" came a furtive whisper. I recognized the voice of Old Crab.

The exorcist unbarred the door and let him in.

"Well?" Old Crab said as he looked at Jinlan and then at the exorcist.

The exorcist smiled and winked at him. "Young Crab is a lucky boy," he said. "Just look at her," and he turned to Jinlan. "Long legs. Round belly. Soft breasts. Nothing at all like the sows customarily produced in Gao Village." He ran his hands over her.

The look on Old Crab's face said that he agreed.

"Do you have a cigarette?" the exorcist asked.

Old Crab pulled a pack from his pocket and handed one to the man. He gave him a box of matches and said, "You've had your fun. Now it's my turn. Go outside and watch the door. I'll let you in after you finish smoking."

"When I am finished?" the exorcist asked and chuckled. "I'll be back in one minute. That's more than enough time for you."

"Don't rush me," Old Crab said. "I'm the team leader!" Before he could continue, the exorcist burst out laughing and exclaimed, "Okay! Okay!" He let himself out and stood under the overhang of the roof and smoked. Old Crab shut the door and turned to Jinlan.

I feared the exorcist might walk around the building, so I scrambled back home. I went to my room and waited. Two or three minutes later I heard Old Crab banging his gong. "The fox spirit is gone," he shouted. "You can come outside."

———

During the next weeks preparations were finalized for the wedding of Jinlan and Young Crab. The ceremony was scheduled to take place during the Moon Festival. Jinlan resumed her duties, leading the water buffalo out to graze. I accompanied her several times but never told her what I'd seen. She never mentioned it, either. I wondered if she'd been given a potion in addition to the acupuncture, perhaps, to render her unconscious and incapable of remembering what had been done to her.

When we talked, Jinlan was wistful. She never spoke of her approaching wedding. She talked constantly of Shuizi.

"Jinlan," I asked, "how are you going to avoid marrying Young Crab?"

"Will you keep a secret?" she asked, and her eyes sparkled.

"Yes," I said. "You are my best friend, Jinlan."

"I'm going to have Shuizi's baby. We're going to run away."

"Where will you go?" I asked.

"Shuizi's father has a comrade in Shenyang. He saved the man's life when they fought the Americans in Korea. He carried the man to safety when he was wounded. They stay in touch. We're going to live with him. I'll have our baby there. Shuizi's father has made the arrangements."

"I'll miss you, Jinlan," I said. I put my arms around her neck and began to cry. "Will you ever come back?"

"Not until Old Crab is dead," she said through her own tears.

"But Old Crab is never going to die," I bawled. "You'll never come back."

"I will," she said. "And when I do, I'll bring my baby and let you hold him."

"If you have a girl, Jinlan," I said, "promise me you'll keep her. Promise me you won't throw her away."

"I promise," she whispered. "Don't worry."

Two days before Jinlan was to marry Young Crab, Jinlan and Shuizi disappeared. Old Crab and Young Crab were furious. They organized search parties during the next weeks and combed the surrounding countryside and visited nearby villages.

Jinlan's parents were inconsolable. They could not understand how their daughter could do such a disrespectful and faceless thing to her parents. They suggested that the exorcist had failed to cast out the fox spirit and that Old Crab had lied to them. Old Crab resented their suggestions and demanded that they return the engagement money. He should have known that their daughter was a little whore, he said. The very idea that his son would marry such a girl was absurd.

———————

Later that year Old Crab announced that his son would marry the daughter of a team leader from a nearby village. The wedding was to take place after the Spring Festival. In the meantime, there was more exciting news for Gao Village. We were told our sheds would soon have electricity. Ever since we'd lived in the village there had been only a single electric line that was used exclusively for the loudspeakers. We used kerosene lanterns and candles to illuminate our homes. The commune requested that each village send one individual to the headquarters for training in electrical installation. Old Crab sent his son to the class. After one day in class, Young Crab was given the title of electrician and put in charge of bringing electrical lines into Gao Village.

A high-voltage line ran from the commune to the village. Young

Crab went from hut to hut, installing wires for lighting. Old Crab, of course, was the first to have his home wired, even though his was not the hut closest to the power source. Old Crab supervised the work of his son and helped out when asked. One afternoon they went to the shed of Shuizi's father, the last shed in the village to be wired. The men punched a hole in the mud wall and pulled the wire through and fastened the end of it to an overhead beam. Old Crab asked Shuizi's father to stand on a bench and strip the wires while he went to his hut to retrieve an outlet for a bulb. Shuizi's father stood on the bench and began stripping the wires. Several times he accidentally cut the wire along with the insulation. Young Crab watched and finally said, "Let me do it."

Meanwhile, instead of returning home, Old Crab ran to the edge of the village, where the main power switch had been placed. He looked around to make sure no one was watching. Then he flipped the switch to turn the power on, left it on for several seconds and turned it off. After that he went home and retrieved the outlet and returned to Shuizi's father's shed. On the way, he ran into Shuizi's father. "What took you so long?" Shuizi's father asked.

"I couldn't find it," Old Crab lied. "Are you all right?"

"What could possibly be wrong with me?" Shuizi's father asked.

When they reentered the shed, they found Young Crab lying on the floor. Shuizi's father turned him over. His eyes were open. He had a look of surprise on his face. His hands were black. And he wasn't breathing. Shuizi's father felt for a pulse and said, "He's dead. How can this be?"

Old Crab fell to his knees beside his son and blurted out, "My son! My son! I killed you!"

"What do you mean you killed him?" Shuizi's father asked.

Old Crab covered his face with his hands. He moaned. "Why *my* son?"

Other villagers heard the cries and came into the shed. They asked what had happened but Shuizi's father could not explain it. "One minute he was installing the wires, and the next minute he was dead on the floor." People shook their heads. It was a mystery. No one could explain the blackened hands. Maybe the fox spirit had returned, some of them whispered. Maybe the fox spirit had taken revenge.

The next day the villagers buried Young Crab. Representatives from the Communist Party came from the brigade and commune headquarters and praised the young man and his father. Old Crab was inconsolable.

With the electricity routed to our home, we were finally able to listen to our radio. It was a novelty in the village. People crowded into our shed and sat with us listening to it. It was a Three Goats (San Yang) brand and had five large tubes in it. It was our treasure. None of the villagers could understand how a little box could make so much noise. They'd never heard anything like it.

At night Papa tuned it to the Voice of America to hear the news in English from outside China. He helped my older brother and me with our English by letting us listen to it with him. Though Papa was sometimes short on patience, the radio was an endlessly patient teacher.

Our English improved. But the English teacher did not stay long in my school. As soon as Party policies changed, she returned to Nanjing. One day she packed all of her belongings and walked to the road and disappeared, heading in the direction of the bus stop. We learned that she later became a factory worker. It seemed to me that everyone from outside the village, from the day they arrived, sought a way to get out and go back to the city. Learning from the peasants was like living in a prison.

43

My older brother and I cultivated a garden in a bare patch of land at the outskirts of the village. It was considered barren soil, and no one else wanted it. Old Crab assigned it to us. We tilled the soil and enriched it with buckets of muck from our own sewer pool. My brother became an expert at spreading water and sewage over the little plot. After school each day we tended it, and before long we had the most productive garden in the village.

An uncle, my mother's fourth brother, was an agronomist. He mailed us seeds of very sturdy vegetables from Tianjin. Our crops were huge compared to those of others. We grew turnips that were five pounds each. Yet before long the largest turnips and bok choy began disappearing each night. Only when we cultivated crops around our home would the villagers not steal them. Those were growing on graves, and village superstitions and ghosts kept our crops secure. It was all so strange. The peasants were supposed to be the ones who understood agriculture. They had lived on this soil for hundreds of years. But within a few months we were growing larger crops because we had better seeds and we knew how to care for the crops scientifically. They watched us and learned from us. The reverse of what was supposed to happen, happened.

I was required to work in the fields every weekend as I grew older. One day I was spreading manure in the rice field with another girl when I became very tired. I felt faint and said I needed to go home. My friend said she was tired, too. At the same time our families needed the work points. When no one was looking, we threw manure in each other's hair, then announced we had to go home because of the accident, and wash our hair. So we got the time off and the work points and headed home. I was fifteen and growing increasingly impatient with village life. I skipped work many times, and I was getting bored with school. Papa felt it might be a good idea for me to get out of the village for a short time. His uncle lived in Nanjing, the nearest large city. He was old and lived alone. Papa had learned by mail that he was not well. "You can visit him, stay with him and see the big city," Papa said. I was excited by the prospect.

I took a bus to Nanjing. It was merely a truck with a canvas top. I crawled in the back where nearly fifty people were crammed inside, some sitting and some standing. I stood and hung on to a rack overhead. Four hours later the bus stopped on the outskirts of Nanjing, where I transferred to a city bus. I found the old man in a dingy and dark apartment. It was a single room with a bed, a chair and a table. He was in bed.

"Grand-uncle, I'm Wu Yimao," I said. "I am Wu Ningkun's daughter. He learned that you were sick, and he sent me here to visit you."

"Come in, child," he said in a weak, wavering voice and motioned for me to approach him. I handed him a letter of introduction from my father. He read it and beamed.

"I have six children," he said. "And no one has come to see me in a long time. I am afraid I will die soon. I feel it in my bones. And now you are here. I am happy to see you."

He told me the wife of a friend in Nanjing came once a week to bring him food and to clean. He could no longer walk alone outside the apartment. He gave me a little money he kept hidden under his bed. He told me where a nearby market was and said I could buy us some fresh vegetables. He had a single electric burner and some pots. I got water from an outside faucet and prepared a vegetable soup for him.

All the while I was cooking, he talked. I slept on the floor beside his bed that night. In the morning I gathered up his dirty clothing and his bedding and washed them. I helped him sit on a stool near me so he could talk while I did the laundry. Then I hung everything on a line to dry in the sun. After dinner he held my arm and I took him for a walk around the block. He had not been outside in months, he said. He loved the smell of the fresh air. I told him I could stay for only two days before returning home. He asked about my father, and I told him about our life in the countryside.

He showed concern. The next morning he wrote on an envelope a name and an address in Beijing. He folded a note and put it in the envelope. "This is a letter to my daughter," he said. "She is married to an influential man. Li Zhisui, her husband, is the private physician of Mao Zedong." He paused for the words to register. "Maybe she can help your family."

I cooked another meal for him, folded his clean clothes and made his bed, and bade him goodbye. There were tears in his eyes when I left. "I will never forget you," he said. "You are a good-hearted girl."

Mama had been trying for years to find a way for us to get out of the countryside. She and Papa discussed petitioning Anhui University to accept him back as a teacher. Mama was employed by the county and could not appeal to another work unit, but Papa had no unit, no organization to which he officially belonged. Only Mama could travel, however, to the places where she felt she might influence someone to transfer us from the countryside to the city again. Papa wrote up a long petition making his case. It said he wished to be rehabilitated politically and get his job and salary back in Hefei. Mama went to Hefei several times, carrying his petition. The travel expenses strained our budget.

Yet my parents thought it was worth the sacrifice. "We must grab every opportunity to get out of here," Papa told us.

When I arrived home I described my stay in Nanjing to my parents and gave Papa the letter. He read it. He was delighted. "This might be a ticket out," he said. It was decided that Mama would go to Beijing to appeal directly to Li Zhisui for help.

She visited him in the middle of a blistering Beijing summer day. She saved her bus fare and walked four miles to Li Zhisui's house from the residence of a cousin where she was staying. When she arrived she was exhausted and thirsty. She knocked on the door, and the wife of the physician—my father's first cousin—answered. Mother had seen her on several occasions in Beijing and recognized her right away. Their eyes met but the woman showed no sign of recognition.

Mama smiled and said, "I am Wu Ningkun's wife. It's been a long time since I last saw you."

The woman responded gruffly, "And who is this Wu Ningkun?"

"He is your cousin. We've met," Mama said. "Don't you remember him? Don't you remember me?"

The woman stared at her coldly. "I've never seen you before in my life. And I have no idea who Wu Ningkun is. You'd better go away."

"But you grew up in the same house. You played together in the same courtyard. You must remember."

"You are wrong. I don't know what you are talking about," the woman said.

"But . . . your father is my husband's uncle."

The woman's stare was icy and anxious, even frightened.

"My daughter cared for your father in Nanjing. She was there last month. He gave her your address. That's how I found you. I have a letter from him for you."

More silence.

Li Zhisui, Mao's private physician, appeared in the hallway behind his wife. My mother recognized him. "Dr. Li," mother said, looking over the shoulder of his wife. "I am here to ask for your help."

The physician said nothing. He stared at her with a combination of curiosity and alarm. Then he disappeared.

Mama held out the letter but the woman pushed it away. "You should go," she said, "before I summon security."

Mama's spirits sank as she stood at the door. She fought back tears. "May I have a drink of water?" she said. "I've come a long way to find you. It's hot and I'm thirsty."

"I think it would be better if you just left," the woman said.

Mama gave her a last look of desperation before she turned and walked away.

44

Mama did not give up. She came home from Beijing empty-handed but she went back and forth to Hefei many more times, seeking help. She visited government officials and university administrators, making a case for my father's restoration in the university. The Anhui University officials expressed displeasure at her appeals and refused to invite him back. But then, almost miraculously, with the assistance of a few sympathetic figures in the provincial government who remembered and admired Papa, she learned of a vacant teaching position in Anhui Teachers University in the city of Wuhu. At the end of 1973 Papa was informed he'd been awarded the vacant position.

My parents worked swiftly completing the required paperwork for our move. Every document had to be signed and sealed by the entire county bureaucracy. Everything was finally completed three days before the Spring Festival began in February.

We started packing. We used a small trunk Papa brought from the United States to carry some of our clothes. It was old and worn but still serviceable. A faded Beijing address was painted neatly across the top of the trunk. One of Papa's friends at the University of Chicago, Lee Tsung-Dao, had written it on the trunk in July 1951. We stuffed the rest of our belongings in other trunks and bamboo baskets. I had mixed emotions about leaving. I'd had a few good experiences in Gao Village, along with my many sad and tragic memories.

In my spare time during the fifteen days of Spring Festival, I visited the families of the friends I'd made. I took several pieces of candy to the shed of Little Rabbit's family and gave them to her brother, who was over five years old. Nobody mentioned Little Rabbit. I thought about visiting Chunying in Bao Village one more time. But I decided against it. I wasn't sure I'd be welcome. Instead I visited her parents. I asked about Chunying. Her mother smiled from ear to ear and announced, "She had a boy!"

"Please tell her I didn't have time to visit her before I left. But say I heard about her good fortune. Tell her how happy I am for her."

Her mother nodded. "I'll tell her."

On the third day of the Spring Festival, I visited Jinlan's parents. I wished them good fortune during the New Year. Jinlan's name was not spoken. And I didn't ask about her.

Finally I walked to the shed of Shuizi's father. He was alone, preparing tea for himself. I entered his shed and wished him a happy New Year.

"And the same to you," he said. "Can you have a cup of tea with me?"

"Of course," I said, surprised to be treated like an adult.

I seated myself on a bench and he handed me a steaming cup of tea. We said nothing at first but merely smiled and sipped tea. At last I asked, diffidently, "How are Jinlan and Shuizi?"

He gave me a look of surprise. "Why do you ask me such a question?"

"Because Jinlan is my best friend. I spoke with her before she ran away with Shuizi. I know what they did."

He looked into his teacup, unsure how to respond. He was silent for several seconds.

"You did a brave thing," I said. "I admire you."

He smiled but still said nothing.

"Tell me," I said, "did Jinlan have a boy or a girl?"

"You know a lot, don't you?" he said.

"Yes, I do."

"She had a boy," he answered. "And she had a girl."

It took a moment for me to grasp what he said. "Twins?" I asked.

"Yes," he said. He rose and went to his bed, reached into the pillowcase and pulled out an envelope. He extracted a small photograph and handed it to me. In it, Jinlan sat beside Shuizi. Each of them held a baby. All four of them were bundled up in padded winter clothing. Jinlan and Shuizi were smiling.

My eyes teared when I saw her. "This is the second time I've ever known of anyone having twins," I said. "It's wonderful. You must be very proud, Grandpa."

He laughed. "I am."

As I stood to leave he reminded me, "This is a secret, Yimao. No one in this village must know."

"I can keep a secret," I told him.

Old Crab called on us during our last day in Gao Village. He'd been drinking heavily.

"So, you are going to be city people," he said. "You think you're flying out of my hand and going straight to heaven."

"We're going to miss you," Mama managed.

"Shit!" he said and spat on our floor. "You're glad to be leaving." When no one corrected his assertion, he added, "Well, you have to give me a going-away dinner tonight. And we have to have one last drink."

Knowing he was still capable of causing problems for us, Mama agreed and asked him to return later.

Early that evening he was back, wearing a clean shirt for the occasion. "I'm thirsty" was the first thing he said upon entering our shed.

Papa opened his last bottle of liquor and filled a cup for Old Crab, who emptied it in one swallow and thrust it out again.

As he poured a second cup for the team leader, Papa asked, "May we bring one of the doors with us?"

"What for?" Old Crab grumbled.

"Lumber is precious in the city," Papa said. "And we can use it as a bed in our apartment. If you remember, you borrowed our other bed after we arrived here."

"I need all the doors," Old Crab said. And that settled it.

After dinner Mama and my brothers and I continued packing, but Father was required to sit at the table drinking with Old Crab and listening to him complain about work points and lazy peasants. Around midnight Old Crab was too drunk to talk. The cigarettes and liquor were gone. He stood, staggered back a few steps, steadied himself and said, "I've got to be going now. Lots of work tomorrow." But before he departed he circled the room looking at what we were packing. He pulled back the cover on a basket and spotted my copy of *David Copperfield*. "I need this for toilet paper," he snarled.

He tucked the book under his arm and stumbled through the door. Seconds later I heard voices outside. The voices of two men. Angry voices. There was an exchange, a shout, and then it was quiet. One of the voices was Old Crab's. And I thought the other was Shuizi's father.

"Did you hear that?" I asked Mama.

"What?" she said.

We listened but there was no sound. "You're tired, Maomao," she said. "We have a long day ahead of us. Go to bed."

The next morning—moving day—I rose early and went to our latrine. The flies were making an unusually loud hum. As I drew near the brick steps, I saw something white at the edge of the muck. I made out what appeared to be two bare feet protruding from the dark pool. I rushed back to our shed and told my parents what I'd seen. Mama ran to summon some of our neighbors. The word spread quickly of my ghastly discovery. Villagers came running. Some gasped and backed away. One of the women let out a long scream and dropped to her knees. Jigui came hobbling on his crutches.

Two men grabbed the ankles and pulled the body out. It was horribly discolored, but by the clothing and the shape of the head, we could tell it was Old Crab. His body was stiff and black. Thousands of flies descended on the corpse as it lay beside the sewage pool. Old Crab's wife fell to her knees beside his body and howled. Jigui dropped his crutches and got down beside the body and slowly waved his Little Red Book above his head, crying, "Here! Here! My papa will help you! My papa is the people's savior! My papa will make you well!"

The villagers stared at Jigui silently, almost as if they believed what he said—that the Little Red Book could restore life. Mama helped Jigui stand and led him aside and whispered something to him. Because of her kindness toward him he always listened to her. He nodded as she spoke and then went home chanting, "Old Crab will be well. Chairman Mao is his savior."

I noted my copy of *David Copperfield*—still clean—not far from Old Crab's body. I picked it up and concealed it from the others. As I pushed away from the crowd, I saw Shuizi's father approaching. While everyone else was in shock, he was composed and unbothered.

"Old Crab drowned in our shit hole!" I blurted out.

I cannot be certain of what I saw next, because a ray of morning sunlight flashed over his shoulder and momentarily blinded me. But I am almost sure he winked. Two men came to our hut a short time later and removed the doors to make a casket for Old Crab. Several hours later a truck arrived to take us to Wuhu. Some of the villagers helped carry our belongings to the main road and assisted us in loading them. I climbed into the back of the truck with my brothers and looked at the village that had been my home for five years. I wanted to burn it into my memory for all time. The same strange sense of wonder went through me as when I'd arrived here from the outside world. Was it all real? Or had it been just a long nightmare? Could I be awakening at last? I saw several men crawling over the roof of our shed, throwing down bundles of straw and lumber for their own use. "Look what they're doing," I said to Mama and pointed.

"Everything will be gone in an hour," she answered.

As the truck pulled away, the villagers stood beside the road and watched us. Some waved. We waved back as they disappeared in the dust.

An hour later we arrived at the ferry dock. Our truck was the last one onto the ferry late that afternoon. As we crossed the Yangtze River, my brothers and I stood at the boat railing and looked at the other shore. The sun was setting behind us. The water shone like gold. None of us said a word. None of us looked back.

45

On the other side of the river, my brothers and I climbed up into the back of the truck and sat among the bundled family possessions while our parents rode in the cab with the driver. It was only a few minutes' drive to the university campus. I was astonished by the traffic on the wide streets and the clamorous confusion of sounds: the rumble of passing trucks and cars along with the constant ringing of thousands of bicycle bells. Cyclists streamed around us when we slowed, like a river rushing around a rock, and moments later we roared past them on straight stretches of the street.

Crowds swirled along the sidewalks and scooted back and forth in the street behind us. Amber lamps illuminated the night, and pinpricks of light glowed in the windows of the squat apartment buildings along the streets. There was noise and activity but nothing ominous, nothing at all like the mass night marches of the Red Guards that I remembered from Hefei. Here no one appeared to pay any attention to us as we passed. People went about their business, seemingly fearlessly, not organized, not marching, not chanting or carrying signs. Children clung to their parents or ran beside them. I'd forgotten how luminous and harmless and alive the night might be. I was thrilled by the promise of our new life.

Our driver found his way to the campus and pulled up beside a dozen other trucks at the motor pool. He jumped out, stretched, rubbed his eyes and told us, "It's been a long day. I'll see you in the morning."

"Where are we supposed to sleep tonight?" Mama asked.

"I'd recommend somewhere close to the truck," he said over his shoulder as he walked away. "If you don't, your stuff won't be here in the morning."

Papa looked at Mama, shrugged, and asked, "What now?"

"First," she said, "these children are hungry. We need to get something to eat." It was decided that Papa would stay with the truck and Mama would take us to find a street vendor.

My brothers and I walked along the sidewalk with Mama. We passed through the university gate and followed the noise and the lights to a nearby bustling street. I was barefoot. It felt strange to be walking on the smooth concrete and tar rather than on dirt paths. I noticed that everyone else on the street, even the children, wore shoes.

Pedestrians stared as we passed, some even stepping aside as if they feared we carried some contagion. A girl about my age stood at a bus stop with her mother and gawked at me. When we were beside them, she looked up at her mother and said, "Look at the country bumpkins, Mama!" Her mother glanced over at me, looked at my bare feet and frowned.

We soon found a street vendor selling steamed buns. I stood close to his stand and breathed in the yeasty scent as Mama bought several. She gave us each one and saved the others for later. We returned to our truck. When we were finished eating we unrolled some of our blankets, and Mama had us squeeze together in the cab to sleep. She and Papa made a bed for themselves on the ground next to the truck.

We awakened at daylight to the buzz of traffic beyond the nearby university gate. Mama stayed with the truck, and Papa took my brothers and me in search of a student dormitory with a latrine and running water. We found one nearby. After we returned to the truck to safeguard our goods, Mama took her turn.

Shortly after eight, I accompanied Papa to the university housing office. He identified himself to an official-looking little man behind the reception desk, showed his transfer papers and requested living quarters. The man examined the papers a moment and looked at Papa and me with undisguised displeasure. He asked Papa a couple of questions and then took the documents to a woman at a desk in the back of the office. In a low voice he told the woman what Papa wanted and went over the papers line by line with her.

Even though they were on the other side of the room and spoke softly, I could decipher some of their words. "Rightist," I heard the man say. "And American spy," the woman added. I looked up at Papa and he smiled down at me as if he'd heard nothing unusual. The woman called someone on the telephone and described Papa's papers. After about ten minutes the man returned to the reception desk, unsmiling and unfriendly, and dropped Papa's papers on the counter without saying a word. He returned to his desk. The woman wrote down an address on a small piece of paper and brought it to us. Papa read it and thanked her. Even as he spoke she turned up her nose and went back to her desk.

Nonetheless, I was excited by the prospect of moving into our own quarters on campus. Papa and I wandered around looking for the address written on the paper. He was confused by street names and numbers. But I was so enthusiastic and giddy that I sidled up to strangers on the sidewalk and asked them for assistance in locating our new home. Most of them seemed puzzled. They wanted to help but knew of no such address.

When we finally arrived at the designated address, we discovered a temporary shed that had been put up for construction workers on the campus. The walls were reed mats supported by long pieces of bamboo. The low roof was a pile of straw. The whole flimsy edifice rested against a section of the university wall. The door consisted of a dozen lengths of bamboo lashed together with a straw rope.

We stared at it in shock. "I think they wrote down the wrong address," Papa muttered. Yet tacked to the door was a sign someone had scribbled on a large sheet of paper: "FOREIGN LANGUAGES DEPARTMENT, WU NINGKUN."

"There is no mistake, Papa," I said angrily. "But we are not going to live here. This is even worse than Gao Village!" I snatched the note from the door, tore it up and threw the pieces into the air. Papa tried to stop me because it was an official notice and he was afraid I might be causing trouble.

But it was too late. The pieces of paper blew away. I was near tears and could not speak. Papa saw frustration and determination in my eyes and said, "Okay, Maomao, you are right. We can't live here." On the way back to the housing office, he said to me, "That couple is not going to change our assignment. I have to find someone higher up."

We went to the administration building and located the office of the university provost. A man about Papa's age sat behind a desk going through papers. When he saw us, he stood. Papa introduced himself and produced his papers. Without even looking at the papers, the provost smiled and extended his hand.

"I am afraid there has been a mistake," Papa said. "Someone assigned my family to a reed lean-to. I have three children. We can't live there."

The provost looked at the slip of paper, balled it up and threw it in his wastebasket. His lips tightened and he slapped the top of his desk in exasperation. "You're absolutely right," he said. "A mistake was made. I'm sorry. This is ridiculous. I only wonder if the man who assigned you to this place could live there."

"It was a woman," Papa said.

The provost flashed a knowing smile. "I see," he said. He sat down and made several phone calls. His voice was stern and critical as he issued orders and requests. When he was finished he smiled at us and said, "I've found you a place that's livable, Teacher Wu. Welcome to our university."

We hurried back to the truck. The driver had arrived, and Papa gave him our new address. As we pulled up to the address, Mama muttered, "Can this be possible? This is a church!"

It was indeed a church that had been converted into residential living quarters. We had never seen anything like it. My brothers and I climbed down from the truck and walked around the building, staring in disbelief. It was about eighty by twenty feet. It had a steep cathedral ceiling. At the front and back were eight tall and narrow stained-glass windows. Along one side of the structure, the lower portion of windows had been knocked out and replaced by eight doors. Each door led to the living quarters for a family.

We were assigned number 2. Papa pushed open the door and we followed him inside. Rough brick walls about four feet high had been constructed between each of the living units inside. Reed mats were strung up over the walls and suspended from the broad ceiling beams fifteen feet overhead to give privacy to each unit.

"This is unbelievable," Mama murmured as she walked the length of the single room. Her voice echoed throughout the building. "God must be watching over us."

As he stared at the high ceiling and the reed mats, Papa answered, "And He can hear every sound we make."

The light spearing through the mosaics at the peaks of the stained-glass windows was breathtaking. Splashes of blue and red and green covered part of our wall. I held my arm in a ray of light, and my filthy white shirt turned a deep emerald. I touched it and said, "I like it here. I like it a lot."

"Let's bring in our things," Mama said. "We're home."

46

After we'd settled in, Mama cooked some rice and we had dinner together. We spoke in low tones, acutely aware that everything we said could be heard by everyone else in the building. And when no one in our quarters spoke we could pick up on several other conversations around us. It was an odd experience and it took time for us to adjust to it.

My bed was placed beside the brick wall near the rear of our quarters. When I went to bed that night, I lay quietly in the dark, listening to the voices of others in the building as they prepared to sleep. When there were no more voices, I heard something very near me, just on the other side of the wall separating us from our neighbors. It was soft, labored breathing. I listened and thought I heard sniffles. Someone was sitting or lying in the dark only inches away from me on the other side of the wall.

I whispered, "Are you there?"

The sniffling stopped. There was no sound. I sat up and put my ear against the reed mat.

A girl's voice came back: "Yes."

"Are you crying?" I whispered.

"No," she choked. Then she said, "You moved in today, didn't you?"

"Yes."

"I heard you."

"What's your name?" I asked.

"Chen Yuanyu. What's yours?"

"Wu Yimao."

"How old are you?"

"I'm fifteen," I whispered. "How old are you?"

"I'm sixteen," she said.

Another voice from her side of the wall said, "Shut up and go to sleep!"

I lay back down and said nothing more to her that night. The following night we spoke for a few minutes. I told her I'd see her in school and we could talk more then.

On our third day in Wuhu I went to school. I carefully braided my hair, washed my face and put on clean trousers and a flowered blouse. My heart was pounding with excitement. The school, which was called Fuzhong High School, was affiliated with the university. It was about one mile from our new home. Yiding and I brought the official papers Papa had given us authorizing our transfer. The school grounds were alive with hundreds of students running around, carrying books, talking or playing. They were nicely dressed and freshly scrubbed, unlike the students in the countryside. We hurried to the administration office and handed in our papers and received our classroom assignments.

By the time I arrived at my classroom, most of the students were seated at their desks. I immediately noticed the large number of girls. Of about eighty students, at least half were girls. I was delighted and smiled brightly. In the countryside I'd had few girl classmates.

The teacher was writing on the blackboard. I stepped through the door and the students stopped talking and stared at me. The teacher, wondering what had caused the sudden silence, ceased writing and turned to me. She was short—only about five feet tall—slender and middle-aged. She had short hair and wore round plastic-rimmed glasses that made her stern expression seem almost forbidding. I said cheerfully, "Good morning, Teacher." I looked around for an empty seat. I wanted to hurry to sit down and join the other students.

She glared icily at me without responding. As I started to walk to a seat, she stepped in front of me. She glowered and pointed to my feet. "Where are your shoes?" she asked. "Go home and put on shoes before you come into my classroom."

I was puzzled. In the countryside I never wore shoes unless it was snowing or cold. Shoes were for special occasions. I looked around at the other students and noticed that every one of them was wearing shoes. I was deeply shamed. I felt my face burn. I bit my lip to stop myself from breaking into tears. The students continued staring at me. Some tittered. My body tightened. I looked at the floor.

"Go," the teacher ordered. "Now." She extended her hand, palm down, and flicked her fingers at me as if expelling a fly.

I backed out of the room. The teacher shut the door in my face. She said something to the class, and her words were followed by an explosion of laughter from the students. I left the school grounds and wandered around almost in a daze. I didn't know what to do or where to go. I didn't own a pair of shoes, and I didn't have the money to buy a pair. I couldn't ask my parents to buy me shoes. After the expense of moving to Wuhu, we had almost no money. Mama had depleted our savings searching for a position for Papa, and they would receive no pay for several weeks.

I ended up meandering through a street market several blocks from the school. Peasants from nearby villages sold their wares without government approval on this black market. They bargained boisterously with hundreds of city people. I walked around the market, listening and watching. Before long I found myself standing in front of a dingy storefront. A handwritten sign in the window read, BUYING OLD NEWS-PAPERS, OLD BOOKS, OLD RUBBER SHOES, EMPTY TOOTHPASTE TUBES,

AND HAIR. I went in. It was so dark I had to blink several times before I could see clearly. The room was small, only a few feet square. It smelled like charcoal and decaying food and tobacco. My first instinct was to turn and walk away.

Yet I hesitated. Through a haze of blue tobacco smoke, I saw the shopkeeper sitting on a stool at a small round table. He stood and hobbled toward me. He was very old and hunched over. He wore an old-fashioned gray gown and a black skullcap. A long-stemmed pipe protruded from the corner of his mouth. He was a few inches shorter than me, his ancient wrinkled face at the level of my chin. He reached out slowly, as if not to frighten me, and gently touched one of my long braids.

"Are you here to sell your hair?" he asked in a wavering, shrill voice.

I stepped back, just out of his reach. I paused before whispering, "Yes."

My heart was crying no, but my lips said yes. The word seemed to pop out on its own. The old man returned to the table and picked up something and said, "Come here." I stepped into the shaft of sunshine that entered through a small window. I saw him holding a pair of large iron scissors. He grasped one of my braids, lifted it in the air, twisted it, examined it closely, tested the weight and thickness, and said, "Oh, goodness, this is thick and heavy. Very good."

I didn't say anything. I was still thinking about leaving the shop without selling my hair.

"Four yuan," he said. "Two for each braid."

I pulled my braid from his grasp and stuck out my chin and declared, "Five yuan for both."

His brow wrinkled as he considered my offer. "Okay," he said. "Five yuan."

He grasped my left braid and pulled it taut. He held the blades of the scissors at the top of the braid and began slicing. I closed my eyes. The scissors squeaked as they opened and closed. I was hurting inside and I wanted to scream. But I stood still.

"Such good hair," he said, as one braid came free and he threw it toward a bamboo basket. He held the other braid, pulled it straight and cut. As it fell loose I opened my eyes and watched him toss it also. He laid the scissors on the table, opened a little tin box, withdrew a five-yuan note and handed it to me. I folded the bill into a small square and clutched it tightly in my fist. I looked over his shoulder and saw my beautiful braids draped over the edge of his basket. My heart ached. I turned and stumbled out of the shop. I felt almost naked without my braids.

I returned to the market and moved from stand to stand until I found a vendor selling shoes. I spotted a pair of black plastic shoes for four yuan and fifty fen. I thought they might last longer than cloth shoes, and they were cheaper.

"I'd like to buy shoes," I said to the clerk.

She gave me an unfriendly look. "What size?" she snapped.

I had no idea what size. I had not purchased shoes in five years. "I don't know," I said.

She looked at my bare feet. "Thirty-eight!" she said. She pulled a pair from a pile and dropped them on the counter.

I held one against my foot and saw it was far too large. "Not my size," I said. "I need smaller ones."

"Are you buying shoes or not?" she said impatiently. "Do you even have money? You don't look like you have money. Buy these or leave."

I thought for a moment and concluded I could grow into them. Perhaps it was wise to buy shoes too large. I opened my fist and dropped the five-yuan note on the counter.

She gingerly picked up the wadded bill as if it were too dirty for her. She smoothed it and held it to the light to see if it was real. She slapped my change on the counter and turned her back to me. I dropped the shoes on the ground and easily slipped into them. It felt strange walking in shoes for the first time in years.

I returned to school without my braids but with new shoes. Outside the classroom, I used my fingers to comb through my hair and make myself presentable. I took a deep breath and pushed the door open and entered the room. All eyes turned to me. The teacher moved several steps in my direction, recognized me and immediately lowered her gaze to my feet. Proudly, I put out my plastic-shod left foot. At that moment, it seemed to me, the teacher suppressed a smile. She asked for my papers. I handed them to her. Her eyes widened when she saw that one of the documents I carried was my Communist Youth League membership.

She pointed to an empty chair and said, "Sit there." Students leaned out of their seats to look at my feet as I passed. Seeing my new shoes, they smiled and whispered to those who could not see. I sat down between two other girls. Each smiled at me. I smiled back. The recitation resumed. I'd memorized the lines long ago and joined with the others:

> The world is yours, as well as ours, but in the last analysis, it is yours. You young people, full of vigor and vitality, are in the bloom of life, like the sun at eight or nine in the morning. Our hope is placed on you. The world belongs to you. China's future belongs to you.

At lunch recess, the teacher called me aside and told me that a meeting of the CYL was to take place after class. "Since you were already a member at another school, you are in this chapter now." So I stayed after school for the meeting.

There were seven CYL members in my class. They welcomed me to their ranks warmly. In only a few hours, thanks to my plastic shoes and my CYL membership, I'd gone from being an outsider to being an insider. Our group leader was named Zhou Yongzhong, meaning "forever loyal to Chairman Mao." Three girls and four boys made up the group. I was asked what my CYL title had been in the countryside. I said I had no title. "We were all just comrades." But in the city, I was told, each member had a title and a delegated function. There was a group leader, a class monitor, a political commissar, an arts and activities commissar and so on. The group decided I should be the study commissar of my class, which was the least political position. I would keep the job until I was proved red enough. My duties, they said, were to collect student homework and take roll in the morning for the teacher.

That night when I went to bed, I again heard soft cries from the other side of the wall. "Yuanyu?" I whispered.

"Yes."

"I didn't see you in school today."

"And I didn't see you."

"When can we meet? Can you show me the street market?"

"Yes."

"Why do you cry at night, Yuanyu?"

Before she could answer, a voice bellowed, "Shut up!"

From other quarters near the end of the building a man's voice rang out, "Let us sleep! Be quiet!"

Neither of us spoke for several minutes. "See you tomorrow!" I whispered as low as possible. Yuanyu scratched an acknowledgment on the reed mat that separated us.

The next day at school was quite exceptional for me. Everybody was dressed nicely. Though it was clear I was a peasant, with my frayed and ill-fitting shirt and trousers, nobody mentioned it. But they looked at me with curiosity, as though I were some strange creature. They knew I was a country bumpkin and many still shied away from me.

Yet I stood before the class that morning and each morning after that and called the list of names to take attendance. I shouted out each name. There were eighty-two students in the class, and each responded, "Here!" If anyone was absent or late, I marked down the name for my report. Students took notice. Country bumpkin or not, I wielded authority in the classroom and I was a member of the CYL. At the end of the semester I drew up a list of those who had been absent or late. The list was put on the wall for everyone to see. Because of my position the other students warmed to me quickly. Test results were posted on the bulletin board, and when I scored at the top of my class consistently, this focused additional favorable attention on me.

At the end of the first school year the teachers handed out report cards with their comments. They customarily wrote something like "Can Hold High the Banner of Mao Zedong Thought." Or "Studied Hard." But my teacher added one special comment: "A Country Girl Who Learned to Wear Shoes."

47

One of our duties as CYL cadres was to visit the families of students in their homes. We were supposed to communicate with the parents regarding what was happening in school. At the same time we were directed to observe the home environment for any "irregularities" and, if we found them, to report them to higher cadres in the league. At least two of us were required to go on each home visit. My first home visits were uneventful and not memorable. Parents were commonly very formal in greeting us and in listening to our reports on their child's performance in school. Nothing seemed amiss in the homes—no suspicious books or pictures and nothing else to indicate that the parents were anything other than model citizens.

During my fourth weekend of home visits, however, I was shaken by our final call of the day. Accompanied by another girl—Xu Yuqing—I completed half a dozen routine home visits. Late in the afternoon we were supposed to visit the home of a girl named Zhou Jing. Her name meant "crystal." She was among the top students in our class. She never volunteered to answer a question in class, yet when called upon, she inevitably had the correct answer. She was very shy and quiet and had no close friends.

We had difficulty finding where she lived, even though we had the address. We finally found her quarters in a dormitory for Wuhu Textile Factory workers. The workers were housed in large barracks-like buildings. These were long, squat, brick-walled, tile-roofed structures. There were dozens of doors along the side of the building. Each door opened to a family's living quarters. We knocked on the door of Zhou Jing's apartment, and she answered and invited us in. We stepped into the small, poorly lit room. There was barely space for two beds, a stack of trunks in one corner and a coal stove in the other. I noticed right away that the room was neat and clean. The beds were made, the floor was swept and a picture of Chairman Mao was hung high on the wall.

Zhou Jing sat down on one of the beds and asked us to sit on the other. After sitting down I noticed a woman standing in a shadow in the corner. When we were seated, she quietly came forward and sat beside Zhou Jing. I flinched as she approached. Her appearance was utterly horrifying. The entire right side of her face was a purple and blue twisted scar. The eye on that side was bloodshot and watery. The left side of her face was quite beautiful, and the eye on that side was entirely normal. I felt my jaw drop open. I felt light-headed and was tempted to rise and leave.

We sat silently. The woman looked at me and then my partner. She saw the look of shock on our faces. Finally she said in a low, almost toneless voice, "What?"

"I am Wu Yimao," I said. I had to clear my throat before I continued. "And this . . . this is Xu Yuqing. We are cadre from Zhou Jing's class. We are here for a family visit," I said in a tremulous voice.

Zhou Jing said self-consciously, "These are my classmates, Mama."

I was so stunned by the woman's appearance that I simply could not continue. I sat gaping at her face, that unnerving combination of beauty and ugliness.

After a long, awkward silence, Xu Yuqing said, "We would like you to know that Zhou Jing has been excellent in her studies. And she participates in school activities productively."

"It's good to hear this," her mother said. "Thank you for coming.

We have never had visitors before. So excuse me for being nervous. You are cadre. You are important people."

She waited for us to reply. But neither of us said a word. When the woman realized we were tongue-tied, she continued. "Let me tell you, since you are cadre, what life is like for Zhou Jing and me." She looked straight into my eyes, as if telling her story to me alone. "Look at my face," she said. Of course, I could do nothing else. "I was not born like this." She watched for our reaction. We were glued to every word and we wanted desperately to hear her story. But at the same time it was painful to see and to hear. Her left eye blinked. The right eye did not move but maintained a steady gaze.

"When I was your age I didn't go to school. I wanted to. But I could not. I am from a poor family. I was sent to work in the factory when I was twelve. I worked at the textile factory throughout my teenage years. I was good at my job. And I was a pretty girl, as you can tell from the left side of my face. In fact, the textile factory employed many pretty young girls. But I was considered the prettiest of them all.

"At the end of the shift each evening, there were always boys waiting at the gate to flirt with us. I had many handsome boys chasing me." As she said this, there was a glint in her eye, and the hint of a smile crossed half of her face. She had been emotionless, but as she remembered what she once looked like, she came alive.

"I had several marriage proposals. But I always thought I could do better. I turned them all down. I waited for someone special.

"Because I was a good worker I was soon promoted to supervisor. I walked around the shop checking everyone else's work. One day one of the large machines froze. I had been working there so long I knew a lot about weaving machines. And since it took forever for the mechanic to arrive when there was a problem, I decided to fix it myself.

"I began poking around inside the device, trying to see where the problem was. Suddenly it started, like a wild animal that had just awakened. I have only a vague memory of what happened next. All I remember clearly is that one second I was looking inside the machine, and the next I was in the hospital.

"I was told that the machine, inexplicably, kicked into life. It caught one of my long braids and pulled it in and ripped off my entire scalp. Half of the skin on my face went with it.

"I was lucky, they said. Someone else stopped the machine or it would have torn my entire head from my body. Many times since then I have wondered if that might not have been better. Who can tell?"

When she said this, Zhou Jing touched her hand, and she grasped it and squeezed it. Each began sobbing. The woman released her daughter's hand, dabbed at her tears with a handkerchief, composed herself and continued.

"I was in the hospital for seven weeks. They would not let me look in the mirror. My face was wrapped with bandages. I was fed through a tube. I had no idea what to expect. I hoped for the best. I never could have imagined how horribly I had been injured. I could, however, watch the expressions on the faces of the nurses and doctors who attended me when my bandages were changed. They were sickened by what they saw.

"And so the day arrived when the bandages were removed and I was allowed to see myself. A nurse handed me a mirror, and I held it up and looked at myself. Who is that? I wondered. Who is that? I put the mirror down. I must be having a nightmare. I waited for a moment and held it up a second time. I moved my lips to make sure it was me in the mirror. It was. I nearly passed out. I had gone from being the most beautiful girl in the factory to being the ugliest girl in the world. I had become a monster.

"Boys stayed away from me after that. There was no one to talk to me, approach me or of course date me.

"You can never imagine how lonely and empty my life became. My girlfriends—the ones who remained my girlfriends, anyway—worried that I might take my own life. A friend of a friend, however, said she knew this man who worked at Anhui Teachers University. He was an instructor there. He had a bad family background and he could find no wife. He had few friends. My friends said, 'Listen, he is a nice person. He will not mind your looks. He will see what is inside you. He wants to meet you.'

"I bought a wig. I bought a scarf. I did what I could to look, well, human. Human! And I steeled my emotions and agreed to meet him.

"He'd been warned about my looks. He didn't express shock. He was kind. We got along well. He could look into my face—what remained of it—and talk to me, sweetly. I told him the story of my life. He listened sympathetically. When I cried he dried my tears.

"He came back to me. And after we'd seen each other for several months and talked for hours, we decided to marry. He brought me something I thought I'd never have again. He brought me happiness.

"Within weeks of our marriage I became pregnant. But then the Great Leap Forward began, and my husband found himself in political trouble. He was labeled a rightist. They came for him and took him away to prison. One week after he was taken from me, Zhou Jing was born. She never met her father. One year later, in 1959, I was told he'd died in a camp in the Northeast. They didn't tell me how he'd died. They just sent me a piece of paper saying he was dead.

"He was a good man with a bad fortune."

I was mesmerized by her words. In many ways she was describing my father and our family. I wondered if her husband had been in the same camp with my father. The difference was that my father had survived and her husband—Zhou Jing's father—had not.

I began crying, and so did Xu Yuqing. The mother continued her tale dispassionately, in a low, slow monotone. It was as if she were describing the life of someone else. She seemed to have become numb to the terrible sting of her own words.

"Those were famine years. We had no food. We had no relatives to turn to. A friend introduced me to the cook in our factory. He was very red, she said. He was from a working-class background. But more important, he could feed us.

"He stole food every day, smuggled it out after his shift and brought it to us.

"When he proposed marriage to me, I said yes immediately. What choice did I have? Yet no sooner were we married than he began beating Zhou Jing. Whenever he was unhappy about something, he turned on her and beat her. She was just a little girl. I tried to stop him. I pulled him away, but then he beat me, and when he'd finished beating me, he beat her again.

"Zhou Jing inherited her father's intellect. She wants to read all the time. She is very quiet. She rarely speaks to anyone. She lives in her own world.

"She is in love with books. But she needs money to buy her books and clothing. If she asks, her stepfather becomes enraged."

As her mother spoke, Zhou Jing held her head lower and lower and wept quietly. Her tears fell to the floor and her body convulsed.

"In the last year, it became worse," the mother continued. "When he feels like it he squeezes her breasts and touches her between her legs. But there is not a thing I can do about it because nobody believes me. He is a worker with a good background. I am the widow of a rightist. I complained once to the Party secretary of his work unit. The man became enraged. 'No one with his good background would do that,' he growled at me. 'Stop imagining things. If you continue making up rumors about revolutionary workers, I'll have you arrested.' That was his advice.

"You two are in the Communist Youth League. Can you help us? Can you help me? Can you help my child?"

At that she bowed her head and wept.

I didn't know what to say. There was nothing we could do. Zhou Jing just sat across from me, holding her head in her hands, crying.

Zhou Jing's was a cruel fate. But I could not change it. Xu Yuqing and I stood. We thanked Zhou Jing and her mother. They didn't look at us or say a word. They sat together on the bed, desolate and inconsolable. On the way home neither of us could stop crying. We sat on a bench under a lamppost and consoled each other.

In the next few weeks I was extra nice to Zhou Jing in school. I tried to draw her out. I gave her pencils and notebooks. One afternoon I pulled her aside and handed her my treasured copy of *David Copperfield*. "Keep this, Zhou Jing," I said. "It has kept me company when I was lonely. Maybe it will be your friend."

Following graduation, Zhou Jing was sent down to a distant village. I thought of her often after that. But I never saw her again.

48

While I adjusted quickly to the routine of school, life at home inside the church was not without unpleasant surprises and difficulties. The church had been built on a small rise called Fenghuangshan (Phoenix Mountain). It was surrounded by apartment buildings. A single public latrine in the neighborhood was shared by nearly two hundred families. It was a five-minute walk uphill from the church to the latrine. Our only source for fresh water was a single faucet outside the church. The water did not flow on a regular basis. Some days and some hours there was water. Some days there was not. Often there was so little pressure that the water merely dripped from the faucet.

One of our neighbors in the church was a low-ranking cadre who desperately wanted to be promoted. He was fifty years old and extremely thin. He looked like a walking skeleton. His cheeks were sunken, his skin was sallow, his hair was thin and white. For years he'd striven to rise within the Party, but something had held him back. We were cautioned by our neighbors that in order to ingratiate himself to other Party members, he had become a sneak and an informant. From the day we moved in, he took a special interest in my parents.

We often entertained visitors. The cadre was always curious about them. He intercepted them when they arrived or left and struck up an awkward conversation. He asked their names, their occupations and the nature of their business with us. Then he hurried back to his apartment to write a meticulous report for higher Party cadres. He could also listen in on our conversations inside the church. The church was designed for good acoustics and not for privacy. Whenever anyone even expelled gas in one of the units, we all heard it—and giggled. The cadre seemed tireless and was alert twenty-four hours a day. His copious detailed reports went into my parents' files. And those files grew thick with his observations and suspicions.

We learned of his activities because one afternoon, when he was rushing off to a Party meeting carrying a thick sheaf of papers, a page from a report came loose and fluttered to rest a few steps from our front door. I found it when I returned from school. I saw the names of my parents and a list of the hours of the day and a summary of their activities and conversations. I gave it to my father. He read it. He showed it to Mama. They were unsure what to do with it. They did not want to be caught with it because they would doubtless be accused of theft. So they tore it into small pieces and burned it in our stove. Later that day I saw the man lurking outside the church, head down, scanning the ground for something. He looked up at me and scowled. I smiled and went back inside to do my homework.

While the cadre was a disconcerting annoyance, the Chen family who lived next to us was never a threat. The father was employed in the university barbershop. The mother worked at Wuhu Textile Factory. They had three children. The oldest, Yuanyu, was the one I'd heard crying through the reed wall. Night after night, we would whisper to each other through the wall until someone in the building shouted for us to shut up. She attended my school, where she was one grade ahead of me. We became fast friends. She was about my size, a very pretty girl, with small eyes, full lips and fair skin with freckles. We each had two brothers. We got up at the same time every morning. Whoever awakened first tapped on the mat softly to awaken the other. Then we dressed and grabbed a basket for grocery shopping and walked to the market together. The government market was cheaper than the black market, but the quality of the food was bad and it was rationed. Most of the time we went to the government market. There was always a long line. We stood in line together, and while we waited, we talked and combed each other's hair.

The first morning we walked to the market, Yuanyu leaned close to me and whispered, "Do you see him?"

"See who?" I asked, since hundreds of other early shoppers surrounded us in the street.

"Our crazy neighbor. He's following us."

I looked back but noticed nothing out of the ordinary. "I don't see him," I said.

A moment later Yuanyu turned quickly and then said, "He hides sometimes when he thinks you know he's there. Wait for a minute and then look again."

I did as she said and I saw him: a strange figure darting back and forth to conceal himself from us. Our eyes met for a moment before he crouched behind a group of pedestrians. He was a young man, his hair was tousled, his shirt was fastened only by a single button and he had a silly guilty grin on his face.

"I think I saw him," I said. "Who is he? What is he doing?"

"He's a lunatic," she answered. "His family lives in the first apartment at the very front of the church. His father is the snoopy cadre."

"Is he dangerous?" I asked.

"I don't think so," she said. "Just crazy. He follows me every day. Sometimes he walks close behind me and runs away if I turn around. Sometimes he stays at a distance and hides behind trees and buildings."

"Why?"

"I don't know. I told my mother. She told me to ignore him. If I complained to someone else, I'd probably get into trouble because of his cadre father."

By the time we got to the market he was gone.

"He's kind of scary," I said as we stood in line. "How did he get that way?"

"People say he was a student at the university," she said. "His parents spent a lot of money giving favors to the authorities to admit him to school. They finally succeeded. And because he is over six feet tall and not very bright, the university put him in the PE department to play basketball.

"There he met a tall, athletic girl and he fell in love with her. She was a student in the art and music department. People said she was one of the most beautiful girls in the university. I never saw her, so I can't say. But they also said many boys had crushes on her. She got a lot of attention.

"She would not talk to him, but he became more and more obsessed with her. He sent her letters and tried to talk to her, but she ignored him.

"Eventually, he became so desperate that something in him snapped and he went crazy. He stopped going to school and he began walking around talking to himself all the time. He became, well, strange."

"Sometimes when I'm at home I can hear him talking to his parents like a normal person," I said.

"But he's not normal," Yuanyu said. "Believe me, he's not. He's crazy."

After that I discovered him following me several times. Sometimes he'd walk only a few inches behind me. If I looked back at him, he'd either glare defiantly at me or stop and look at the ground sheepishly. Sometimes he seemed to want to threaten me, and other times he seemed threatened by me.

When I told my mother about him, all she did was to caution me to stay away from him because his parents wielded political influence. He had furious temperamental outbursts interrupted by long periods of nearly catatonic silence. He had good and bad days. On good days he sat outside the church, unmoving and expressionless. On bad days he howled and screamed and pounded on the walls.

One morning after shopping I walked to the public latrine. There were two rooms in the facility, one for men and the other for women. On the women's side were two rows of holes in the floor. No dividers separated them. I had lowered my trousers and squatted over one of the holes when he suddenly walked in and squatted over the hole opposite me. He leered at me with a big mischievous idiot's grin. I pulled up my trousers and ran home. As I ran I could hear his footsteps and his breathing close behind me. I hurried into our apartment and slammed the door behind me. I was trembling and out of breath and feared he might burst through the door.

"What's wrong?" Mama asked.

I found a piece of paper and wrote down what had happened. I was afraid if I spoke that the boy's father would overhear me.

Mama read my words and pursed her lips and nodded. She opened the door a crack to see if he was outside. But he was gone. The boy became even crazier after that. One morning he took his family's full night bucket and flung it against our door. We jumped when we heard the loud clatter. Moments later, we smelled the result of his fury. We were afraid to look outside. We heard him scream, "Damned rightists! We know what you're up to! This is only the beginning! The war has just begun."

We stared at one another in dismay and fear as he raved. It reminded me of the Red Guards in Hefei. I was afraid that everything was coming back to destroy us. But we weren't his only targets. He was indiscriminate in his hate. He wandered around at all hours, pestering and accusing people. One evening he walked away and didn't return. His parents looked for him most of the night and in the morning filed a missing person's report. He didn't appear the next day or the next. He never came back. We were relieved by his disappearance. But we dared not express such feelings. On the way to school one morning, about a week after his disappearance, Yuanyu stopped and turned around to look at the people walking far behind us. "I can't believe he's really gone," she said.

We resumed our walk, and she told me how happy she was that the boy was gone. "Me, too," I said. "I wonder what happened to him?"

"Why wonder?" she asked and laughed. "When something good happens, never ask why."

Yuanyu and I did nearly everything together. We walked back and forth to school except when I had CYL meetings. She was not a member of the group. We carried our family laundry to the water faucet and sat on small stools and did the family wash while we chatted. There was a big tree in front of the church where we hung the clothes to dry. We climbed high into the branches when we were finished hanging the clothes and let our feet dangle and watched the world below us. One afternoon while we were sitting in the tree, several policemen appeared and ordered everyone off the street. "Go inside and close your doors, and don't come out again until we tell you to," they shouted.

A man asked, "What's happening? Is something wrong?"

"A foreign dignitary is visiting Wuhu," a policeman answered. "He's come all the way from the United States. We don't want him to be bothered. So just get inside. And stop asking questions."

Yuanyu and I stayed very still and the policemen didn't see us. We remained safe in our perch while everyone else disappeared into their dwellings.

Two policemen stationed themselves near the base of our tree. It became very quiet on the street. We could hear the policemen talking.

"Who is this dignitary?" one asked the other.

"A famous physicist. He's Chinese but he lives in America," the other answered.

"Famous for what?" the first asked.

"He won a Nobel Prize," came the reply. "Didn't you read that in the *People's Daily*?"

"What's his name?" the first asked.

"Yang Chen-Ning," he answered. "But this is hard to believe.

Another Chinese physicist won it with him. Two Chinese! Lee Tsung-Dao is the name of the other one. He also lives in America." When I heard the name Lee Tsung-Dao, my mouth dropped open and my eyes widened. Yuanyu noticed my surprise but remained silent.

A line of police cars appeared with their lights flashing. Behind them was a long black limousine, the biggest car I'd ever seen. The dark curtains in the windows were drawn shut. Behind the limousine were more police cars. They rushed past below us and the two policemen strained to look inside the limousine. Moments after the motorcade had passed the policemen walked away. People soon emerged from their living quarters and the street came alive again.

I scrambled down the tree with Yuanyu. "You won't believe this, but we have a trunk in our place with Lee Tsung-Dao's name written on it," I told her breathlessly. "And he wrote it himself."

"Really!" she exclaimed.

"He was my papa's classmate in America a long time ago," I said. "He helped Papa pack for his trip back to China."

I ran home and found Papa sitting at a table reading. "Papa," I whispered, restraining my excitement. "Didn't you see who's here?"

"Who?" he asked.

"Yang Chen-Ning! And the policemen said that he is the friend of Lee Tsung-Dao."

Papa's face paled.

"Papa, they said he is an important man now. They are both important and famous."

"My dear old friend?" Papa murmured in disbelief. "Here?"

"Yes. I saw the limousine."

Papa's eyes filled with tears. "Here? In Wuhu? Now?"

"Yes," I said. "With policemen guarding him."

Papa smiled a sad smile and held his head in his hands and said nothing more.

49

Nearly every night I heard Yuanyu's father beat and berate her. He blamed her for anything that went wrong in the house; even when her brothers didn't do as well in school as he expected, he blamed Yuanyu. When he was finished, her mother often complained. Yuanyu lay next to the wall and cried, and I could hear her only inches away from me. The sound clawed at my heart. I asked her why her parents behaved that way. She answered very simply, "Because they hate me."

"Why?"

"I wish I knew," she said. "Sometimes I think I'm adopted and that's why they hate me. I think maybe someone gave me to them, maybe during the famine. And now they regret it. Maybe I have a real mother somewhere else. Maybe she misses me. I wish I could find her."

"Why would you say that, Yuanyu?"

"Because everyone else in my family has big eyes and no freckles. Haven't you noticed? I have narrow eyes and freckles. I don't look like anyone else in the family. How can this be, Yimao?"

"I don't know," I told her.

"Maybe that's why they hate me," she said. "There's no other reason. I cook and I shop and I clean and I do the laundry and they hate me."

Like me, Yuanyu received straight A's in school. But this didn't impress her parents. They were concerned only with how her brothers did.

Each night I heard the shouting, the criticism, even the beating and her pleas. Sometimes when we met in the morning I noticed that her eyes were red and her arms and face were bruised. She asked to borrow my long-sleeved shirt to hide her bruises. I felt so sorry for her. But there was nothing I could do. As the school year drew to a close she told me wistfully that she could hardly wait to graduate and get away from her home. "I'll miss you terribly, Yimao," she said.

"I'll miss you, too, Yuanyu," I assured her.

"But there is nobody else I'll miss."

"Promise me," I said, "that after you graduate and go away, promise me that you'll write to me whenever you can."

"I will," she said. "Will you write to me, too?"

"Every week, Yuanyu. I promise."

That summer Yuanyu was sent to work in a Production and Construction Corps in the countryside. It was made up of "educated youths" who were all high school graduates. She wrote a letter to me once each month, telling me what her life was like there. "It's hard work, Yimao," she wrote. "And sometimes I get very tired. But nobody beats me. I'm glad I'm here. I miss you very much." I wrote back to her immediately describing school and my friends and activities. And in every letter I told her that I missed her, too, and wished she lived closer.

After several months the tone of her letters changed. She told me that the boys in the Production and Construction Corps liked her. "They come from all over China," she said. "And there are several of them who like me and talk to me after work and even help me on the job to make my life easier. I am liking it more and more here, Yimao."

Her letters came less often, and in the spring, they stopped. I wrote a half-dozen letters to her after that but there was no response. I stopped writing and waited and hoped for the day she'd come home and we could sit in the tree together again and she could tell me stories about her life in the countryside. I planned to remind her that she'd broken her promise to write to me. But before I made her sad, I'd also tell her I forgave her and that my feelings about her had never changed.

Our educational curriculum was organized around the principle of Mao's "open-door schooling." The Great Helmsman dictated that all students must not merely learn academic subjects in the classroom but also learn from workers, peasants and soldiers. Central to the fulfillment of Mao's decree was our assignment to work four weeks at a time in local factories.

My first assignment was to a large Popsicle factory on the outskirts of the city. Old women and children sold the Popsicles on the street. They carried little wooden boxes and banged on them with a small block of wood, proclaiming, "Milk flavor, bean flavor, banana flavor, three, four and five fen." Popsicles were a special treat, a rare affordable luxury. So when I learned I had been assigned to the Popsicle factory, I was excited. I imagined that when I worked there, I'd be able to eat all the Popsicles I wanted.

The factory supervisor was a middle-aged woman who wore baggy blue overalls and a military-style cap. Twenty of us were assigned to her facility. She ordered the boys to work with Master Worker Sun and the girls with Master Worker Wang. There were eight girls in my group. Master Worker Wang took us to a large room with three long tables placed end to end in the middle. She dragged in a big bamboo basket filled with red beans and spread them out evenly on the entire length of the tables.

"Your job is to pick the rat shit out of the beans so it doesn't get into the Popsicles," she said. "The rats crawl into the beans and eat them. You must be alert because the rat shit is similar in size, shape and color to the beans." She surveyed the beans on the table and picked out a red bean and another particle that looked like the bean and held them up to us. "This is a bean," she said, showing us what she held in her right hand. "And this is rat shit," she said, thrusting out her left hand. She threw the bean back on the table and dropped the rat shit into an old tin can next to her on the floor. "The beans are a bit redder than the shit," she said. "So be careful. If you have doubts, keep in mind that they don't taste the same." After the shock of her words registered on our faces, she broke into a broad toothless grin. "Just use your fingers. That should be enough."

"Master Worker Wang," one of the girls said, "are there gloves for us to wear?"

"Gloves?" she snarled. "Aren't you supposed to rid yourself of your bourgeois thinking? Do you see me wearing gloves?" She held up her bare hands. When there was no response, she left and closed the door behind her.

That was it. We stood quietly at first, looking at one another. We could hardly believe that this was what Chairman Mao wanted us to learn from workers. Separating rat shit from beans with our bare hands? Xu Yuqing broke the silence finally and ordered, "Don't just stand there. Let's get started. We must do what Master Worker Wang tells us to do." She dipped her hand into the pile of beans and withdrew a fistful and began examining them. The rest of us began pawing through the beans, feeling for rat shit. Some of the girls were repelled by the exercise, but we had to do it. And we had to do it bare-handed.

"I know one thing for sure," I said after removing a dozen little balls of rat shit.

"What is that?" Xu Yuqing asked. "What have you learned today, Comrade Wu?"

"I have learned that I am never going to eat any Popsicles, Comrade Xu."

There were giggles around the table. We separated beans from shit for four weeks. Then we attended classes in math and chemistry and

English for a short time. The level of instruction was elementary. In English class, we memorized mispronunciations of the alphabet. We were taught to wave our fists in the air and proclaim, "Lang Li Wu Qi Men Mao," which we were absolutely convinced was "Long live Chairman Mao" in perfect English. After a few weeks of this it was decided we had more to learn from workers. This time we all marched off to a truck factory. I was assigned to work with a welder. She was a friendly woman with a very red round face and an unusually musical voice. She greeted me with a smile. "Welcome," she said. "My name is Master Worker Jiang. You are a high school student, and no doubt you are a big intellectual in this humble factory. What are you doing here wasting your time? You should be studying."

"I am here to learn from you, Master Worker Jiang," I replied timidly. "You are supposed to teach me how to weld."

She burst out laughing. "And what will you do after you learn how to weld?" she asked.

"I don't know," I said.

"What a waste!" she grumbled. "Anyway, as long as you're here, follow me."

She led me to her work area in a corner of a huge room. The odors from the chemicals she was working with were overpowering. My eyes watered and sharp pains shot through my head. Master Worker Jiang, however, seemed oblivious to the smells. She held a metal mask in front of her face and welded a small spot on a piece of iron. "Put this on," she said and handed me the mask. "Hold this with your left hand." She thrust a welder's gun into my hand. Then she had me weld a spot. It looked simple. She gave me a piece of scrap metal to practice on. I tried to do what she had done, but my work was uneven and messy. She laughed and said, "Ah, you're just a kid. You're too weak. You'll hurt yourself. You don't have to do anything. Just sit down over there."

"But aren't I supposed to do something?"

"No, there's nothing you can do here," she said.

The factory was organized on new theories called "the no-government theory" and "the iron rice bowl." As far as I could figure, this meant there were no bosses and nobody worked.

I noticed that beneath her open overalls, Master Worker Jiang was wearing a colorful sweater. Embarrassed by my inability to weld, I changed the subject and said, "That's a beautiful sweater."

She smiled at my remark and her eyes flashed. "I made it myself," she said. "Maybe there is something I can teach you. Bring some needles and yarn tomorrow, and I'll show you how to knit a sweater."

The next morning I brought knitting needles and yarn with me to the factory. Master Worker Jiang sat next to me on a short welding stool and patiently showed me how to create fancy stitches and designs and to put flowers into the material. Day after day we sat together and knitted. She brought her own knitting and made a sweater for her husband. Now and then she paused to do some welding, but only to make a washbasin stand for her home. Since it was a government factory and government materials, she was stealing. I didn't say this, of course. I noticed when we left the factory in the evening that many of the other workers were taking articles home—a small fish tank, a table, a chair. They were slowly looting the factory.

One afternoon I was talking with a student who worked in another department of the factory. I stood next to a table and asked her, "What are you doing here?"

She smiled and held up a book and replied, "Reading. What do you do?"

"I knit," I said. We talked for a time until I wandered back to my department to resume my knitting.

I finished the sweater while we were in the factory, and my classmate was successful in getting a good deal of reading done.

50

One year after we arrived in Wuhu, Yiding graduated from high school and was sent down to the countryside as an "educated youth." There were limited choices each student might make as to where he would be sent. My parents tried to learn something about the living conditions in different areas of the province in order to help Yiding find a good commune. Yiding, for his part, tried to comfort my parents. "I'll be okay," he assured them. "I learned how to work in the fields in Gao Village." But they were worried. They signed him up for a commune in Dangtu County, thirty miles south of Wuhu. When he departed, I was sad for him. I knew that the same fate awaited me in a year. I didn't go to see him off. It was just too painful for me to say goodbye at yet another official departing ceremony.

I completed my final year of high school and on March 23, 1976, I was sent down to the countryside with the other educated youth. I was seventeen. There was no graduation ceremony. The day the academic year ended was like any other day. The political atmosphere at that time was a bit stricter than the previous year. I did not have a choice. All I knew for sure was that I was going to Jingxian County. No other details were provided. I stayed awake the night before I left. I packed a small suitcase with my clothing and a few books. My parents and Yicun came to see me off. It was a beautiful morning. The sky was blue. The sun was shining. The clouds were white. The parting ceremony was like all the others I'd seen. The only difference was that I was the one leaving in the long parade for a glorious future in the countryside.

There was a rally at the city bus terminal. A dozen weathered and rusted buses were lined up waiting for us. Red paper flowers were tied to them. The flowers symbolized honor and celebration because this was supposed to be a great patriotic undertaking. Some parents were already there when we arrived, helping load their children's luggage. A group of students from some middle school halfheartedly pounded gongs and drums. Many parents were crying and holding their children's hands. I tried to put on a good face and not cry and struggled to find something appropriate to say. I told my little brother that since Yiding and I were both gone, it was his responsibility to care for our parents. I reminded him to be a good student and go to market for Mama every day.

At eight o'clock the mayor of Wuhu appeared on a stage. He was a short fat man with thick glasses. He wore a perfectly pressed gray Mao suit and a little matching cap. He spoke with a heavy local accent. He gave a brief speech about what an honor it was to be sent down. "To be able to answer the call of the Great Helmsman," he proclaimed, "is a great thing. You should put down your roots in the countryside and carry out the revolution there for the rest of your lives." When he was finished, there was a burst of singing and the renewed clatter of drums and gongs.

The bus drivers started their engines. The air filled with fumes. As we lined up to board, the sky quickly darkened and a light rain began to fall. People covered their heads. I was surprised at how emotional I became. I broke down and began sobbing as I said goodbye to my family. Mama decided to ride the bus with me because she was worried about where I was going and what might happen. She climbed aboard behind me. But the Party cadre was waiting for us in the aisle. He spotted her right away, trying to conceal herself in the crowd. He shouted, "No parents are allowed. Only the educated youth."

Mama pleaded, "My daughter is not in good health. Please let me accompany her." The cadre shoved her down the steps and out the door.

There were forty of us on the bus. The noise from the singing and drums and gongs outside was deafening. Everyone gathered around the buses, waving, screaming and crying. I looked at my mother and father and brother and waved weakly as we pulled away. Some of the parents in the crowd ran alongside, reaching up to touch their children one last time, banging on the side of the bus, trying to keep up as long as they could. As the bus gained speed, they fell behind. I pressed my face to the window and continued waving and sobbing as my parents and my brother disappeared in the exhaust and the dust.

I slumped in my seat and was jolted from side to side as the bus carried us through the city and out into the countryside. The Party cadre sat stiffly in a seat behind the driver and stared dispassionately out the window. In the countryside the road was rutted and full of potholes and sometimes sloped from side to side. The driver swerved back and forth and slowed and accelerated like the captain of a small junk navigating troubled water. The springs were useless in protecting those inside from the ravages of the road.

Each time we hit a pothole, the entire bus trembled and shuddered and sounded like a can filled with nails. The students clutched the sides of their seats in an effort to steady themselves. My queasy stomach couldn't take it, and before long, I felt my breakfast rise into my throat. I yelled to the cadre that I was going to throw up and staggered into the aisle. The cadre told the driver to open the door but not to slow down or stop. I stumbled to the front of the bus and descended the stairs. I stood on the bottom stair and grasped the side rails and leaned out the door and vomited. Another girl, who was the only other student from my school on the bus, ran to stand behind me and hold me around the waist to prevent me from tumbling out the door. The cadre watched with contempt.

I thought that I'd never return to my family. I'd be a peasant, like the peasants of Gao Village, for the rest of my life. Wuhu was not the escape I once hoped it would be. It was merely a brief interlude between miseries. I knew that the life of a peasant with a black-family background was not worth living again. I wanted to jump out of the bus and fall under the wheels and end everything. I leaned a bit farther out the door and my schoolmate tightened her grip around my waist. "Careful," she warned. "You don't want to hurt yourself." When I turned and looked up at her, I saw tears in her eyes and thought she must be reading my mind.

Three hours later we stopped outside a small town. The cadre announced, "We are stopping here for one hour for lunch." Everyone filed past me and stepped outside. But I could hardly move. Everything hurt. I lay down across the rear seat of the bus to rest. When the other students returned, the cadre stood in the aisle and held up a large envelope. "Listen, everyone!" he shouted. "This is the list of your names and the communes to which you have been assigned. The bus will make drop-offs at each commune along the way. So pay attention. I want no mistakes."

He began reading. This group was dropped off at this commune and that group at that and so on. I didn't hear my name. The others appeared to recognize the name of the places to which they were being sent. Those in the same group grabbed hands in congratulations that they would be together.

When the cadre was finished, I said to my schoolmate, "I didn't hear my name. Would you ask him where I am assigned?"

She moved to the front of the bus and asked the cadre, "Can you tell me where Wu Yimao is assigned?"

The cadre went down the list and seemed puzzled. He thought for a moment and said, "Oh, yes . . . I remember. She is the one nobody wants. She has family problems. She's from a *black* family."

I'd been an active member of the CYL for two years. I'd participated in all activities, earned good grades, and been a class cadre. I'd almost forgotten that the shadow of my family background was forever following me. At his words, I remembered, and the remaining pathetic residue of my youthful hopes and illusions was immediately and thoroughly dissolved. The past sucked me down like quicksand.

"It was decided at the last minute that she would go to Xiyang Commune, Luo Village," the cadre said. "It's deep in the mountains. A good place to bury someone of her kind. We will not have to worry about her anti-revolutionary activities because she will be in such a desolate area."

His sharp words were tipped with poisonous glee. The other students stared at me as if I were a spy in their midst. I felt like a character from one of the popular operas of the time—a true enemy of the people working from within. Now I had been identified, and they were exiling me to the remotest mountain area. Poetic punishment for a spy. Again I felt the urge to jump from the bus and end my life. But I had neither the energy nor the courage. The bus stopped again and again, and the students stepped off in twos and threes, carrying their luggage. Finally, I was the only student left. The bus continued on for fifteen minutes before the cadre told the driver to stop. He turned to me and said gruffly, "You—get out here!"

I picked up my bag and stepped out and collapsed to the ground. The cadre strode to a nearby building. It was a small single-story brick structure with a gray tile roof. He found a man inside and brought him out. "This one is for you," the cadre said, pointing at me with his foot as if selling a pig in the black market. The man who accompanied him was only about four and a half feet tall. He was slim and wiry and had the stub of a cigarette in his mouth. His eyes bulged out and the few teeth he had were black. He walked up to me and said, "I am Production Team Leader Huang of Luo Village."

His accent was thick and I could hardly understand him.

He picked up my bag and started to walk away. "I'm so tired," I said to him. "Can I rest for a minute? I've been throwing up all the way here."

"No," he answered without looking back. "We can't wait. We have a long way to go. If we don't get to the village by dark, we may run into a tiger."

I thought he might laugh, that he was trying to scare me. But he didn't stop and he didn't laugh.

I struggled to my feet and whispered weakly, "Well, let's go, then."

I followed him up the winding mountain path. He was clearly accustomed to climbing the steep trail. He moved deftly and I had a hard time keeping up with him. Now and then he looked down at me and spat on the ground. "Useless damned city girl," he said. "Why did they send you to me? What in the world am I going to do with you? Another mouth to feed."

With every twist in the path, he cursed me and cursed his fate.

As the sun settled beyond the mountain peaks, the lush greens and blues of the landscape faded to a monochromatic dull copper. The outcroppings of steep rocks shimmered above broad patches of russet undergrowth. The silhouettes of trees sprouting from bare rocks stood like a scattered column of attentive sentinels ascending into the clouds.

I climbed wearily into the thinning air, pausing often to gasp for breath. I felt no sense of wonder or exhilaration at the gorgeous scenery around me. I was thinking only that every step I took separated me further from the rest of the world, from my friends, from my family, from a happier future I'd imagined for myself in a city. Everything I loved faded in the valley far below. After a two-hour ascent, we passed through a low-hanging cloud, and as we emerged from it, I saw the village laid out on a flat brown terrace of land. "We're here," Team Leader Huang called to me. He waited for me to catch up with him and then led me into a small mud hut and dropped my suitcase on the dirt floor.

"Cuihua, I've got someone for you," he shouted.

"Who is it?" came a sleepy reply.

"It's Team Leader Huang," he answered.

A young woman appeared. She was about my age and height. She was slim and had a long narrow nose and wide eyes. She was combing her hair. She looked at me curiously and said, "I'm Sun Cuihua. I'm an educated youth from Jing County. And who are you?"

I introduced myself, relieved to have a companion here.

"We did not know you were coming until yesterday," Team Leader Huang said. "We have to go to the commune headquarters tomorrow and get you a bed. Tonight you sleep with Cuihua." And with that he left.

I sat down on my bag. "Are you hungry?" Cuihua asked. "I can get you something to eat."

"Not hungry." I sighed. "I'm tired and I don't feel well. I need to lie down."

There was a single wooden board on four legs that served as the bed for both of us that night. And there was a thin blanket. I got in and squeezed close to the wall. Within seconds I was in a deep sleep.

Team Leader Huang awakened us the next morning. He was with another man from the village. "We are going to the commune head-quarters," he said. "The government has given us rations for each educated youth. You get a sickle, a hoe, a shovel and a shoulder pole along with your bed."

"Must I go with you?" I asked. "I'm still tired and sore. My legs and back hurt. I can hardly walk, Team Leader."

"You don't have to go," he said. "You'll just slow us down anyway. You don't have to work in the field today, either."

I thanked him for his understanding.

Much to my surprise, the men returned about three hours later. They carried my supplies and the materials to make a bed for me.

"Look what we found on the road," Team Leader Huang shouted from a distance and pointed back down the mountain. I strained to see the path below. A lone figure—a woman—trudged toward us. She looked up at us and waved. It was my mother. I rushed down the path to her.

"How did you find me?" I asked breathlessly.

"After I was pushed off the bus," she said, "I tried to find a way to follow you here. But nobody was coming this way. The public bus would have cost me three yuan. I tried to find a free ride. Finally, a friend of a friend of a friend said she knew someone at the post office, and he let me ride on the mail truck. I came here just like a package. I asked for you at every stop and people kept telling me, 'Farther up the mountain, farther up the mountain.' "

She was exhausted from the climb. But she was also very excited to see me. The two men hung a bamboo partition at one end of the hut to give me a room. Cuihua, Mama and I put my new bed together in my new room. We talked most of that day. Mama said life would be hard here. She cautioned me to be careful and to do what I was told. "The times will change," she said. "Someday this will end. And when that happens, our new lives—our real lives—will begin. I know it is hard for you to believe this. But you must. Never give up hope. Never!"

Cuihua and I listened to her words, catching fragments of faith from them.

"Be sure you eat enough food," Mama said. "And don't work too hard."

We cooked rice, and the three of us ate dinner together. Afterward Mama and I sat outside and watched the sun set. She asked me many questions about my journey. I didn't want her to worry about me, so I said it had been uneventful. She watched my face as I spoke. I was not sure she knew I wasn't telling her everything.

"Maomao," she said, patting my hand, "there is something you need to know before I leave you here. Do you remember what happened when you were in the hospital in Hefei?"

"I remember. You told me never to talk about it."

"Have you?"

"No."

"After I arrived and saw your condition I baptized you. Do you know what that means?"

"No. I only remember it was wet."

"Maomao," she said and then lowered her voice to a whisper, "I am a Christian. And you are, too."

"I don't know what that is. How did you become one?"

"When I was fourteen, my brother and sister—your third uncle and second aunt—took me to a church with them. They had become Christians years earlier. They attended a Catholic university in Beijing and were converted there. At first I thought it was fun. I'd never seen or heard anything like it before. I was enthralled by the ritual, the chanting and the singing, and the incense and statues. I returned with them the following week. They explained what it meant. They taught me that there is a God and that there is a Son of God and a Mother of God. They showed me that there is another world. I know this is hard for you to understand, particularly now, in this world. But you need to know these things. They will help you stay strong."

I listened intently and was moved by her solemnity.

"When I was fifteen," she continued, "I was baptized by a priest in Tianjin. A priest normally baptizes. But when I saw you in Hefei, I thought I was going to lose you, so I baptized you myself."

"And that is how I became a Christian, Mama?"

"Yes."

"Why?"

"Because I want someone to watch over you when I am not with you. Because I don't want to lose you ever to those who pulled us apart and tormented us. Because there is a God who watches over you."

"Why is this a secret? Why can't I tell anybody?"

"Because they hate us and fear us—the Communist Party. After their revolution, they began arresting Christians."

"Did they arrest you?"

"Not me, because I was young. But they warned us to stop believing in our God. They said we were 'prisoners of superstition.' They told us, 'Wash your minds and get rid of your religion.' In 1951 policemen came to our house in Tianjin—the same house where you lived with

Grandma when you were a little girl. They ransacked the house. They took away your second aunt. They beat her and put her in prison. She is still there today. She refused to deny her God. She has been in prison for twenty-five years because she is a Christian."

"What if they find out about me?" I asked. "I'm in enough trouble already."

"They won't. Nobody knows. But you must never confide in anyone else."

"I won't."

"Remember," she said, "if you ever feel you need help, Maomao, if you become sick, if you should think that you can't go on living, remember what I am saying. There is a God. Close your eyes and ask Him to help you. He will."

"Where is He?"

"He's up here in the mountains with you. And he's down in Wuhu with us, too. Until you learn more, just whisper, 'God help me!' "

I really didn't understand what she was saying. I gave her a perplexed look.

She read my face and said, "Someday this will make sense to you. But for now, in this chaos, even though it is hard to grasp, you need to have trust and faith."

"I will," I assured her.

In the morning I received permission from Team Leader Huang to walk Mama down the mountain. The bus came, and she climbed aboard. I waved goodbye until she was out of sight. Then I felt completely lonely and lost. "God help me," I said. I waited for a voice or a sign. There was none.

I adjusted to the cycles of village life. Because we were in the mountains, the sun did not appear over the eastern peaks until nine in the morning, and it set about five in the afternoon. The days were short and the nights were long. Each morning Cuihua and I boiled a cauldron of water and filled a thermos. We cooked rice for breakfast. We had rice and hot water for lunch and dinner. This was our daily diet. The lack of iodine in the mountain springs and the restricted diet—vegetables did not grow well at that altitude—meant that many of the villagers suffered from what they called big-neck disease, or goiters. Most had prominent or bulging eyes, another symptom of dietary deficiencies.

I worked with the villagers every day in the terraced fields from dawn until dark. We planted rice, picked tea leaves, and chopped down trees and bamboo. I learned to carry a long stick and swish it through the underbrush in front of me on the way to and from work in order to scare away the poisonous snakes that infested the region. One of the feared snakes was called a five-step serpent by the villagers, indicating that anyone who was bitten could take only five steps before dropping dead. Another feared snake was the bamboo-leaf green serpent. This one blended into the bamboo and might strike from either above or below. Its bite was just as deadly.

Only when it rained or snowed heavily were we allowed to stay home. Weeks blended into one another, every one pretty much like the last. And I always asked God for rain and snow. One rainy day while I was washing my soiled clothing in a big wooden basin, I sensed someone standing behind me. I assumed it was Cuihua. I turned and noticed a pair of high-topped white sneakers. These were unusual, since most of us in the mountains went barefoot. I looked up and saw a nicely dressed and handsome young man smiling down at me. His face was bright red. He was blushing. I stood up. My hands were wet and soapy. I didn't know what to do with them. Cuihua came into the room and saw the visitor and said, "Wu Yimao, this is Teacher Zhu. And Teacher Zhu, this is Wu Yimao, the new educated youth from your hometown, Wuhu."

"Hello, Teacher Zhu," I responded.

"Please, don't be so formal," he replied. "Call me Zhu Yiping."

Hearing him speak in the Wuhu dialect sent a shudder of delight through me. Here was someone from home. I wrung my hands together nervously. "I heard there were some new educated youth here, so I dropped by to say hello," he said. "Are you getting accustomed to

the altitude and the mountain life? Everything here is up and down."
He laughed. I was uncomfortable talking with a young man my own
age who stood so close to me and spoke so informally. I'd never had a
conversation like this before. I had difficulty hiding my uneasiness.

"How long have you been here?" I finally managed.

"Four years," he answered. "Four *long* years."

"And you're a teacher and not a peasant?"

"Yes," he said, "that's an interesting story. I'm from a black family. I
was sent here to be a peasant. Some time ago, while I was working in
the field, a small tractor driven by a peasant backed over my foot. He
came close to killing me, but he only broke several bones. I stayed in
bed for two months. It took me several weeks after that to walk without
pain again."

"Why didn't they send you home as a handicapped person?" I
asked. "I thought that was the policy."

He laughed. "Oh, you are new here! Believe me, if injury were a
way of getting out of here, every educated youth in the mountains
would be standing behind a tractor! A broken foot or a broken leg is a
small price to pay for going home. But no way. Sorry. They know that.
They just wait till we get better and then give us another assignment.
Yimao, they're never sending us home. They waited until I could walk
and saw I'd be no use working in the fields, so they assigned me to the
school."

He shuffled back and forth across the room and showed me that he
still favored his left leg. "See," he said, "it never healed right. But up
here, nobody cares."

His words unsettled me. I once more sensed the dread that I would
never leave this place except by death.

Zhu Yiping remained and talked with us the rest of the afternoon.
He started back to his village before darkness set in; waving his snake
stick in front of him, he still had a slight limp. "How do you get around
on these mountain trails?" I called after him. He turned and smiled and
shouted, "Badly!"

We kept a large water jar inside the hut, and we had to fetch water for it every few days. When I first arrived, Cuihua fetched it for both of us from a nearby well. Soon I was taking my turn getting our water. I carried two wooden buckets to the well, which was about twenty feet deep. I could not see the bottom. I was afraid I might fall in. I knelt at the edge and braced myself on the rock wall surrounding it. After I threw down the bucket I pulled it from side to side with a long rope, but I failed to fill it with water. I pulled it back up, uncertain what to do. Just as I was about to give up and go home, Zhu Yiping came along. "Cuihua told me you were here," he said. "Let me help you." He picked up the bucket. "Keep it upside down when you drop it. If you don't, it will float." He filled each of my buckets for me. He handed me his snake stick and he carried them on a shoulder pole back to our hut, and I followed him.

Cuihua was waiting for us. She watched from the door. "You're almost a family now," she said. "You two look like a husband and wife."

I was embarrassed. I could think of nothing to say. Yiping also reddened and put down the buckets and said, "The water is for both of you, Cuihua. And I really don't fancy having two wives." It was perfect, and all three of us burst out laughing.

Yiping visited us regularly after that. Sometimes he brought rice with him, and we cooked dinner together and talked late into the night. I learned he had only a middle school education but studied classical Chinese literature and poetry on his own. We shared a love of poetry. I told him I'd brought several books of poetry with me, and he said he had done the same. He carried them with him after that, and I got out my large book of Tang Dynasty poetry and we sat together long into the night reading and reciting to each other. Some evenings, as he intoned the ancient poems of love and loneliness, I listened and followed his recitations with my finger on the page. I warmed at certain passages and my heart quickened. I wondered if he was trying to speak directly to me through the poems, or if he merely loved the words on the page.

One evening he stood near the window, catching the last light of the day, holding a volume of poems in one hand and gesturing with the other as he read:

> Last year this very day
> I found in this doorway
> Her face and peach blossoms
> Mirroring each other's beauty
> I wonder where
> The face has gone
> Only the peach blossoms
> Still smile in the spring wind.

My heart crept into my throat. I forgot the fatigue of the day and the hopelessness of life. His gentle expressive voice lifted me and carried me away. I dreamed with my eyes wide open. I recited from memory:

> You ask me why I live on Green Mountain
> I smile in silence with a quiet mind.
> Peach petals blow on mountain streams
> To earths and skies beyond humankind.

Yiping watched me as I spoke. I was so embarrassed I had to turn and face the window as my words spilled out.

When I was finished, he began to recite from memory:

> Over far-flung wooded plain wreaths of smoke weave a screen,
> Cold mountains stretch into a belt of heart-rending green
> The dusk invades the tower high
> Where someone sighs a longing sigh . . .

He momentarily forgot the rest of the popular Li Bai poem. I waited while he rolled his eyes, trying to remember. I began to say them, and he remembered, and we finished the poem together:

On marble steps she waits in vain
But to see birds fly back again
Where should she gaze to find her dear
She sees but stations far and near.

"Li Bai must have passed this way," he said. I cleared my throat, blushed, and told him I agreed.

When we spoke about growing up, I learned that Yiping and I had shared similar experiences and had many common emotions and memories. We were lonely and homesick. Our souls had been tattered by the years. Our childhoods had been stolen. We comforted each other with our words. Yet we had to be cautious. We knew that in the past, passion was a political sentiment—a feeling we feared when we detected it in the voices or the faces of others. Passion was the private monopoly of those who persecuted others. We had experienced only sorrow, timidity, fear, frustration and regret. But now, here, we sensed a passion in our hearts. We hardly dared look at each other for fear of bursting into flames. We were all embers beneath our skin. Yet we kept a wall between us. We did not touch. We did not hold a glance too long. We knew when to stop. It was not easy. But we knew and we kept our distance.

I looked forward to Yiping's visits. I combed my hair, washed my hands and face before he arrived. Cuihua laughed at my giddiness. I sensed she was growing jealous, and I'd read that jealousy always led to serious trouble. I decided to be even more careful about the time I spent alone with Yiping.

One afternoon when I was returning home from working in the fields, I heard crying and screaming. I ran the last short distance to our hut. Cuihua was in the midst of a circle of people, rolling around on the ground, her fists doubled up like a baby's. She was screaming in a desperate high-pitched voice.

"What's wrong?" I asked a woman.

"Cuihua fell into the latrine," she said.

In the mountains, rather than simply digging a hole in the ground for the latrine, as they did in the lowlands, they sank a large jar in the ground with the lip extending about half a foot above the surface. They placed two planks across the opening. Relieving yourself was a balancing act. You had to stand over the jar with one foot on each plank. If you shifted too much one way or another, the plank moved and you might lose your balance. I always found it frightening to use the device; every time I squatted over the jar, I was afraid.

Cuihua's long hair was caked with raw sewage. She was embarrassed about falling in and having to summon several villagers to fish her out. I found the scene comic and tragic at the same time. The villagers were all talking and laughing. Team Leader Huang appeared and asked what was going on. He stepped to the center of the amused circle and said, "Cuihua, get up and wash yourself. Everyone knows you're a city girl. In the countryside we get dirty now and then."

"Get dirty now and then!" Cuihua screamed and struggled to her feet. "Look at me! This isn't dirt! This is the shit from your villagers. I can't live here anymore. I have no face here. I might as well die!"

"You're not going to die," Team Leader Huang said.

"I want to go home to recover from this, Team Leader. I need two weeks. I deserve it. I've earned it."

Team Leader Huang scowled at her but was not unsympathetic. "Okay," he said. "You can have one week away."

Cuihua broke into a big smile and hurried toward the river to wash. The next morning as I left to join a group of women picking tea leaves higher in the mountains, Cuihua walked down the mountain carrying her bag, singing to herself.

Several weeks each year the villagers picked tea leaves. As I worked beside them, I saw how incomparably beautiful the mountains were. Thousands of red azaleas bloomed on the adjacent slopes. As the sun crossed the sky, the peaks and valleys in the distance shone as if they had been splashed with fresh blood. From ancient times the tea from these mountains had been offered annually as a tribute to the emperors. Traditionally, it was harvested only by women. I arose before sunrise and climbed with the others high into the mountains. Each of us carried a bamboo basket to hold the leaves we picked. We gathered just the top three leaves of each branch of the bushes. Because of my dexterity, I was able to pick with both hands, and this amazed the others. We worked all day but still gathered only about a pound of leaves each.

After five days of this work, I became increasingly weak. I fell far behind the others climbing up to the tea bushes. I had to sit down and rest many times during the day. On Saturday I stayed in bed rather than report for work. No one missed me. I stayed in bed the next day. I didn't cook for myself and I grew even weaker. I ran out of water and was too ill to go to the well. I became dehydrated. I wondered when someone might notice my absence. Cuihua was supposed to return on Sunday, but she didn't. And she didn't come back the next day. On Tuesday afternoon Yiping stopped by. He hadn't seen me in over a week. He said he thought I'd gone home when Cuihua left. He was shocked to see my condition.

He hurried to the well to retrieve fresh water. I was so thirsty I begged him to give me a sip before he boiled it. He comforted me and told me to wait. He built a fire in the stove, boiled the water for me and cooked rice porridge. After I sipped some water I managed to sit up in bed. I had little appetite but he encouraged me to eat. He sat on the edge of the bed and spooned warm porridge into my mouth. When he touched my neck and looked into my eyes, I found my affection for him deepening. I had fallen in love. It was a wonderful feeling. At the same time, I knew that it was forbidden. After I'd eaten, he moved to a stool and read poems to me. He returned to his home that night and came back to care for me the next day.

I was concerned that Cuihua had not returned, but I valued the time I could spend with Yiping as he nursed me back to health.

I could tell by the way he looked at me, by the selection of the poetry he read, by the way he lingered in the hut into the night, that without saying so directly, he had fallen in love, too. I sat silently on a stool and watched and listened to him read, noticing the way he gently turned the page, the way he moved his arm or his fingers in making a particular point. The music of his voice enchanted me. He could read my heart in my eyes, and I read his feelings in his words.

Yet neither of us knew what to do next. A growing affection between us was doubly bad because we shared a common background—a black family. If we were discovered or even suspected of crossing forbidden lines of emotional attachment, our punishment was likely to be far more severe than that of children of the red families. We heard of the offspring of red families in the mountains who fell in love and married and settled down and lived like peasants. But they fully expected that as soon as the political winds shifted, they would be the first to return to the city. We knew that if we ever settled down in the mountains, all hope was lost of ever getting out.

Yiping and I talked sometimes in a fanciful way about returning to our families and even going to college. We assured each other that our time in these mountains, contrary to what we'd been told, would someday end. Our real future, our actual lives, awaited us beyond the mountains back in the city. We also knew without saying so that romance would surely spoil those dreams. We stayed close yet also at a guarded distance. With others around, we separated and blended in so as not to arouse suspicion. When Party members were present, we didn't even look at each other.

Yiping lived with two other educated youths from Wuhu. One day after the harvest, when we didn't have to work, Cuihua and I visited them. After sharing tea, we decided to climb to the top of the highest peak in the surrounding mountains. We packed some steamed rice and poured a thermos of tea, and one of the boys borrowed an ancient hunting gun from one of the villagers. He said he thought he might be able to shoot a bird at some higher altitude and we'd all feast on it.

The ascent was more difficult than I expected. The path rose steeply after a short distance. There were places where we had to proceed on all fours. I was frightened by the heights. I fell behind. Yiping came back for me. He took my hand and helped me climb and advised, "Don't look down."

I was petrified by the narrow steep path. "I don't think I can continue," I told Yiping.

"Of course you can," he calmly assured me. "Just hold my hand and you'll be safe."

And so I grasped his hand tightly and looked only at him and moved on. We climbed through a thin mist. Everything behind us was blotted out. When we reached the top of the mountain, the others were waiting for us. The view was truly breathtaking. We could see for miles and miles over the tops of the clouds.

It was an enchanted kingdom. Below us on other peaks we saw flowers in bloom, patches of pink and yellow and red. Birds were wheeling beneath us, unaware that we stood above them. There was no one in the world but the five of us. The sky above was blue, and the white clouds were huge and thick and floated past us like continents. No one spoke for a long time. Cuihua finally turned to say something to me but stopped and gave me a forbidding look. I realized I was still holding Yiping's hand. I immediately let go and stepped away from him.

We lay down in a circle, our heads nearly touching, and stared up at the endless blue. I closed my eyes and breathed the cool limpid air. The only sound was the gentle breeze whistling over the rocks. Suddenly there was a monstrous explosion nearby. I sat up, my heart pounding. "What's that?" I asked.

The others laughed. One of the boys had fired the gun.

"Look how scared you are," Cuihua said. "Did you pee in your pants?"

I blushed. "I'm not scared. I was just surprised."

"If you're not scared," one of the boys said, "then you shoot the gun." He reloaded it and handed it to me. It was heavy and I had difficulty lifting the barrel. He showed me where to put my hands and how to aim and pull the trigger.

"There," he said, pointing at a bird floating below us. "Shoot the bird."

But I was in no mood to kill any animal on this day. So I aimed at a cloud and closed my eyes and pulled the trigger. There was a loud blast, a flicker of fire, and a powerful recoil. I stumbled and fell over backward. I dropped the gun and screamed as though I'd shot myself.

"Well, you scared a lot of birds," one of the boys said, laughing. "But we won't have any for dinner."

Scores of birds in the crags and rocks and bamboo took flight at the sound of the gun. A huge eagle flew up and circled us. It was so beautiful, gliding through the sky. It soared and then swooped down and floated on invisible currents of wind.

On the spot I made up a poem and recited it.

> The eagle is flying over the mountain
> The sun is sparkling like a jewel
> We are standing on the top of the world
> When the sun sets today
> The eagle will rest in his nest
> And we will all return to a strange place
> Far below us
> That is not our home.

The others listened quietly. Yiping said, "Such sad words spoil a beautiful day."

"Yimao, you're making me cry," Cuihua said. "We should forget our worries today."

One of the boys added, "It's too melancholy, Yimao. How about this?"

> At the top of the mountain
> The eagle soars
> Brave Wu Yimao

Fires a gun
Scares away dinner
And pees in her pants!
We will go down the mountain
With empty stomachs.

We laughed. The somber mood created by my words dissolved. We sat together, our toes touching, and shared the rice and passed around the cup of hot tea. There were few words as we ate. We were deeply affected by our surroundings and our lighthearted and careless comradeship.

"We'd better start down before it gets dark," Yiping said as we finished the rice.

Descending the mountain was even more difficult than coming up. The mist and clouds had thickened and I could barely see the path beneath my feet. Once more Yiping held my hand and encouraged me. When we reached the grassy slopes we sat and slid part of the way down. By the time we arrived at our huts, it was dark. I was exhausted and tired and sore. The next day Cuihua and I climbed to the terraced rice fields with a team of workers. We were so tired we could not keep up with the others. Team Leader Huang asked: "What were the five educated youths doing yesterday? You climb to the top of the mountain without doing anything productive. You don't cut bamboo, you don't collect wood or mushrooms. Why in the world do you waste your days like that?"

It would have been impossible to explain to him what we'd done, how we felt. So we responded with silence.

51

Two weeks after our trek up the mountain I decided to commemorate the Moon Festival with another gathering. I sent invitations to Yiping and his friends and to educated youths in the nearby villages. Two days later ten young men and two young women joined Cuihua and me for the celebration.

We asked everyone to bring something to add to our banquet. Some of the boys shot birds and brought them, and others stole new bamboo shoots from the commune fields. The girls picked a large pumpkin that was still green and carried it to our hut. We cooked a delicious feast together. The boys carried the table outside. The night was illuminated by a bright full moon, so we had no need for candles or lanterns. I bought several bottles of wine from the commune store. Cuihua and I poured real wine for the boys and wine mixed with water for the girls. We gathered around the table to eat. The boys made toasts. And with each new toast they became louder and wilder in their talk. We ate and drank and laughed and took turns remembering our lives in the city. Everyone complained and commiserated about life among the peasants. The light faded. Yiping pulled me aside and asked if I wanted to go for a walk.

We sneaked off together and strolled along the riverbank, talking about our hopes for the future and about how much fun it was getting together with the other educated youths. At a spot along the river was a large rock with a flat smooth surface. Beside it was a tall willow tree. We sat on the rock. The bright moon made the night beautiful, and the only sound was that of the river rushing by. We dangled our feet in the cool water. We were lost in thinking the same thoughts but afraid to move closer together.

Out of the shadows a voice thundered behind us, "Don't move or I'll shoot!" We froze.

Yiping raised his arms in the air and said, "Don't shoot. I'm Zhu Yiping."

"Ohhhhhh, so it's you," the voice came back. And Team Leader Huang stepped forward. He lowered his gun and said, "You frightened me."

"Well, you frightened us," we responded.

"I thought you were ghosts," he said.

"Why would you think that?" I asked.

"You are a Party member. You aren't supposed to believe in ghosts," Yiping said.

"I believe in the Party. But I also believe in ghosts. There is no conflict in that."

I wanted to laugh but suppressed the urge.

"You dumb city kids," he said and shook his head. He pointed to where we'd been sitting and said, "This rock where you are standing is called the Ghost's Dressing Table. The river is like a large mirror here. And when there's a full moon, ghosts come here and sit on the rock and look at themselves in the river and comb their hair. That is why I brought my gun tonight. Most villagers won't come near this rock on the night of a full moon."

"Have these ghosts ever hurt anyone?" I asked.

"People have disappeared in the river. Men and women. And children."

We glanced at the ruffled surface of the water nervously and made our way toward Huang.

"I was on my way back from a monthly Party meeting," he told us. "But I had to pass here, and I heard you."

"We're having a banquet," I said. "Will you join us?"

Huang walked with us back to the gathering. As we approached, I saw the others sitting in a circle on the ground. Light from the moon illuminated their faces. I recognized the sad song they were singing about educated youth. Their voices were melancholy. As I listened to them singing, I wanted to cry.

> *I sit beside the kerosene lantern*
> *Bowing my head, missing my home.*
> *The wind blows, the flame wavers*
> *Our life is so miserable*
> *Dear Mom and Dad*
> *Please don't cry for your poor child.*

Huang laughed when he heard it. "Spoiled city kids," he muttered. "You're all like little lost girls." The others continued singing, and Yiping and I joined in.

Team Leader Huang stood to the side, listening and observing. When the song ended, one of the boys poured him a drink. He took the proffered cup and swallowed it in a single gulp. He put down his gun and sat on the ground with us, pulled out a cigarette and lit it, and asked for another drink. After four cups of wine and three cigarettes, Huang had difficulty standing and finding his gun in the dark.

"Going home?" Yiping asked him.

"Yeah," Huang responded, slurring his words. "Time for bed." He staggered away.

After he had left some of the boys complained about his thirst for our wine. "Cheap bastard," one of them said, and the others chimed agreement.

"Cheap bastard with a gun," another said. "Stupid old bastard," another said. "And dangerous bastard!"

We laughed. I looked in the direction that Huang had walked. I thought I saw the glisten of his watery eyes in the moonlight. "Shhhh, he's watching us," I told the others. Everyone became quiet. Then someone began to sing a slow, sad, familiar song about home.

> *My home is on the Songhua River in the Northeast,*
> *There are forests and coal mines,*
> *And soybeans and sorghum cover the mountains and fields.*
> *There live my compatriots and my frail parents.*
> *One miserable day I was forced to leave my hometown,*
> *Giving up all that inexhaustible treasure*
> *Wandering! Wandering! All day long, wandering!*
> *Which year, which month,*
> *Will I be able to return to my lovely hometown?*
> *Oh, Mother and Father, oh, Mother and Father,*
> *When will we be able to joyfully reunite at home?*

———

After working in the mountains for six months, I was granted a home leave. Team Leader Huang issued me a permit to return to Wuhu for two weeks. When I arrived home, my parents were happy to see me but at the same time worried about my health. Because of the diet in the mountains, consisting principally of rice, I had gained weight and was lethargic. Mother went out of her way to buy fresh vegetables and meat. She cooked several special dishes for me and I regained my energy.

I asked about Yuanyu. Papa stared at me for a moment and responded, "You haven't heard?"

"I have heard nothing," I said. I wanted to hear something wonderful about her, a change in fortune or a new position.

"The news is not good," he said.

"What is it?" I asked, assuming he'd merely say she was unhappy working in the countryside or at worst that she was not in good health.

"I talk to her father when he cuts my hair," Papa said.

"Is she coming home? Will I have a chance to see her?" I asked excitedly.

"According to her father, Yimao, she had a boyfriend in the countryside. And—how can I tell you this—she became pregnant. She didn't tell anyone about it for a long time, and by the time it was discovered, well, it was too late to do anything about it. She had the baby. It was taken away from her immediately."

My heart sank. I remembered Yuanyu crying next to me night after night. I remembered her suspicions that she had been adopted when she was very young. Now her baby had been adopted. Or perhaps worse.

"Of course, her parents were told of her behavior—of her problem. When the news arrived they were embarrassed and ashamed. Her father wrote to her and told her he never wanted her to come home again. He told her that she was not his daughter."

"Is that true, Papa? Was Yuanyu adopted?"

"I don't know. He was angry when he spoke. But that's what he said."

"Where is Yuanyu now?"

"I went for a haircut last week, Yimao. Her father told me that Yuanyu is dead."

I held my hands to my face and closed my eyes. "How?"

"She had become pregnant again. She tried to get rid of the baby herself. She took pills. She took too many."

I doubled over and wept.

"Her father denounced and disowned her. He said she was shameless and brought nothing but grief to his family."

I remembered all the times Yuanyu and I played together, walked back and forth to school and the market, sat in the branches of the tree outside and looked down at the world. I could not stop sobbing.

"Why are you crying so hard, Yimao? My goodness, even her mother and father didn't cry. She brought this on herself."

I wanted to say something, but I could not find the words. I didn't think anyone else would understand. I curled up in the chair, sobbing. I knew if I went to my bed and lay down beside the wall, I would only think of her and cry harder. My best friend was gone. My connection to a brief period of happiness was gone.

The two weeks at home flew by. It was difficult returning to the mountains. Yet there was no choice. Mama packed several books in my bags to keep me company. There were no tears this time at my departure. Mama and I exchanged looks of resignation and sadness. I carried with me also the burden of the fate of Yuanyu. As the bus bumped its way out of the city, I stared out the window at the pedestrians and cyclists going about their business, and I was filled with envy and longing and deep sadness.

The day after my return to the mountains, there was a big commotion at a cluster of huts not far from ours. Villagers ran from their huts and hurried down the slopes. "What's going on?" I asked as a woman pushed past me.

"A hunter trapped a tiger," she said.

Cuihua and I joined the others. It was indeed a huge tiger. The hunter displayed it in a cage constructed of thick wood bars, each the size of a man's leg. Inside, the tiger paced back and forth; now and then he paused and looked through the bars at the curious villagers and gave a deep menacing growl.

Cuihua and I stood near the edge of the crowd and stared at the incredible and beautiful beast. I had never seen such brilliant colors or such long claws. I stepped closer to the cage and stooped to look into the animal's piercing black-and-amber eyes. He gazed back at me. I could smell him. I could feel his warm, ragged breath. He stilled. I felt sorry for him. He reminded me of myself. He was trapped like me in this godforsaken place. My condition and that of all the educated youths was as desperate and hopeless as his. We had wild spirits and hopes and longed above all else for a different destiny. I was transfixed by the caged tiger. The villagers mocked him and praised the hunter and laughed when the tiger scratched at his cage. Some flipped pebbles into the cage to anger him. I saw the desperation and the fear and frustration in the eyes of the beast, and I wanted to free him.

52

Winter arrived. Snow covered the mountaintops, and the reds and greens of the landscape became a brilliant white. Schoolchildren were given a New Year's holiday, and Yiping was given permission to return home. I wanted to go home, too. A telegram arrived from my father giving me an excuse to apply for a special leave. It read, "Father hospitalized. Mother broke arm. Hurry home." I was disturbed by the news and went to Team Leader Huang's home. He was sitting down to eat his dinner. In the mountains it was customary for the head of a household to eat alone. His children and his wife were not allowed to sit with him and were nowhere to be seen. He invited me in, and I showed him the telegram and asked him for two weeks of leave.

"It's dinnertime," he said. "Sit down and we can talk about it."

"I need to return to my hut to have dinner with Cuihua," I told him.

"Tell you what," he said. "If you drink three cups of wine with me, I'll grant you the leave."

I needed his authorization, so I agreed. I seated myself across from him at the table. He poured me a full cup of wine, poured one for himself, and offered a toast to a long life. He emptied his cup in one gulp, and I sipped mine twice before returning it to the table.

"Drink the wine if you want your leave," he teased. I forced myself to do as he required and, following his example, tipped the cup back and swallowed the wine. It burned in my throat as it went down. He chuckled mischievously and refilled our cups. He drank his down and insisted I do the same. I felt I had no choice but to obey. My face flushed, and I felt light-headed.

"Team Leader Huang," I said, "I don't think I can have another. Can't you give me the permission now?"

"We have a deal," he said. He raised three fingers in the air. "Three cups of wine. Not two—three!"

He poured a third cup. We clinked our cups together and drained them. My stomach grumbled and I felt I needed to throw up. I was unsure I could stand.

"May I have your permission?" I asked.

He leered across the table at me in the light of the flickering kerosene lantern. "I'll have to think about it," he said.

"Team Leader Huang," I said, slurring my words, "you just promised me if I drank three cups of wine—"

"I'll *think* about it!" he said, his face aglow in the light of the kerosene lamp and his eyes glistening.

"I'm leaving," I said and rose, steadying myself with my hands on the table.

"You don't have to go yet," he said and reached out to grasp my wrist.

I pulled away and opened the door and stepped out into the cold night air.

In a flash he was behind me. His heavy breath was on the back of my neck. "Don't go," he slobbered. His arm snaked around my waist.

I twisted loose and moved aside.

"I told you to wait," he grunted behind me. "I'm not finished with you yet."

I ran across his yard and headed up the mountain toward my hut, gasping, stumbling, red-faced, frightened and embarrassed. When I burst into our hut Cuihua was seated at the table eating. She looked up at me, surprised, and asked, "What happened to you?"

"I tried to get permission from Team Leader Huang to go home," I cried.

She smiled and shook her head. "And Team Leader Huang said, 'If you drink three cups of wine with me. . . .' Right?"

She knew exactly what he'd done.

"Yes."

She shook her head. "That's the requirement for all the girls," she said. "Three cups of wine and his hands all over you for a few minutes."

"I ran away from him," I said and seated myself across from her.

"In that case," she said, "I doubt if he'll ever let you leave."

I broke into tears. Cuihua looked at me and sighed. "We're here to learn from the peasants." She sounded like the authorities when we left our homes. "Learn from the poor and lower-middle peasants!" she proclaimed. When I looked up, she was smiling at me, but there were tears in her eyes.

The next day I found Yiping before he departed and told him what had happened.

"That lecherous old fart!" he said. "Let me see what I can do. I'll take care of it." He smiled at me confidently.

That night there was a familiar soft tapping on my wooden window shutter. I got up and let Yiping in.

"I got you the permit," he whispered proudly.

"How did you do it?"

"My friend is a Party member. He accompanied me to call on Team Leader Huang. I told Huang I'd come to help you get a permit to leave. My friend said he'd been hearing certain things about Huang. He said the other Party members were upset and were considering writing a criticism to the commune headquarters. Huang was frightened. My friend said he'd persuade the others not to write the report, and Huang gave you authorization for a leave."

"What did he say?"

"He said you can go. We have to leave right away," he said, "before the old fart changes his mind."

We beamed at each other. "I'll come for you at daybreak," he said. "Be ready."

A few hours later, Yiping and I raced down the mountain to the bus stop.

"What do you do when you are in Wuhu?" I asked.

"I read. I sleep late. I go for walks. I practice calligraphy. I see movies."

"Do you visit Mirror Lake Park?" I asked. "I've heard it's very romantic in the winter." I was surprised at my boldness, and I blushed.

"I've heard that, too," he said and smiled. "Maybe we can go for a walk there together some afternoon."

We sat side by side on the bus and watched out the window as the world passed by. Each time the bus turned a corner, we leaned in to each other. I felt myself warm as our bodies pressed together. But I dared not look into his eyes when it happened. My home was half an hour's walk from the bus stop. Yiping helped me carry my luggage home. I had been worried about my parents, but Mama and Papa were overjoyed to see me.

Papa had become ill with malaria and had been hospitalized for several days. While caring for him, Mama had slipped on the ice on her way to the market and had broken her arm. Although my brother was able to help them, he was not very good at shopping, cooking or cleaning. A friend sent the telegram, Mama said, because she really could use my assistance and because she thought it might be a good excuse for me to come home. Mama welcomed Yiping also and asked him to stay and join us for dinner. In the following days, I was able to help with chores around the house and visit Papa in the hospital. Yiping came by every morning to accompany me to the market, and he helped me lug home coal that I bought at a government supply store.

After things were settled at home, I visited Yiping at his apartment and met his parents and his sister. We walked together in the snow around Mirror Lake Park. Yiping and I spent nearly every day with each other during our stay in Wuhu. We ate our meals at his home or at mine. I thought everyone was delighted by our close friendship. I dreaded returning to the mountains. I shared my fears with Yiping and told him I suspected that Team Leader Huang would not leave me alone. Yiping assured me he'd protect me.

When I returned to my hut in the mountains, Cuihua greeted me at the door and said, "Welcome home. You're leaving."

"What do you mean?" I asked.

"Team Leader Huang has transferred you," she said. "He was angry when he found you'd gone home."

"But he gave me permission."

"That's not the way he tells it now."

"Where is he sending me?"

"You'll have to ask him," she said.

I was angry and afraid as I hurried down to Team Leader Huang's hut.

"You cannot stay in my village anymore," he told me.

"Why not?"

"You're a bad element," he said. "They told me that when you arrived here. You proved it to me by going home without my permission."

"But—"

"You're being sent to Tongxin Brigade. You'll be an elementary school teacher. You're leaving tomorrow morning."

Tongxin Brigade was two hours away and on an even higher mountain. When Cuihua heard the news, she said, "You should be happy. No more fieldwork. Now you can be a teacher like Yiping."

I was happy to be leaving the fields. Yet it meant separation from Yiping. And I suspected this was precisely the punishment that Huang wanted for me.

I began packing my things. That afternoon I received another surprise, a letter from my father's sister Auntie Ninghui in Shanghai.

I expected the letter to cheer me up.

Dear Maomao, she began.

    Yesterday I received a letter from your father. He told me you have a boyfriend.

Boyfriend, I thought and blushed. That was the first time I'd heard the term used with reference to any of my friendships.

    Hearing the news, I had mixed feelings. I was happy because you have grown from a baby I once held in my arms and you called me mama, into the young lady you are today. I was sad, however, because of the possible terrible consequences of this relationship in the countryside and what it might mean for your future.

    If you marry someone in the mountains, you will never be able to return to the city. Please think about this. *Think about the misery you will bring to your parents. Think of the misery for you.*

    Heed these words. You are on the brink of a precipice right now. Break off any relationship you have with this boyfriend. Don't be sentimental. You are young, beautiful, intelligent and capable. You have a wonderful future ahead of you. Things will change someday. When they change, if you are settled down to a married life in the mountains, they will force you to remain there the rest of your days. There will be no hope for a return. Stop this horse at the edge of the cliff and avoid disaster. Your poor parents have suffered so much these past years. They are like feathers in a storm, blown from one place to another without any control over their lives. They cannot take any more difficulties. They have already eaten too much bitterness.

    You will have many possibilities in the future. You will meet many men. They will be worth your love. Do not waste your life!

When I finished, I dropped the letter and sat down, trembling.

"What's wrong? Bad news?" Cuihua asked.

I cried and could not speak for a long time. Finally I went to my bed and lay there the rest of the afternoon. Cuihua picked up the letter and read it. "Yimao, your aunt is right."

I responded with more tears.

Late that afternoon I heard Yiping outside, calling my name. I didn't move. Cuihua let him in. A moment later he appeared at my door. He saw I'd been crying. He came to my side and asked, "What's wrong?"

"Yiping . . ." I began, but I choked on my own words. I wanted to tell him everything but did not know where to start. I felt a profound love for him. But I had never expressed my feelings to him directly. When it came to saying anything openly romantic, I had always been tongue-tied. Now, when I needed to tell him, I could not do it. I handed him the letter and watched his expression change from curious to grave as he read. He slumped to the stool beside my bed, sighed deeply and closed his eyes.

Then he opened his eyes and looked at me. "We've been so silly," he said just above a whisper. "Really, Yimao. We both knew what was happening and yet we let it happen. We should have known this was hopeless."

"No," I said. "It is not hopeless, Yiping."

"Shhhh," he said. "Your aunt is a wise woman."

I knew him well enough by now to see he was struggling to maintain his composure. But I did not know if he was telling me how he felt or if he was telling me what he thought I needed to hear.

"Yiping," I said, "what is to be done?"

"What do you want? What are your feelings?"

"I don't know." I paused and added shyly, "I'll do whatever you want."

There was another long silence.

"I know what I want. But it's impossible."

"Why is it impossible?"

"Because we don't want to live the rest of our lives here. Even if we were together, it would crush us. We would someday come to regret it."

"Don't say that!"

"Yes. It has to be said. We are from black families. All the rules are different for us."

I looked at him, and my look told him I knew he was speaking the heartbreaking undeniable truth.

"Yimao, I think I know how you feel. I feel the same. It's like a dream. But . . . we've dreamed too much. We've dreamed too far."

"No," I said. "Don't say that."

"You cannot ignore what your aunt has written. She's right. Your parents have suffered so much. So have mine. So have we."

"Maybe if we just . . ." I stammered.

"Maybe if we just waited," he finished my sentence. "Maybe something will change and then . . ."

"My feelings will never change, Yiping," I sobbed. "Never."

"And neither will mine," he said. "But that's not the point."

He folded the letter and laid it next to me on the bed. He looked straight into my eyes and said, "The truth is, Yimao, that all of us are feathers in this storm. Your parents, my parents, the educated youth . . . and you and I. We control nothing. And we have been denying that. If our dreams are to come true, we have to stop here . . . now."

"No," I choked. "I can't."

He took my hand in his and grasped it tightly and held me with his warm gaze. "Maybe I'm stronger than you. Maybe I'm not as blind as you. I don't know what it is. But I know this much . . ." He released my hand and stood and looked away. "Maybe some other time . . ." he began wistfully. "Maybe . . ."

He never finished. He stood and left the room.

The next morning I rose early and packed my belongings. I tore a page from my notebook and wrote a poem on it.

Even when we are a thousand miles apart,
We will enjoy the same moon together.

I folded it neatly and left it in the middle of the table. On another page I wrote a note to Cuihua and asked her to give it to Yiping.

I pulled on my jacket just as the cock crowed. I stepped outside and took a deep breath of the cold morning air. I carried with me a box of books, a bag of clothing and a badly broken heart.

53

The mountain path to Tongxin Brigade was steep, winding and dangerous. As I left Luo Village I heard the deep distant growl of the tiger in his cage in the mist far below. I was surprised. I thought the villagers had killed him by now. But he was still there, still alive, pacing and snarling and clawing incessantly at the bars of his prison. I turned to look in the direction of Yiping's village many times. But it was soon lost in the morning mist. The road narrowed and wound along a deep precipice. The farther I climbed, the less dense were the bamboo and trees. The birds were singing. There was an ancient roadside resting place with a small pavilion. It had deteriorated badly, but there was a stone bench to sit on. Past travelers had etched their names and thoughts on the stone. I read some of the names and the brief poems. Most appeared to have been carved by Red Guards making their way up or down the trail, praising Chairman Mao for giving them strength, giving meaning to their lives, giving them life itself.

As I climbed, I kept looking for Tongxin Village. Eventually, I spotted a solitary structure in the distance on a terraced plateau. Several dozen children were playing around the building. "This must be the school," I said to myself. "But where is the village?" A river descended on a steep grade next to the plateau that separated the mountain path and the school. A single log, less than a foot in diameter, had been dropped across the river to serve as a bridge. I was hesitant to cross. I stood at one end of the log and looked down at the water rushing past. The water was clean and clear, and I could see the rocks and pebbles at the bottom of the river. I put down my luggage. The children on the far side of the bridge saw me. They shouted happily and ran to stand on the opposite side of the bridge. A young woman, a schoolteacher, I thought, joined them. "Come on," they shouted. "It's easy."

Still I waited. Two boys nimbly ran across the log to me. They picked up my belongings. "Are you the new teacher?" one asked.

I nodded.

"Come on!" he called. "Don't be afraid." The children ran back across the log.

All of the children began laughing at my fear and encouraged me to cross. The teacher called, "It's easy, really. Just don't look down."

I stared at the log and tried not to see the rocks and rushing water below. The drop was about ten feet. I turned sideways and began inching my way across.

The girl approached me once I was safe on the other side. "You're the new teacher?" she asked.

"I am."

"We've been waiting for you. I was told you were coming. I'm Xiang Dongmei."

"I am Wu Yimao."

We went inside the school, followed by the boisterous crowd of children.

Dongmei showed me the layout of the structure. It was divided into four rooms. There were two classrooms, a kitchen and a bedroom-office for the teachers.

Dongmei asked me about my schooling and my life in Luo Village. She wanted to know if I was aware of the dangers of life in the mountains. I told her I was. "Did they tell you why there is a vacancy here?" she asked.

"No one told me anything."

"Until four weeks ago, there was another educated youth from Shanghai teaching here with me. One evening after the children returned to their villages, she went for a walk along the stream. Not far from here she was bitten on the finger by a bamboo-leaf viper. She screamed, and fortunately a peasant was nearby chopping down bamboo. He hurried to her and she told him what had happened. She described the snake. The man told her to close her eyes and hold out her hand. He pressed her hand to a rock and chopped off the bitten finger with his hatchet. He wrapped her bleeding hand in his shirt and carried her back here. A group of peasants took her down the mountain to the county hospital. She recovered there and was allowed to return to Shanghai because of her disability."

I cringed as she told me the story.

"If I had been bitten"—she sighed—"they never would have sent me home. I have the bad family background. The only way I'll ever leave this place is if I die."

"Me, too," I said.

"Black family?"

"Yes."

She pointed to an empty bed against the wall and said, "That was hers. Now it's yours. Welcome to Tongxin School."

As I unpacked, she briefed me on the lessons for the children. They were divided into two classrooms. Grades one, two and three were in one room and four, five and six in the other. She said she would be teaching political studies and math and I would be teaching Chinese and music. In the morning she taught the higher grades and I taught the lower grades. In the afternoon we switched.

That evening and for many evenings after, Dongmei and I talked late into the night. We soon got along like sisters. Dongmei was nineteen and from Shanghai. We were about the same height and weight and had similar experiences growing up. Her family, too, had been terrorized by Red Guards. She loved school and dreamed of going to college someday. But her assignment to this remote region convinced her that those dreams would never come true.

I told her about my life. I told her about Yiping and my mixed feelings—love of him and fear for the consequences. She suggested I write to him and explain everything. I tried to write to him many evenings but ended up crying so hard I could never finish. I waited instead for a letter from him. None arrived. When I found I could not put my feelings into words, I thought about walking to his school to talk with him about our relationship and our future. Yet I was afraid to be so bold, fearing I'd get into trouble or be embarrassed or rejected. I waited and hoped.

I tried to clear my mind. I began taking walks up the mountainside by myself, always carrying a stick to scare away the snakes. It was peaceful. Tall bamboo and trees surrounded me, lush and green and shimmering with life. The clouds floated low overhead, and mist filled the valleys below. I found a solitary spot at the edge of a steep rocky height. I sat there, dangling my feet over the edge, staring down into the valley and nursed my broken heart.

He is my true love, I thought. I will never love another. He's the love of my life. I wept. The first and the last. I didn't know what to do.

As days turned into weeks, my thoughts changed. They became darker. I began thinking about stepping off the cliff, plummeting down through the clouds to the rocks below. My life was so miserable. My heart ached so much. Why not just end it? A single step, a single act of will, was all it took. And then I'd free myself from this turmoil and find peace of mind.

Late one afternoon I stood at the very edge of the precipice and stared down at the mist and the green and gray world far below. I closed my eyes and gathered my courage and was about to take the final step when a voice cried out behind me, "Yimao! Stop!"

I opened my eyes and stepped back.

Dongmei ran to me. "Don't!" she cried. She took my hands in hers and held them tightly. "Life is hard. But we have to live it," she said. "We have to. Our fate is better than this. Our lives are going to be better than this. I do not know when or how, but everything will change. This is not the end."

"No, it won't change," I cried.

"It will. Believe me, I've felt like you. I've sat on this very spot, too, and looked down into the dark valley. I know what you were thinking."

"I hate my life," I sobbed. "I'm tired. I don't want it anymore."

That night we cried in each other's arms and slept in the same bed.

I decided not to tempt myself again and didn't go back to the cliff. Time passed slowly. We taught and talked and sang. We tried to cheer each other up. Yet I remained depressed. Soon my mood began affecting Dongmei rather than the other way around. Her optimism and confidence slowly eroded. My darkness was seeping into her soul. She became quiet. She sat alone outside in the dark. We went through the motions of teaching. The children provided a much needed diversion during the day. We spoke to each other less in our quarters at night. Slowly, along with me, Dongmei lost hope.

"We are going to grow old and die here," she said to me one evening as we sat on the log bridge and looked down into the river.

I was thinking the same thing.

"There is a way, though. If we were Party members, we would have a better chance of going home. Party members have priority."

"How could we become Party members?" I asked. "With my background and yours, it is impossible."

"Well, it is not impossible," she said. "We might try. It's better than rotting here, isn't it?"

"It is," I agreed.

"There are two ways for people with a bad family background to become Party members," she explained. "One of them is the basket Party member. That means we bring baskets full of presents to the Party secretary. And after he gets enough presents, he will recommend Party membership for us and fix the records. Basically, we buy it."

"We don't have much to give as presents," I said. "And we don't have any money."

"You're right," she said and laughed. "But there is another way." She hesitated and studied my face before continuing. "It's called loose-belt Party member."

"And what is that?"

"That means you sleep with the Party secretary."

"I what?" I asked. I wasn't quite sure what she was talking about.

"You don't know?"

"I don't think so."

"You take off your clothes. You get into his bed. You do what he likes. And before long, you are a Communist Party member. Then you may make it out of here."

I was shocked. "I could never do that, Dongmei," I said. "Could you?"

"I'd do anything. Just look around us, Yimao. Really, now, wouldn't you? When you've been here as long as me," she said, "you'll feel the same way. Just wait."

A week later she visited the Party secretary. He lived in a village about thirty minutes down the mountain. She told me she intended to fill out an application to become a Party member. She washed, borrowed my white flowered blouse, looked at herself in the mirror, pinched her cheeks to make them red, and left.

I lay awake and waited for her. As the night passed, I began to worry. I walked to the bridge to see if she might have fallen. I could not see in the darkness.

Just before dawn, she returned. She was crying.

"Are you okay?" I asked. "What happened?"

She said she didn't want to talk. She crawled into her bed.

The next night she returned to the Party secretary and the next. Each time she returned home crying.

On the fourth night she went to see him again but returned home in less than an two hours. This time she was fuming.

"What's wrong?" I asked.

"That bastard," she said. "That filthy bastard. He wouldn't see me tonight to consider my application."

"Why not?" I asked.

"Because he was with another girl from another village. And he said my application had been denied."

"I'm sorry," I said.

"That liar," she said. "I hope he gets bitten by a snake! I hope a tiger eats him. I hope he falls off a bridge! I hope a rock falls on his head! I hope someone cuts him up!"

"What will you do now?" I asked.

"I don't know," she said. "There's nothing more to do. It's hopeless. It's even worse than hopeless."

54

One day the children came to school very excited about something. They told us a fortune-teller was wandering through the nearby villages. He was telling people their future.

When Dongmei heard this, she turned to me and said, "I have to see him!"

"Me, too!" I said.

"Where is he now?" Dongmei asked the students.

"On the other side of the bridge," they said. "We just passed him on the way to school."

Dongmei and I hurried outside and saw the lone figure in the distance beyond the bridge. We crossed the bridge and called to him. He turned and watched us approach. He was a surprisingly young man for a fortune-teller—in his mid-thirties, perhaps—and quite good-looking. He had large piercing eyes and a long stringy beard. He held a staff and carried a bedroll and a small wooden box that contained his instruments for telling fortunes.

The children followed us and gathered around.

"We want you to tell our fortunes," Dongmei said to the man.

He studied us for a moment. "Five fen," he said. "Each."

"All right," she said. "We have that."

He sat on his bedroll, opened his box and pulled out a worn and soiled deck of ancient cards—long and narrow, with strange-looking faces and symbols printed on them. He sorted and shuffled them and laid them facedown carefully on the box top. He looked at Dongmei and said, "Teacher, take three cards."

She turned excitedly to me. "He already knows I'm a teacher," she said. She picked out three cards and handed them to him. He looked at them and closed his eyes and mumbled a long sonorous mantra. The children who had seen him work his wonders before whispered that he was getting guidance from the gods.

It was quiet for several seconds and then he spoke. "Ah, I see. You are very unhappy here. You are from far away."

"Yes, yes," Dongmei said. "Shanghai."

"Yes, Shanghai," he said. "And you want to go home."

"Yes, I do. Very much. When?" she asked.

The fortune-teller closed his eyes and appeared to be listening to distant voices that he alone could hear. He nodded acknowledgment. He opened his eyes and looked straight into Dongmei's eyes. "You will go home," he said.

"When?" she asked.

"Soon," he said.

She grinned broadly.

"And you will never grow old," he said. "Not like me."

"Oh." She sighed with relief. "But you are not old."

"Never grow old," he repeated. "Not . . . like . . . me."

"Forever young." Dongmei laughed. "How perfect."

I picked three cards and handed them to him. Again he chanted and meditated before speaking.

"Will I go home, too?" I asked him.

"Yes, you will go home, Teacher," he responded. He closed his eyes and listened to his distant voices for a minute before continuing. "But you will grow old. You will grow old far away."

Before I could respond to his prediction, Dongmei burst out

laughing. "Poor Yimao," she said. "You will lose your beauty. But I won't."

The children all laughed and danced around us.

The fortune-teller watched me. I felt there was something he was not saying. The deeper meaning of his words, perhaps. What had he seen? Could he really tell the future?

"Is there more?" I asked.

He gathered up his cards and put them back in his box. "No more," he said. "I cannot reveal the gods' deepest secrets. If I did, I'd lose all my power."

We paid him and thanked him, and all of us returned to the school laughing. Dongmei was happier than I'd seen her in weeks.

———————

Several days after the meeting with the fortune-teller, Dongmei and I ran low on rice. I offered to go alone to the commune headquarters to pick up the month's ration. Dongmei was not feeling well. She reminded me to watch out for snakes. A crowd had gathered at the commune headquarters. There was a loud buzz of conversation and everyone was crying. A woman approached me, weeping and trembling violently. I stopped her and asked, "What's wrong? What's happening?"

"Haven't you heard?" she wailed.

"Heard what?" I asked.

"The sky has fallen. Our beloved Chairman Mao has passed away in Beijing," she choked before hurrying on her way, inconsolable.

The crowd was frightened and disoriented. No one could really understand the news. Many disbelieved it and said it was impossible. Chairman Mao dead? How could this be? He was supposed to be immortal. The thought of his passing had never crossed the mind of anyone. Mao was supposed to live ten thousand years! Had he really lived less than eighty-three? I had difficulty getting anyone's attention inside the store. But finally, I succeeded in acquiring forty pounds of rice. I hoisted it to my shoulder and hurried home. I never stopped to rest and I ignored the fatigue in my legs. When I at last saw our little school in the distance, my heart began to race. I put down my burden on the far side of the bridge and shouted, "Dongmei! Dongmei! Good news!"

She stepped outside and shaded her eyes as she tried to make me out in the distance. "What is it?" she called.

"He's dead!" I shouted, laughing as I spoke. "Chairman Mao is dead. The Red Sun has set!"

She ran to me and caught me in her arms, and we spun around laughing.

"That fortune-teller was right," she said. "We *are* going home, Yimao. This is what we've been waiting for." We burst into tears of joy.

We stayed up all night, singing and reciting poems and dreaming about the future. Dongmei said that when she got home, she'd visit all of her relatives and then start studying for college. "I think I'll be a doctor," she said. "What about you?"

"I think I'll be a professor," I told her. "A professor of English literature, just like my father. But let's never lose contact, Dongmei. We have to get together at least once every year, no matter where we live."

"We will." She laughed.

The entire nation seemed to collapse into a long night of grief and mourning. Funereal music played from every loudspeaker in every village. People wept openly. Dongmei and I were given instructions to bring our students to the commune headquarters to participate in the official memorial ceremony. We set out early in the morning. Because our school was the farthest of the mountain schools from the commune headquarters, we were among the last to arrive. As we approached the headquarters, we saw children from all the surrounding villages and hundreds of peasants gathered in a gloomy assembly. Dirges blared one after another over a loudspeaker and echoed up and down the mountains.

A large portrait of Chairman Mao draped in black with white flowers around it had been raised above a platform. All of us were ordered to face the picture and bow. Nearly everyone was crying. Some were wailing and flailing their arms about in the air, utterly stricken. Others were merely somber and wept silently and dabbed handkerchiefs to their cheeks. I tried to squeeze out a few tears but could not. Inside me there was too much excitement and joy. As speaker after speaker stood and praised Mao, I wanted to laugh out loud and dance. Dongmei and I exchanged mischievous glances occasionally. Each of us knew what the other was thinking.

It had taken us two hours to walk to the site. My students were exhausted. Some of them sat down during the tedious ceremony. I didn't want to be charged with teaching disrespectful or disloyal students, so I went among them, pulling them to their feet and turning them to the portrait. When the ceremony ended and the groups began to break up and go their separate ways, I caught a glimpse of Yiping. He was busy with his students not far away, and he hadn't noticed me. I felt my heart pounding and my face growing warm, and I wasn't sure what to do. Several hundred grieving people stood between us. As the crowd began to break up, some were pushed in one direction, the rest in another. Yiping and I were carried in opposite directions. Students on either side of me held my hands and arms. I began to cry when I saw Yiping turn and start down a path in the midst of his students. I tried to call his name but no sound came out. Several adults sought to comfort me, assuming I was weeping for Chairman Mao. But I wasn't. I wept for Yiping.

———

Despite our expectations of a sudden change in our lives, day followed tedious day and nothing seemed to happen. But Dongmei and I did not give up. We embraced new hope tightly. Word at last came from Beijing that a new policy was about to be instituted. University entrance examinations would be administered throughout the country. The rules assured that students would be admitted to the universities partly on test scores rather than solely on family backgrounds. Because of the massive number of high school graduates from the previous decade who had not been allowed to continue their education, only the top 2 percent of those taking the examination could be admitted to a college or university.

Educated youths throughout the nation began to cram tirelessly during the next weeks, brushing up on their studies. Each knew that his or her life hung in the balance, that a top score on the exam really would dramatically alter the future. Because few reference books were available, highly prized hand-copied editions and commentaries were passed from hand to hand in the mountains. Almost miraculously, Dongmei's parents in Shanghai mailed her three old textbooks they'd salvaged from somewhere. The mathematics, physics and chemistry texts were valued by us more than copies of Mao's Little Red Book had been by the Red Guards. After teaching each day we spent hours together in our room studying. Some nights we went without sleep. As dawn was breaking we quizzed each other on our studies. Both of us coached and encouraged the other.

More than three hundred educated youths in the commune took the two-day examination in early December at the county high school. Each of us was seated at a desk, a pink test participation slip on the right corner of the desk. Before I began writing I asked God to help me. Then I asked Him again. I reminded Him that I was a Christian. I decided to take no chances. I closed my eyes and asked Buddha, my ancestors, the Earth Father, the Earth Mother and Chairman Mao to help me. And to be sure I did not insult God, I asked Him a third time for help. When I was finished praying to every known deity, I picked up my pen, opened my examination and began writing.

On the way back to our quarters after the exam, Dongmei bubbled over with enthusiasm. But I was somber. "I know I did well." She laughed. "I could tell. Now all I have to think about is which university I'll attend. I want to go back to Shanghai. Fudan University is my first choice. My parents are going to be so happy."

I wasn't as optimistic. The exam had been very difficult. "Well, Fudan is a good choice," I said. "But I'm not sure I'm going anyplace."

"Cheer up!" Dongmei said. "We studied together. I know you did well, Yimao. I'm sure you'll get your first choice of schools, too."

We had not yet received notice of our scores when school was dismissed for the Spring Festival in January. In the more relaxed atmosphere of post-Mao China, educated youths were given longer leaves to go home for the holiday. While I was celebrating the arrival of the New Year with my family, a letter arrived from the commune notifying me that I had scored high enough on the examination to be admitted to Anhui Teachers University in Wuhu, where my parents taught. It was my third choice of schools. My brother Yiding was notified that his score had qualified him for admission to the same school. Not only were we leaving the countryside, we were coming home.

Because of the good news, I lingered for two extra days in Wuhu before returning to Tongxin. On the way back I stopped at the commune headquarters and met half a dozen other educated youths who were returning from their holiday and picking up supplies. There was little joy among them. I learned that I was the only educated youth in the commune who had been admitted to a university. I realized this meant that Yiping and Dongmei hadn't passed. I suddenly had mixed feelings about my good fortune.

None of the others congratulated me. They cut short our conversations and commiserated only with one another. I pulled aside a young woman from a neighboring village and asked her, "Why is everyone avoiding me? I've done nothing wrong."

"You remind us of our broken dreams," she said.

"I'm sorry," I told her. And then, "I'm worried about Dongmei. I need to get back to our school."

"Dongmei's not there," she said.

"Where is she?"

"Yimao, after learning of her score yesterday, Dongmei jumped from the ledge at the top of the mountain. Several villagers in the valley saw her fall."

My legs weakened, and I collapsed onto a bench. "Oh, Dongmei, Dongmei, Dongmei . . . no . . . no," I wept. "Dongmei! Why did you do this? Why wasn't I here to save you?" The girl comforted me but the other educated youths merely watched from a distance.

After I'd recovered somewhat from the shock of this news, I climbed up the steep path to the school one last time. I crossed the bridge deftly and went inside the school. I expected to be greeted by Dongmei—I simply refused to believe that she was gone. Her clothing was laid out neatly on her bed. The textbooks we'd studied together were stacked in the corner.

I sat on my bed once more and called out her name, as if I might summon her from wherever she had gone. As I lay down to rest, my face touched a sheet of paper on my pillow. It was a page from one of the notebooks we'd used when we prepared for our examinations. My name was scribbled across it in Dongmei's handwriting.

Yimao, it read.

I heard the good news. Congratulations. I am so happy for you. Do you remember the fortune-teller and how we laughed at his words? Well, he was right. I don't want to grow old here and I want to go home. If you ever think of me, remember the days and nights we spent here laughing and dreaming. Forget the sadness and the tears.

I remember the night you recited the poems for me that you'd recited for Yiping. Your recitation of Li Bai was my favorite.

> *You ask how I spend my time—*
> *I nestle against a tree trunk*
> *And listen to autumn winds*

In the pines all night and day.
Shantung wine can't get me drunk.
The local poets bore me.
My thoughts remain with you,
Like the Wen River, endlessly flowing.

Say goodbye to the children for me and tell them all to study
hard. My thoughts remain with you, Yimao.
Endlessly flowing.

Dongmei.

When I finished reading her words, I felt as if I were suffocating. I went outside to breathe. I paced back and forth from the bridge to the school, weeping. Every few minutes I looked up the path leading to the top of the mountain and called her name. Only the mournful echo of my own voice came back. Classes resumed the next day. I gathered the students in one room and told them I was the only teacher. I did not know if they had been told about Dongmei. I said, "Teacher Xiang asked me to tell you all to study very hard. And she thinks about you every day." My words were met by silence and tears.

An official from the brigade headquarters came by that afternoon and told me that a new teacher would be arriving in two days. "I know you are leaving us," he said. "But I'd like you to stay until he gets here."

I agreed. "I have a request," I said. "Can I see Dongmei before I go?"

He gave me an uneasy look. "I'm afraid not," he said. "They never found her. Some villagers saw her jump. But the valley is deep there. It is impossible to find her."

I broke down again at his words.

Two days later I left Tongxin School. On the way down the mountain, I decided to take a detour and find Yiping. As I neared his village I passed around the settlement where the captured tiger had once been caged. I wondered what had happened to him. I noticed that the stack of stout beams that had been his cage were piled outside the shabby hut of the hunter. I recalled the wide-eyed peasants gaping at the trapped animal, his deep growl like distant thunder, and his ominous persistent scratching. How I pitied him. I wondered if he'd escaped and if he was free again in the mountains. I hoped he was.

At the last moment I changed my mind about visiting Yiping. What was the point, after all? He wasn't leaving the mountains, and I was. Meeting him would shatter us both and remind us of the tragedy of our forced separation. It was far better, I felt, to carry Yiping in my heart, to remember him as he was when we recited poetry and climbed through the clouds hand in hand. I turned around and walked slowly back past the dismantled tiger cage and descended to the valley floor.

As I neared the base of the mountain, I sensed an unseen burden being lifted slowly from my shoulders. My steps quickened and became lighter. A fresh morning breeze caressed and cooled my face. I felt like a feather falling from the sky, fluttering peacefully to the earth. I arrived at the bus stop and sat on my bag and waited. When I heard the engine of the bus laboring in the distance, even before I could see it, I rose. When it choked to a stop a few feet from me, I climbed aboard and found a seat.

I watched out the window as we pulled away. Despite the joy of this moment, which I had dreamed about for so many years, my heart ached for those I was leaving behind. I looked up for the last time at the green peaks and the terraced rice paddies, the tea bushes, the drab huts, the huge heavy clouds hugging the mountain and the rich blue patches of sky. I whispered goodbye to the children, to the peasants, to all the educated youths who remained behind. I whispered goodbye to Dong-mei and Yiping.

Then I lowered my eyes, leaned forward, cradled my head in my hands and wept. My tears fell like raindrops on my bare feet and began to wash away the hard mountain soil.